Coaching

Coaching
A REALISTIC PERSPECTIVE 8th Edition

Ralph J. Sabock and Michael D. Sabock

ROWMAN & LITTLEFIELD PUBLISHERS, INC.

Lanham • Boulder • New York • Toronto • Oxford

ROWMAN & LITTLEFIELD PUBLISHERS, INC.

Published in the United States of America
by Rowman & Littlefield Publishers, Inc.
A wholly owned subsidary of The Rowman & Littlefield Publishing Group, Inc.
4501 Forbes Boulevard, Suite 200, Lanham, MD 20706
www.rowmanlittlefield.com

P.O. Box 317, Oxford OX2 9RU, UK

British Library Cataloguing in Publication Information Available

Library of Congress Cataloging-in-Publication Data
Sabock, Ralph J.
    Coaching : a realistic perspective/Ralph J. Sabock and Michael D. Sabock. – 8th ed.
        p. cm.
    Includes bibliographical references and index.
ISBN 0-7425-3634-3 (cloth : alk. paper) – ISBN 0-7425-3635-1 (pbk. : alk. paper)
1. Coaching (Athletics) 2. Coaching (Athletics)–Vocational guidance. I. Sabock, Michael D., 1955- II. Title.
GV711.S22 2005
796'.07'7–dc22

2004010055

Printed in the United States of America
⊗™ The paper used in this publication meets the minimum requirements of American National Standard for Information Sciences—Permanence of Paper for Printed Library Materials, ANSI/NISO Z39.48-1992.

This edition of *Coaching* is dedicated to
men and women of the coaching profession,
past, present, and future.

CONTENTS

Chapter 10 Final Preparation for the Season 217

This book is for you and your contemporaries who are preparing for or have just begun a coaching career. The title reflects its primary thrust. It is a book dealing with the coaching profession rather than a cookbook approach on how to coach. There is a vast difference between the two. No one can tell you the right way to coach, as each of us is unique and so is the situation in which we find ourselves. The person who knows all the answers to the right way and only way to coach has yet to be born.

Experience has shown that few professionally prepared coaches get into difficulty because of a lack of knowledge regarding the skills of a sport. Rather, they get into trouble because of mistakes resulting from a lack of understanding of what coaching is all about. Therefore, much of what follows is an attempt to point out what coaching will demand of you physically, emotionally, and mentally. The book also explores a number of potential problem areas, along with some suggestions for dealing with them and, most important, preventing them. Finally, the book outlines guidelines and principles that should be helpful to you in organizing a program that will give youngsters under your tutelage the greatest opportunity for success in athletics.

It makes no difference what sport you coach or intend to coach, and little difference as to the level—the material in this book is applicable. Naturally, the relevance and importance of specific material will be affected by your own experience and the situation in which you find yourself. There are also some generalizations throughout; therefore, some flexibility in your thinking will be necessary in applying the information that follows.

Be cautious about disregarding some of the information as being irrelevant or unworthy unless you have already experienced life in the coaching profession. There is, after all, a huge gap between the classroom and real life, and until you've experienced both, you'll want to avoid making snap judgments about the material in this or any book on coaching.

Coaching is fun, exciting, sometimes difficult, always time-consuming, and never dull. It is the epitome of a "people" profession. That is to say, your "product" is human beings, taught by you, using the sometimes highly emotional experience of athletic participation as a tool. This feature is what will set you apart from all other professional men and women. No one will ever be able to set a price tag on the value of the work you do in preparing youngsters to become productive citizens. Therefore, do not search this book trying to find specific coaching techniques for hitting a ball or "pumping iron." You will not find any. You will find a realistic description of the coaching profession—which is what sets this book apart from all others.

The information that follows is a result of years of experience, input from other coaches, and reactions from my students over a long period of time. It is through this book and young men and women like you that we hope to make a worthwhile contribution to the coaching profession.

We wish you the best in life and hope you become one of the most successful coaches ever.

Ralph J. Sabock
Michael D. Sabock

> If I can supply you with a thought,
> You may remember it or you may not.
> But if I can make you think a thought
>   for yourself,
> I have indeed added to your stature.
>
> Elbert Hubbard

ACKNOWLEDGMENTS

We would like to express our thanks to Brian Siegrist of the Penn State Athletic Media Relations Office; to Mike Korcek of the Sports Information office at Northern Illinois University; to Ron Bracken, sports editor of the *Centre Daily Times;* to Lori Jones and Craig Horitz of the *Centre Daily Times;* to Dr. Robert Baker, Ashland University; to Dr. J. W. Yates, University of Kentucky; to Tom Caudill, Muskingum College; to Ron Pavlechko, State College High School Athletic Director; to Chris Gegares, Principal of Crestwood High School; to Jackie Estrada, Collegiate Press.

Finally, our thanks go to Cheryl Norman for her superb help in preparing the manuscript over the years.

1

COACHES, ATHLETES, AND ETHICS

Every book dealing with coaching should begin with a chapter on ethics, because nothing else will matter if you, as a coach, do not have a positive set of ethical values. All your knowledge of a sport, your teaching ability, and your goals and ambitions will eventually turn to ashes and your obligation to the youngsters you coach will have been violated if you fail to demonstrate personal and professional integrity of the highest order.

> The best chance you have of making a big success in this world is to decide from square one that you are going to do it ethically.
> —*Allen Greenspan, Federal Reserve Board Chairman*

I do not believe anyone can be a dishonest, unethical person and still be a good coach. To deliberately break rules, to cheat, to be unethical is to violate a basic trust that is inherent in fulfilling the role of coach. Indeed, the more any individual breaks trust the more it becomes part of that person's being, and when faced with moral dilemmas his or her first impulse is to cheat.

Unfortunately, a lack of ethical and moral behavior exists in all facets of our society, more so than ever it seems. As a result, some educators and parents are now insisting that values be taught in our schools again, simply because desir-

> Integrity has no need for rules.

able attitudes such as scruples, ethics, honesty, and integrity have been ignored for too long. Some believe we are now in the throes of a moral cesspool. Athletic coaches are in an excellent position to influence this situation in a positive way, simply because they are the foundation, the rock, on which athletic teams are built.

Despite the fact that some of the greatest problems in the history of sport have been and will continue to be caused by rules violations, the topic of ethics is regularly given slight attention or completely ignored in many textbooks, classrooms, coaching workshops, and clinics.

Obviously, ethical behavior in athletics has been a concern of educators for many years; it is not some recent discovery or new problem area. Human nature and society being what they are, it would appear that the issue of ethical behavior in competition and coaching will continue to be of great concern as long as athletic programs exist.

> An absorbing interest of the public and students has created an atmosphere not always purest. . . . There has been evident improvement in the rules; what is needed most is to improve in the ethical standards of all persons interested in athletics. Conformity to athletic rules is too much of a technicality and not enough of a principle— athletics, like every other form of amusement or business, must eventually rest on sound ethics. It is unfortunate in the extreme that the public mind is so eager for amusement that it becomes indifferent to the ethical conditions surrounding the game—it is a manifest waste of energy to spend time in denouncing athletics; what is needed is efficient leadership by men to whom principle is dearer than anything else. . . . We shall never reform athletics simply by rules, we shall reform it only when we have inspired young men to cling to high ideals and to be governed by sound ethics.
>
> *—President Oxley Thompson, The Ohio State University, 1904*

Some believe that ethics, fair play, and honesty are suffering more abuse in athletics today than at any time in our history. The literature and news media regularly report recruiting violations, altered transcripts, cheating, questionable coaching tactics, and abuse of officials on all levels of sport.

Throughout the world of athletics, *sportsmanship*, *ethics*, and *honesty* have become synonymous. Defining these terms is as easy as looking in a dictionary, but getting everyone to agree on the true meaning of such words as *standards, principles, moral duty, good, bad, right,* and *wrong* is quite another matter, and this ambiguity is where much of the problem lies. It is virtually impossible for any group of people with varying backgrounds to agree about the meaning of these terms.

ETHICAL STANDARDS

In actuality there are only three kinds of ethical standards: high, low, or none at all. *Webster's Ninth New Collegiate Dictionary* offers definitions of *ethic* and *ethical* that seem appropriate for each of us in the coaching profession:

> The discipline dealing with what is good and bad and with moral duty and obligation.

> A set of moral principles or values.

> Principles of conduct governing an individual or group.

> Conforming to accepted professional standards of conduct.

While all of these definitions are appropriate, the one that is of prime importance to coaches is the last one. Of course, it is also the one that causes the most friction between coaches, because of the unclear meaning of "accepted professional standards of conduct." You would be hard pressed to find a unanimous interpretation of this phrase among coaches. Nevertheless, coaches should still be able to agree on some basic expectations of themselves

> Those who ignore history are bound to repeat it.

and others. For example, coaches are expected to teach their teams to play by the rules, to teach fair play, to teach good sportsmanship, and to observe rules and their intent.

Within this context lies another troubling factor: the vast differences in interpretation among coaches as to where they draw the line between clever strategy and unethical conduct. This difference probably causes more conflict and antagonism between coaches than any other factor, because what one coach believes to be a great strategy might be perceived as unethical behavior by another.

Sportsmanship Versus Gamesmanship

Ethical behavior on the part of a coach involves not only observing the rules of a particular game but also, and more important, behaving according to the true spirit of the game, or according to the unwritten rules that are an integral part of every sport. These rules are concerned with the conduct of a coach or competitor and have been established and observed through the years under the heading of *sportsmanship*, or fair play.

Violating the spirit of a game is often referred to as *gamesmanship*—doing something simply to upset or psych out an opponent in order to win. For example, in golf it is not against the written rules to make noise or accidentally develop a coughing fit while an opponent is putting. However, everyone is expected to be quiet at this time because it is in the spirit of the game to do so.

Similarly, a track athlete shouldn't play "silly games" at the starting line in an effort to upset other runners. According to the spirit of the game athletes should simply line up and run the race to see who is fastest; mind games are not part of a race for true sportsmen.

Taunting an opponent, having an in-your-face attitude, and trash talking have become commonplace on all levels of competition today. Consequently, rule makers have adopted rules directed at curtailing or eliminating this kind of unsportsmanlike conduct. The irony is that conduct of this sort could be eliminated overnight if head coaches made it clear to athletes that such behavior is unacceptable and will not be tolerated—*period*.

In all game situations, officials are involved to see that the written rules are obeyed. But observing the unwritten rules, as dictated by the spirit of the game in each particular sport, is governed by each coach's personal philosophy of coaching and standards of ethical behavior. Some coaches take great delight in studying the rule book to see how far they can bend certain rules without breaking them. Even though they often violate the true meaning of the rules, they justify their actions by stating that, according to the book, they have not broken any rules. In their minds, this is good coaching, because it involves the strategy of making the rule book work in their favor. They feel they have outsmarted the opposition. Actually they are beating the rules, even though technically they are not. Some believe that such strategy is clever coaching even though it violates the spirit of the game. Others think this behavior isn't fair because, in their opinion, beating the rules has no place in athletic contests.

Teaching Ethical Conduct

For years coaches have been claiming that sport is a builder of strong character and honesty in those who participate, and this claim remained unchallenged for years. Sports have always had critics, but they were usually people outside the realm of sports competition. Today we are in an era of accountability. Critics demand proof or some evidence that coaches are doing the good things they claim to be doing in athletics. The number of cheating violations taking place in athletic programs across the country makes this evidence increasingly harder to produce.

> The measure of a person is not money or possessions, but a person's real wealth is character.

Participation in athletics can provide one of the greatest opportunities for youngsters to learn honesty, integrity, dignity, the need to obey rules, and ethical behavior. However, young people can also learn the opposite of all these values through athletics.

One of the difficulties coaches encounter in attempting to teach or expect ethical conduct is the fact that everyone comes from varying backgrounds and experiences with differing views as to what is right or wrong, fair or unfair, acceptable or unacceptable behavior.

Nevertheless, the fact remains that it does not matter one bit if you are a coach or an athlete, famous or unknown, rich or poor; there is no excuse for cheating, stealing, lying, or deliberately harming another person. These attitudes and actions simply cannot be tolerated in a civilized society and certainly not in an athletic program. This is an area that demands every coach's attention.

Ethical behavior is not inborn. Children must be taught right from wrong, and in athletics it is the sole responsibility of you, the coach, to teach it. Just observe young children at play: They rarely show sportsmanship or generosity in their games. Children may take advantage of an opponent, make up rules for their own benefit, and possibly have temper tantrums when they lose. It is only when youngsters begin to mature and to observe adult behavior in athletics that they learn what sportsmanship means.

Athletics provides excellent opportunities for youngsters to develop moral values. Athletic competition is loaded with circumstances involving ethical behavior. These instances are real and immediate and demand some action or decision from the participants.

For centuries, education has been concerned with the development of moral and ethical values in students. There is no invention or secret formula known to humankind that can ensure a good and solid society if personal integrity, honesty, and self-discipline are lacking.

Athletics can be a significant factor in developing young people's ethical values. It all depends on you, the coach, and whether you make a conscientious effort to teach youngsters the importance of high ethical standards by word or, more important, by deed. If you can instill these qualities in young people through sport, you can rightfully say that sport does build strength of character for those

> To educate a person in intellect alone and not in scruples is to produce a menace to society.
> —*Theodore Roosevelt*

who have the courage to participate. These lessons will be remembered long after game scores have been forgotten. It is also this kind of teaching that will enable you to live with the unhappy message the scoreboard sometimes carries, because you know that the outcome of a single game is not the beginning or end of the world. Good character is formed by living under conditions that demand good conduct.

Competition and Winning at All Costs

High school athletes are at a stage where they urgently need to feel important to their peers. They need to have friends and to feel themselves loyal members of a group for which they have real enthusiasm. The craving for excitement and adventure is normal; yet today's world gives a youngster fewer opportunities than ever before to satisfy it. The drama and excitement of competitive sports, the demands for efficiency and excellence, for courage and self-discipline, meet many needs of adolescent boys and girls.

Plato said, "You can discover more about a person in an hour of play than in a year of conversation." Competition brings out both the best and the worst in people. Competition is part of life, and we face it from the

day we are born until we die. The infant vies with brothers and sisters vying for attention from mother, and the child competes with brothers, sisters, and play-mates for access to toys. School-age children compete with each other for grades in school, to make the honor roll, to draw the best picture, or to write the best paper. Young people compete with each other to see who's the coolest or the best dressed, and they go on to compete for girlfriends or boyfriends. Youngsters learn to compete for first chair in band, for parts in plays, for a place on a team,

and for a teacher's attention. As they grow up, they face competition for a mate and a well-paying job.

Wherever there is life, there is con-flict, and life without rivalry, anxieties, and strains simply does not exist. As long as games are played, there will be a winner and a loser, and it is everyone's lot to play both roles.

Many would have us believe that ethical violations occur in athletics mainly because of coaches' desire to win. If it weren't for this single factor, why would anyone bother to stoop to unethical behavior, they ask, because the outcome of a game wouldn't matter.

To a degree this is true, but a parallel can be drawn with the common mistake people make in saying that "money is the root of all evil." The real saying is that "the love of money is the root of all evil." Money itself has no moral properties.

And so it is in athletics. Wanting to win is natural. It is only when winning becomes the sole purpose of athletic competition that violating ethical conduct becomes a temptation some cannot resist. Doing what is right in the face of temptation is not easy. It re-quires not only courage but the ethical commitment to do what is right no matter the consequences.

The following excerpt, from a letter sent by a former student now coaching on the Division I level, further illustrates this point:

> And what a business—so many illegal things go on . . . I feel I'm in a dilemma at times. I hope to be a head coach someday but the moral and ethical question is a big one—do I want to cheat to win? . . . I could ask myself that as an assistant—

especially with recruiting. I haven't cheated yet and I don't want to, but the unspoken rule here is either win or look for another job.

When the outcome of an athletic event is on the line, what will be most important to you, the game or your own integrity? This should not even be a question for you. If it is, you do not belong in the coaching profession—regardless of what other coaches do or what you believe they do. You still have to look in the mirror every morning, and you must remember what kind of lessons you teach your athletes through example alone. Although you need to talk to athletes about values, your words will be meaningless unless *you* live them as well.

In too many instances unethical acts committed in an athletic contest by a coach or player are explained away simply by saying, "I hate to lose; therefore I play (or coach) hard all the time." This is plain rubbish—there is no excuse for unethical conduct.

Actions Speak Louder Than Words

Can ethical behavior be learned through sport? The answer is yes, but the lesson is not automatic, and it cannot be assimilated through osmosis. Ethics must be taught by the coach. There is no other way. To teach ethics, you must be personally ethical. For example, the coach who holds illegal practice sessions before the rules allow is teaching dishonesty, plain and simple.

> Unless you are honest in small matters you won't be in large ones. If you cheat even a little, you won't be honest with greater responsibilities.
> Luke 16:10, *The Living Bible*

There are no degrees of honesty. You cannot be just a little dishonest or a little bit unethical. A person is either honest or dishonest, ethical or unethical. There are no shades of gray. When you give lip service to the rules and then violate them yourself, you are advocating cheating—not by what you say but by what you do. When you say one thing and do another, your students will disregard the words and assume that your actions are a truer indication of your beliefs. All the words in your vocabulary will not change this fact.

Coaches have been heard to say that they don't *want* to violate any rules but feel they must because their opponents do. Therefore, to give their athletes a fair chance to compete, they have to cheat, too. This is not a reason, nor is it good logic. It is simply an excuse to break the rules. Coaches who actively practice this kind of reasoning do so because (1) They are ambitious and anxious to move up the coaching ranks on the basis of their team's won-lost record, (2) they are afraid for their jobs, or (3) they are dishonest. What-

> If something is right but a lot of people don't do it, it is still right.
> If something is wrong but a lot of people do it, it is still wrong.

ever the reason, behavior of this sort is unethical. It is such conduct that makes a mockery out of the claim that sport builds character. Sport by itself can neither build personality traits nor tear them down. It all comes down to you, the coach, and what is taught by your actions. Talk is meaningless when contradicted by action. Don't ever forget this.

ETHICAL DILEMMAS

Many situations in athletic contests demand that coaches or athletes react to or make decisions involving honesty and ethics. You need to recognize these situations because they become important "teachable moments" for you and should not be ignored. Many of these incidents will not be covered in a rule book, but they do challenge fair play or the spirit of the game.

An *ethical dilemma* is defined here as a situation in which a person is faced with a difficult choice and in which no clear-cut answer or action exists. People in athletics are faced with these kinds of circumstances regularly.

To help you clarify some of your values and to learn how others think, consider the following situations. Some have nothing to do with athletics, as you will see, but they do have a lot to do with your own personal code of conduct. No attempt has been made to tell you what course of action is correct; you will have to figure that out for yourself. Don't waste time arguing over whether these situations should have arisen in the first place. They did, so the question is: How would you deal with them?

1. While in the supermarket you notice a well-dressed woman in front of you. As she pulls her hand out of her coat pocket, she drops a $50 bill on the floor without realizing it. She goes into another aisle, and there is no one in sight as you pick up the money. Will you keep the money, or will you call after her to return it? Why?

2. In a girls' softball game, a runner trying to steal second base was called out. The second baseman dropped the ball but recovered it quickly. However, the umpire did not see this, being blocked out by the runner and the dust. The runner told the umpire that the second baseman dropped the ball. The umpire then asked the second baseman whether she had indeed dropped the ball. This situation raises two questions: Should the umpire have asked the second baseman? Since she did, how should the player respond? Why?

3. One of the good clothing stores in town is having a big sale. You visit the store and purchase a sweater. The sale price is not on the tag, so the clerk has to figure out the price. You pay the bill in cash and leave the store. As you are walking down the street, you begin thinking about the cost of the sweater, and it occurs to you that the clerk actually charged you $10 less than she should have. The clerk does not know you, and you probably won't be in that store again for six months or more. Anyway, chances of the error being detected and connected with you are slim to none. Would you return to the store and point out the mistake? Why? What would you do if the same clerk had overcharged you? Why?

4. In tennis, players are responsible to officiate their side of the net. During a crucial match, player A makes an obvious bad call in her favor. How would you as the other player respond? Would you complain to player A, ignore the call, or make a bad call yourself to get even?

5. During the waning seconds of a football game, the team with the ball needed to stop the clock but had no time-outs left. An assistant coach quickly sent in a substitute with instructions to fake an injury. On the next play the boy faked a neck injury, which brought the game to a halt. Medics came on the field and took the boy to the hospital in an ambulance. The boy went through a series of x-rays, after which he finally confessed to his frantic parents and doctor that he had faked the injury. What is your reaction to this behavior on the part of the coach? What do you think the young man learned?

6. The score in a women's field hockey game was 0–0 when a player broke loose down the field and flipped a shot into the lower corner of the net. The officials signaled a goal, whereupon the players on both teams moved to midfield to line up for the face-off. The girl who had scored the goal went up to an official and said, "It wasn't a goal, I hit the ball off the back of my stick." This is illegal in field hockey. The startled official thought for a minute, reversed her decision, declared no goal, and gave the ball out of bounds to the other team at their end of the field. When questioned after the game, the girl said she knew the official hadn't seen it, but she thought it wasn't right that her team should have the goal counted. If you were the girl's coach, how would you react to the player and the official?

7. You are in your first coaching job in the role of an assistant. The head coach is a veteran in the profession, the situation is great, and you wouldn't mind being head coach there someday. Through midseason the team is struggling; for some reason it just isn't clicking. Naturally, the critics have noticed this, and, as usual, some grumbling is heard around town. One evening several members of the power structure in the community come to see you—unofficially, of course. They tell you they believe the head coach is no longer effective, and they are going to work to remove this person. They say they would like to see you take over as head coach and ask if you would be interested. How would you react?

8. You are a graduate assistant at a prestigious Division I university. You call a high school coach to tell him/her that one of the university coaches plans on

attending their next athletic event to look at a super prospect. The coach tells you that would be a waste of time because the youngster in question just got hurt in practice and will not play, which is not public knowledge. This team's opponent happens to be coached by a friend of yours who gave you your first coaching job. If your buddy had this information, it would significantly alter his preparation for the game, which in turn would give his team a better chance to win. The question is, Do you pass this information on to your friend, or do you keep quiet? Why?

9. The final event of the girls' dual track meet was a relay. As the anchor runners from both teams crossed the finish line, the second girl yelled to the starter that the other team had passed the baton out of the exchange zone. If this was true, the winning team would be disqualified and lose the race. Because of an oversight, there had been no inspector at the exchange zone. Consequently, the starter called the third and fourth runners of the winning team together and asked them if their exchange was in the zone or out. If the official was justified in asking the questions, what kind of response should the two girls give?

10. During a junior high championship track meet, a coach was told that one

of her very good runners could not compete because the coach had left her name off the entry form. The girl burst into tears because she was so disappointed. The coach was upset because it was her fault, so she decided to enter the girl in her regular events anyway by using the name and number of one of her teammates who was officially entered in the meet. What lesson do you suppose the girl learned through this? Do you see anything wrong with what the coach chose to do, or was she justified in her action?

11. Many basketball coaches teach their players that when there is a scramble for the ball and it goes out of bounds, a player should get it and prepare to put it in play even if he or she had touched it just before it went out of bounds. The reasoning is that if the official wasn't sure of the call, he might give it to this player. No rule is being broken because the call is the official's decision, and if the official makes a mistake, it is his or her fault—correct? Or are these coaches teaching a tactic that really isn't ethical?

12. At the outset of a high school basketball tournament, one of the coaches decided her team would have a better chance to advance to the finals if they could play in the losers' bracket (double elimination). So she played her junior varsity team the whole game and kept the varsity team on the bench. Naturally, the team lost and moved into the losers' bracket. The opposing coach was very angry. She charged the other coach with making a travesty of the game and violating coaching ethics. The other coach said she broke no rules and therefore her tactics constituted smart coaching. What is your reaction to this?

13. While you are driving on a bypass around a large city, an armored truck passes you at a high rate of speed. When the truck gets in front of you, the back door flies open, a bag falls out, and suddenly the air is filled with money. The truck keeps going, but a lot of cars come to a halt, including yours. People gather up money and drive away. You find yourself with $15,000 in your hands, with virtually no chance of ever getting caught. That evening an announcement is made on TV requesting that people turn in whatever money they picked up and promising that no questions will be asked. What would you do?

14. You are one point away from winning the conference championship in tennis—a dream about to come true. Your opponent hits what appears to be a winner deep to your baseline with such speed that you cannot return the shot. But, there is a legitimate question in your mind about the ball being inbounds or out. You honestly couldn't tell and neither could anyone else. If you call the ball out, the match is over and you are the champion—call it in and the match continues. It is your call; what will it be, and why? Would your call be influenced by the score or by the fact that no one else would ever know if the ball was in or out?

15. A college quarterback was 13 yards short of breaking the career passing record of a great former player. However, it was the last game of the season, there were only 70 seconds left in the game, and the other team had the ball. When the ball was snapped to start the next play, the defensive team dropped to the ground and allowed the ball carrier to score, untouched. After the ensuing

The world needs men and women

- who cannot be bought;
- whose word is their bond;
- who put character above wealth;
- who are larger than their vocations;
- who do not hesitate to take chances;
- who will not lose their identity in a crowd;
- who will be honest in small things as in great things;
- who will make no compromise with wrong;
- whose ambitions are not confined to their own selfish desires;
- who will not say they do it "because everybody else does it";
- who are true to their friends through good report and evil report, in adversity as well as prosperity;
- who do not believe that shrewdness and cunning are the best qualities for winning;
- who are not ashamed to stand for the truth when it is unpopular;
- who can say "no" with emphasis although the rest of the world says "yes."

God, make me this kind of person.

—Leonard Wagner (*Hymns for the Family of God*, Paragin Associates, Inc., Nashville, p. 532) kickoff the quarterback completed two quick passes to establish an all-time passing record for college football. At this point, the opposing coach was livid with anger. He branded the action a disgrace to football, a lack of class on the part of the other coach, and a humiliating experience for his team. It was not clear who told the defense to collapse. No rules were broken. Was the spirit of the game violated? Were coaching ethics involved? Why?

16. At the end of a busy week you decide to treat yourself and a friend to dinner in a local restaurant. After paying your bill, you discover the cashier gave you back too much change. What will you do?

The preceding examples represent only a few of the vast number of ethical dilemmas that people face on a regular basis. This list could be multiplied many times over by anyone who has coached any kind of athletic team for any period of time.

Is it possible to practice one kind of ethics in athletics and another in one's personal life? If you believe in preparing youngsters for life through participation in athletics, it follows that ethical values have to be consistent whatever the circumstances.

Unless your answers to these dilemmas reflect complete honesty and integrity, you cannot expect your players to exhibit these qualities in similar situations—especially during the excitement of a highly competitive contest. This is one area in sport where the opportunity for character development is particularly great. But this lesson must be taught by you; athletes will not automatically learn from the situation itself—if they do, they might learn that dishonesty can be justified if it will help win a game.

Most people would agree that dishonesty is not a desirable quality. Many people believe that character is "caught" rather than taught and that each experience a boy or girl has at home, at play, or in school shapes that youngster's standard of conduct, good or bad. The coach who assumes that athletes will develop high ethical standards merely by participating in athletics is greatly mistaken. This process is not automatic.

PROFESSIONAL ETHICS

Professional ethics can be defined as a coach's conduct in fulfilling the obligations of the position in relation to other people in and out of the school setting. Professional ethics for a coach fall into five distinct areas.

Coach to Teacher

Teachers have reciprocal responsibility to each other. Problems of professional ethics can arise when a student speaks critically of a teacher to the coach, when a student speaks critically of a coach to a teacher, or when a teacher or coach criticizes a fellow teacher in front of a student.

Professionally, such criticism is unacceptable. It can cause a great deal of friction and bad feelings within a faculty. Coaches are more apt to be involved in such situations than almost any other teacher in the school because of the role they fill and the informality of their relationship with many students. You should never be outwardly sympathetic toward any student's criticism of a fellow teacher.

Coach to Parent

Conversations between a parent and a coach should be considered privileged communication. When parents talk with you about some specific concern they have for their youngster, they usually preface their remarks with, "Don't tell my child that I talked to you about this, or he will get really upset." Naturally, parents expect their requests to be honored. Even if they don't specifically state the desire to keep a conversation in strictest confidence, you should have enough good judgment to know when to keep a conversation to yourself.

Most conversations of this type come about because a youngster isn't playing in the games or was playing but has now been benched. Naturally, parents would like to know why, because of their interest and because their youngster comes home every night feeling discouraged. The youngster normally does not want the parents to go to the coach, for fear the coach will be annoyed and take it out on him or her.

In one case, a parent asked a coach why his son was benched, only to have the boy come home from practice the next day with tears in his eyes and ask his father, "Why did you call the coach?" The coach had told the boy that he definitely would not start the next game, simply because the coach had a policy that any time a parent asked him about a son's playing time, he would not start the boy in the next game under any circumstance. The boy was crushed.

Coach to Student

Students sometimes feel the need to confide in an adult other than a parent. The logical person is often you, the coach. You might be flattered that a student wants to confide in you and ask for advice. But there is danger in agreeing not to tell the parents something, because you might discover that the problem is of such magnitude that the parents ought to be aware of it. In this situation you will have backed yourself into a corner.

Unless you can convince the youngster to tell the parents, you must either keep quiet or violate a confidence—both no-win positions.

A safe approach to the opening statement, "Don't tell my mother or dad what I'm about to tell you," would be to say, "I can't promise that. Let's talk and then decide what is best for you to do under the circumstances."

Coach to Administration

In far too many cases the obligations of a coach to school administrators are clearly defined, whereas the obligations of administrators to the coach are not. There are three main areas of concern in this regard: honesty, loyalty, and support. The fact that coaches and school administrators deal with the public to a degree greater than most other teachers makes these areas essential to both of them.

The implications for the coach are clear. You must be truthful in all your dealings with an administrator. Under no circumstances should you speak critically of a school administrator to the public. Some coaches feel frustrated because they believe a particular administrator is hampering part or all of the athletic program. In desperation, they criticize this person to people in the community, hoping that they will exert pressure on the administrator and get things changed.

Such criticism is not only unethical, it is potentially dangerous to your professional career. In one or two instances, it might seem to work. But even though you may have won a battle, the administrator will eventually win the war, and it will prove costly to you.

One area in which school superintendents frequently violate ethical behavior is in the procedure for interviewing applicants for a coaching position. Unless the interview was a disaster, most applicants are told that they are a fine prospect and will be contacted in just a few days about the position. Each applicant might naturally assume that he or she will be offered the job. Days, and possibly weeks, will then pass by without a word. Finally, the applicant summons up enough courage to call the superintendent's office, only to learn the job was filled quite some time ago, and the school was just too busy to notify the applicant.

This practice could be classified as bait casting. All the legitimate prospects think the job is theirs. They are all kept on the hook until the employing officials find the person they want, whereupon all the rest are simply dropped. The fact that the superintendent promised to be in touch often means nothing; this practice is not unusual.

Another violation in this area of professional ethics occurs when coaching responsibility is taken away from a coach. In many states, since coaching is strictly an extracurricular activity, this assignment can be taken from an individual at any time by the superintendent of schools. There is no obligation to explain why.

More than one coach has settled down at the breakfast table to enjoy a cup of coffee and the morning paper only to read in the sports section that he or she was fired the night before. More than one coach has learned that his or her coaching job is gone by looking at next year's teaching contract and discovering that no coaching assignment is indicated. And more than one coach has been dismissed without any explanation other than, "We think it is time for a change." These are painful but real examples of a lack of professional ethics on the part of some administrators.

Coach to Coach

This last category of professional ethics includes interactions between coaches within a school, as well as between schools. The greatest single factor causing antagonism between coaches in the same school is the conflict that occurs when one coach expects his or her athletes to concentrate only on a specific sport at the expense of all others. This pressure is selfish, puts athletes in a difficult situation, and angers colleagues.

It is not unusual for conflict to develop between coaches in different schools as well. This occurs primarily because one coach views conduct by an opposing coach as unethical. Nothing will infuriate you more and stay with you longer than your perception of unethical behavior by an opposing coach. When coaches begin to feud, the games often become bitter grudge matches, which complicates the matter further. This kind of behavior on the part of coaches makes a mockery of the claim that they serve as positive role models for youngsters to emulate. Ideally, the winningest coach should also win the trophy for sportsmanship.

The Representative Assembly of the National Education Association adopted a Code of Ethics and Bill of Teacher Rights as a guide for the teaching profession. Since all teachers should be members of a united profession, the basic principles enumerated apply to all persons engaged in the professional aspects of education—elementary, secondary, and collegiate. This code is reprinted here (on page 16) by special permission of the National Education Association.

I have to live with myself, and so
I want to be fit for myself to know.
I want to be able as days go by,
Always to look myself straight in the eye.
I don't want to stand with the setting sun,
And hate myself for the things I've done.
I can never hide myself from me;
I see what others may never see,
I know what others may never know,
I can never fool myself, and so—
Whatever happens, I want to be
Self-respecting and conscience free.
—*Author unknown*

DISCUSSION QUESTIONS

1. Debate this statement: "There are no degrees of honesty."

2. Are there such things as situational ethics? If so, give examples.

3. Many coaches pressure or antagonize officials. What is your opinion of that type of coach? Does this behavior have anything to do with ethics?

4. Some coaches encourage their players to bend rules and to attempt to upset their opponents. How do you feel about such tactics?

CODE OF ETHICS
of the Education Profession
ADOPTED BY THE 1975 NEA REPRESENTATIVE ASSEMBLY

Preamble
The educator, believing in the worth and dignity of each human being, recognizes the supreme importance of the pursuit of truth, devotion to excellence, and the nurture of democratic principles. Essential to these goals is the protection of freedom to learn and to teach and the guarantee of equal educational opportunity for all. The educator accepts the responsibility to adhere to the highest ethical standards.

The educator recognizes the magnitude of the responsibility inherent in the teaching process. The desire for the respect and confidence of one's colleagues, of students, of parents, and of the members of the community provides the incentive to attain and maintain the highest possible degree of ethical conduct. The Code of Ethics of the Education Profession indicates the aspiration of all educators and provides standards by which to judge conduct.

The remedies specified by the NEA and/or its affiliates for the violation of any provision of this Code shall be exclusive and no such provision shall be enforceable in any form other than one specifically designated by the NEA or its affiliates.

Principle I: Commitment to the Student
The educator strives to help each student realize his or her potential as a worthy and effective member of society. The educator therefore works to stimulate the spirit of inquiry, the acquisition of knowledge and understanding, and the thoughtful formulation of worthy goals.

In fulfillment of the obligation to the student, the educator—

1. Shall not unreasonably restrain the student from independent action in the pursuit of learning.

2. Shall not unreasonably deny the student access to varying points of view.

3. Shall not deliberately suppress or distort subject matter relevant to the student's progress.

4. Shall make reasonable effort to protect the student from conditions harmful to learning or to health and safety.

5. Shall not intentionally expose the student to embarrassment or disparagement.

6. Shall not on the basis of race, color, creed, sex, national origin, marital status, political or religious beliefs, family, social or cultural background, or sexual orientation, unfairly:

   a. Exclude any student from participation in any program;

   b. Deny benefits to any student;

   c. Grant any advantage to any student.

7. Shall not use professional relationships with students for private advantage.

8. Shall not disclose information about students obtained in the course of professional service, unless disclosure serves a compelling professional purpose or is required by law.

Principle II: Commitment to the Profession
The education profession is vested by the public with a trust and responsibility requiring the highest ideals of professional service.

In the belief that the quality of the services of the education profession directly influences the nation and its citizens, the educator shall exert every effort to raise professional standards, to promote a climate that encourages the exercise of professional judgment, to achieve conditions which attract persons worthy of the trust to careers in education, and to assist in preventing the practice of the profession by unqualified persons.

In fulfillment of the obligation to the profession, the educator—

1. Shall not in an application for a professional position deliberately make a false statement or fail to disclose a material fact related to competency and qualifications.

2. Shall not misrepresent his/her professional qualifications.

3. Shall not assist entry into the profession of a person known to be unqualified in respect to character, education, or other relevant attribute.

4. Shall not knowingly make a false statement concerning the qualifications of a candidate for a professional position.

5. Shall not assist a noneducator in the unauthorized practice of teaching.

6. Shall not disclose information about colleagues obtained in the course of professional service unless disclosure serves a compelling professional purpose or is required by law.

7. Shall not knowingly make false or malicious statements about a colleague.

8. Shall not accept any gratuity, gift, or favor that might impair or appear to influence professional decisions or actions.

5. What would you do if your principal suspended a player from the team for causing a disruption during the school day?

6. What are professional ethics?

7. "You can discover more about a person in an hour of play than in a year of conversation." Interpret this statement.

8. Is going on strike violating professional ethics?

9. Is it ethical to play not to win? Why?

10. When do strategy and ethics come into conflict?

11. What is meant by observing "the spirit of the game"?

12. Give a personal example of a situation involving honesty and ethics in athletics.

13. Several principles are stated in the Code of Ethics adopted by the NEA as a guide for teachers. Discuss how these relate to a teacher/coach.

14. Why are ethics and honesty a problem in athletics?

15. Is a player ever justified in telling an official a call was incorrect in that player's favor?

16. Should officials ever ask athletes questions about something that happened during a game and then base their decision on the response? Why?

17. What is the message in the 1904 quote from President Thompson?

18. What is the best way for a coach to teach honesty, sportsmanship, and ethical behavior?

19. Interpret the statement: "Character is caught, not taught."

20. What would you do if your "boss" asked you to do something you knew was a violation of the rules?

Coaching is truly an exciting occupation, involving the whole gamut of emotions from super highs to heartbreak. And, as you will see, there is a great deal more to coaching than fun and games. This chapter is an attempt to aid you in understanding all that coaching entails so that you don't enter the field with stars in your eyes only to be caught by surprise when confronted by reality—hence the title of this book and the inclusion of this chapter. Keep in mind that a coach is in the "people business," and that is not always easy.

One of the most important decisions you will ever make is what your profession will be—what you intend to do with your life. Perhaps this is not an issue for you because you have already decided. If so, things are somewhat simplified in your case, since everything you do from now on should have purpose.

If you have decided that coaching is what you want to do, so much the better. Read and study as much as you can about coaches and the coaching profession, participate as an athlete if possible, attend coaching clinics, and become as knowledgeable as possible as quickly as possible.

If, on the other hand, you are not sure that coaching is the right career choice for you but you think it *might* be, there is only one sure way to find out, and that is to try it. If you choose to stay in the profession, fine. If not, at least you won't go through life wondering whether you missed your calling because you never gave coaching a chance.

If you haven't yet decided to become a coach but are thinking about it, the first thing you should do is establish some priorities. Take a long look in the mirror and ask yourself what will be most important to you when you begin working for a living. If making a lot of money and acquiring material possessions and stability rank high in your desires, then coaching is the wrong profession for you. These three things are not normally experienced in coaching. On the other hand, if teaching young people, competition, excitement, challenge, giving of yourself, and self-satisfaction attract you, then coaching could be the right choice.

I have come to a frightening conclusion:
    I am the decisive element in the classroom.
It is my personal approach
    that creates the climate.
It is my daily mood that makes the weather.
As a teacher, I possess tremendous power
    to make a child's (student's) life
    miserable or joyous.
I can be a tool of torture
    or an instrument of inspiration.
I can humiliate or humor,
    hurt or heal.
In all situations
    it is my response that decides whether a crisis
    will be escalated
    or de-escalated,
and a child humanized
    or dehumanized.
    —*Author Unknown*

If you do decide to become a teacher and remain one until you retire, you will spend approximately forty years in the profession. If you coach and teach full time, you could be directly responsible for up to 500 students in any given school year, depending on the subject you teach. This adds up to some 20,000 boys and girls during your career.

Do you have any idea of the impact you can make on all those young lives, and of the incredible responsibility you will have over all those years? It is mind-boggling if you really think about it. We are not talking about the scores of athletic events here; we are talking about what happens to young people's lives because you were their teacher. If you firmly believe that one of your primary obligations as a teacher/coach is to help young people grow into healthy, relatively well-adjusted, productive adults, you are on the right track.

PERCEPTIONS OF HIGH SCHOOL ATHLETICS

One of the errors in thinking coaches frequently make is to assume that everyone views the existence and purposes of athletics the same way. This simply is not the case. It therefore becomes important for you to be aware of some common perceptions so that you can be more effective when dealing with the people most involved with high school athletics.

Athletes

Mostly you will find athletes "I" directed. That is to say, many of their basic concerns are self-centered; for example: Will I make the team? Will I be a starter? Will I play a lot? Will I earn a letter? Will I win an athletic scholarship?

Parents

The nature of being an athlete's parent is to view a team with tunnel vision. Regardless of the number of youngsters involved, parents tend to focus only on their own son or daughter. Of course, at the end of this "tunnel" they see a "star." It is safe to say that they lack objectivity. And therein lies the seeds of potential conflict.

Principal

The principal probably holds the most difficult position in any school, and many faculty members really do not appreciate the demands made on that position. Concerns of the principal include curriculum, band, school dances, plays, bus schedules, cafeteria, custodians, discipline problems, teacher strikes, teaching assignments, parent conferences, condition of the school building, leadership for the faculty, faculty evaluations, PTA meetings, special interest groups in the community, and interscholastic athletics, to mention just a few.

An athletic team is just one of many parts of a school community, not the major reason the school exists. Failure to recognize this fact can create serious and needless misunderstanding between you and the principal who, by the way, is directly responsible for every program in the school, including athletics.

Coaches

You will soon discover that a number of demands are placed on you as coach, beyond simply teaching skills and strategy.

About 90 percent of an iceberg is underwater and, therefore, unseen. So it is with coaching a team (see Figure 2.1). While the tip of the iceberg is very important and the most visible, the bottom area, largely invisible and unrecognized by the public, illustrates the parts of coaching the typical fan is unaware of.

Community

In the eyes of far too many citizens of the community, the most important consideration in athletics is the scoreboard—who won. The reasoning of a lot of these people is simple: If you are a good coach our team will win; if the team loses, you must be a poor coach. There is nothing complicated about the issue in the minds of these folks. Of course, these statements are generalizations, but they are fairly typical on the secondary school level.

IS COACHING THE CAREER FOR YOU?

Coaching is anything but a dull occupation—there is no doubt about that—but only for those who are dedicated and who enjoy it. For others, coaching is simply a lot of time-consuming, hard work that pays relatively little. There doesn't seem to be any middle ground. This is not a "ho-hum" profession to be entered into on a whim. Rather, it is one to prepare for because you really want to be a coach more than anything else. The late, great coach Paul "Bear" Bryant said, "The only reason to go into coaching is if you can't live without it."

Lee Corso, a former college coach said, "Coaching is not a job, it's a privilege. Coaching is like being a sculptor. You can create something no one else has created. It's yours; it's from your soul, your work; it's like a painting. That's the thrill of coaching. You don't get bored doing it. You have to set your priorities straight."

FIGURE 2.1
The coaching iceberg.

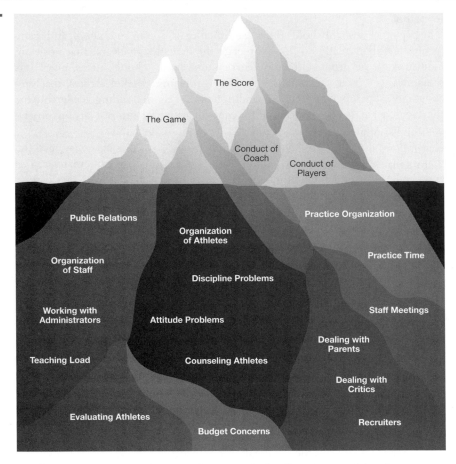

If someone were to ask you to give a reason for choosing coaching for a career, your answer might be similar to one of the following:

1. I like sports.

2. Since I enjoy playing the game, coaching will keep me in close touch with something I really like.

3. I liked my high school coach, so I decided to become a coach, too.

4. I want to be a college coach someday.

5. I needed to declare a major, and since I enjoy athletics I decided to try physical education and coaching.

6. I want the prestige of being a coach.

7. I think I would enjoy the excitement and glamour associated with coaching.

8. You get paid extra money for coaching.

9. I like working with young boys and girls.

10. I want to teach boys and girls to enjoy the game.

11. It looks like fun.

No doubt other reasons could be added to the list, but these are the most typical. Whether each reason is sound will not be discussed here, but everything that follows in this book should help you determine the appropriateness of the factors that influence your decision to prepare for a coaching career.

Cautionary Notes

I should clarify several points before we continue. The first is that coaching is rarely a lifelong occupation. There are a number of reasons for this—time and energy drains, age, health, stress, and getting fired, to mention just a few—but the fact is that most people get out of coaching long before reaching retirement age.

Second, success at and enjoyment of athletics does not necessarily mean you will experience success and enjoyment in coaching. Participating in athletics and coaching a team are two entirely different experiences. This is due in part to the degree of individual commitment and personal responsibility a coach has for the overall success of the team. Many people enter the profession because of an early interest in athletics, and although their reasoning is basically sound, they may need more insight into their true motives, along with a greater understanding of the profession.

Third, the fact is that money, glamour, and fame come to relatively few coaches, and even then not usually for long. The average sports fan and the typical school administrator have notoriously short memories concerning coaches' past records and accomplishments. Coaches rarely have an opportunity to rest on their laurels. A winning team last season makes little difference to fans if the current season is going badly. What happened yesterday is history; in the eyes of the fans, the present is what matters.

This concept is illustrated by a speech from the movie *Patton*. With a little imagination, you can visualize a coach returning to town after that big win, saying:

> For over a thousand years, Roman conquerors returning from the wars enjoyed the honor of the triumph, the tumultuous parade. In the procession came trumpeters and musicians and strange animals from the conquered territory with carts laden with treasure and captured armaments. The conqueror rode in a triumphal chariot with the day's prisoners walking in chains before him. Sometimes his children, robed in white, stood with him in the chariot or rode the trace horses. A slave stood behind the conqueror holding a golden crown and whispering in his ear the warning—that all glory is fleeting.

Will Rogers once said, "Being a hero must be about the shortest-lived profession on earth."

Emerson wrote, "Every hero at last becomes a bore." And so it is with coaches—and athletes, I might add.

The fourth point to be made here is that in most public school situations you will be hired as a coach with the understanding that your first responsibility will be to teach classes all day, every day, and that your coaching responsibilities are to be fulfilled above and beyond this workload. Naturally, there are exceptions, but you should be aware that if it is the love of athletics that leads you into the profession, it is also necessary to have a similar feeling about teaching classes.

The salary structure should give you a good idea about the relationship between your daily teaching responsibilities and coaching. If, for example, the beginning teaching salary is $30,000 or more and the coaching salary is $3,000, you are being paid ten times as much to teach classes as you are to coach. That is precisely the way most school principals view the importance of the two assignments.

To further illustrate this point, compare a sport season that lasts three months and that involves approximately 2.5 hours a day for 10 to 100 athletes, to a nine-month school year involving 7.5 hours a day with anywhere from 100 to 250 students each day. It is not difficult to understand where a coach's primary responsibility lies, at least in the eyes of the administration. Perhaps this is why school administrators say, "First we hire teachers, then we hire coaches." This is not to insinuate that coaches are not teachers, but rather to emphasize a coach's first responsibility—the daily teaching schedule, not an extracurricular activity. This is the rule, and you need to be aware of it to avoid accepting a position with the false assumption that you will only be a coach. Things just aren't done that way in most high schools. The irony here is that in spite of this emphasis, many coaches are still judged by their win/loss record rather than on their classroom record.

The final point to elaborate on is that coaching is many things above and beyond actually coaching a team, regardless of the situation in which the coach works. A high school coach wears many hats during the school year because of his or her unique role in the school community and because of the special relationship that normally exists between coach and athlete. You need to be aware of and to try to develop an understanding of your various roles and responsibilities (see Chapter 5).

Job Security

One of the main concerns everyone has upon entering a new profession is job security. Security in the coaching profession can be described simply as the odds against getting fired. Those who are in the profession are well aware that being fired is always a distinct possibility, and the risk is not necessarily confined to college coaches or to coaches of professional teams. Until coaches are granted tenure, if ever, there will be no job security in the coaching profession.

Longevity in high school coaching depends on a number of factors, some of which you can control and some which you cannot. There are four considerations you should be aware of at the outset:

1. The visibility of the team you coach and how much you win. The greater the fan interest in a particular team (which varies from community to community), the greater the impact on the number of years you spend in that position.

2. Your own ability as a coach. It doesn't matter how many assistants you have. If you are head coach, your ability to deal successfully with all the competencies required of the position will be critical.

3. Your faith in the youngsters on the team and the assistant coaches: faith that the athletes will perform in the excitement of competition the way they were taught in practice, and faith that your assistants are dedicated, loyal, and knowledgeable enough to do an outstanding job of teaching the skills and attitudes necessary for the athletes' success.

To further illustrate this point, keep in mind that you are preparing for a profession in which your success or failure lies in the hands of teenagers playing a game. Whereas salespeople need complete faith only in themselves and their ability to sell a product, and musicians must have faith in themselves to play well, coaches are evaluated by how well others perform as a result of their teaching. Men and women who choose to coach as a way of earning their living are placing their careers in "the hands of God and 16-year-old youngsters," as some coaches have put it. This takes faith. It also sets coaching apart from other professions.

This single factor, more than any other, is probably the greatest difference between a coach's approach to a season or a game and the approach of the young athletes. To the athletes, a game is to be played and enjoyed for the moment. To a dedicated coach, the game is a way of life and his or her future. This difference varies in direct proportion to the coach's level of ambition, which can become a trouble spot in the relationship between coach and team.

4. Cooperation with the school's administration. This requirement is discussed in greater detail later in this chapter; basically, it means that you should not expect administrators to adjust the school program solely to suit the needs of your athletic team. Schools can exist without sport, but sport on the secondary level cannot exist without the schools.

CONSIDERATIONS IN THE LIFE OF A COACH

Coaching high school students can be described with almost any word except boring. Coaching can be a truly great way to earn a living, because every day brings new challenges. Dealing with teenagers who are predictably unpredictable is enough to ensure that the coaching profession will not be boring. Associating with high school students, watching them grow as athletes and as young adults, and sharing the ecstasy of triumph or the disappointment of defeat are aspects of coaching that set it apart from any other teaching position. Coaches who are so eager to climb the ladder to bigger and better jobs that they are unaware of these aspects are to be pitied, for they have missed one of the most satisfactory experiences in the profession: associating with young athletes.

The competition surrounding every phase of a sports season is another factor that ensures coaching will not be monotonous. No sooner is one contest over than the next one takes over in a coach's thoughts. You will rarely have much time to savor a team's or an athlete's victory until the last game or match has been played. The presence of another opponent on the schedule will keep reminding you that what happened yesterday makes little difference today in competitive athletics.

One Day at a Time

There are two days in every week about which we should not worry, two days which should be kept free from fear and apprehension.

One of these days is *Yesterday*, with its mistakes and cares, its faults and blunders, its aches and pains. Yesterday has passed forever beyond our control. All the money in the world cannot bring back yesterday. We cannot undo a single act we performed; we cannot erase a single word said—Yesterday Is Gone!

The other day we should not worry about is *Tomorrow* with its possible burdens, its large promise and poor performance. Tomorrow is also beyond our immediate control. Tomorrow's sun will rise, either in splendor or behind a mask of clouds—but it will rise. Until it does we have no stake in tomorrow, for it is yet unborn.

This leaves only one day—*Today*! Any man can fight the battle of just one day. It is only when you and I have the burdens in these two awful eternities—Yesterday and Tomorrow—that we break down.

—*Author Unknown*

This is also a lesson youngsters should learn: The newspaper that praised them, you, or the team yesterday is in someone's trashcan today.

Frustrations

As in every profession, there are times of frustration. Many things can frustrate coaches, but generally the primary factor is impatience in trying to accomplish a specific goal in the sport they coach. Usually this goal is to have a winning team and the opportunity to organize the program in such a way that winning teams become the rule rather than the exception.

Some of this frustration will be directed toward the administrators of the school if they don't give you a free hand in organizing the program the way you think best. Their unwillingness, or inability, to grant every request you make in order to develop and expand a program can breed frustration. In such situations, coaches have a tendency to assume that the administrators just don't care and are "sitting on" the program. Occasionally this is true, but more often it is not true at all, and the coach, through an understandably narrow point of view, might be making a false assumption.

You can also become frustrated if you are impatient. Normally it takes time to develop a good program, and it might be several years before a varsity team meets your goals. In the meantime, a team can be losing games, which often compounds the feeling. Losing is particularly frustrating when a team comes out on the short end of the score in a game they should have won. Allowing frustration to grow and dwelling on it can seriously hamper your effectiveness as a coach.

Rewards

Coaching can, of course, be a highly rewarding experience—rewarding not in strictly financial terms but in ways that cannot be weighed or measured. Granted, rewards of this type do not pay the bills or put food on the table, but they do create a special atmosphere that makes coaching much more than a job. It is this aspect that will help you avoid the feeling of going to work when it is time for practice. (When practice becomes a chore, it is time for you to consider another occupation.)

These rewards include the inner satisfaction one feels from teaching, being able to share an important part of young people's lives, and occasionally seeing some evidence that your students learned something worthwhile because of you, their teacher. Sometimes you will only discover your influence years after an athlete has graduated, or you may never know for sure how much of an impact you had. The effect that any coach has on a student's life remains largely a mystery. There is no way to measure the influence, but coaches receive enough feedback from athletes and parents to know that through athletics they can, and do, make lasting impressions on young people's attitudes.

Trauma

The life of a coach can be traumatic. This is especially true when an athlete suffers a serious injury. When we care about people, what happens to them also happens to us, and seeing an athlete get hurt cannot be shrugged off easily.

It can also be traumatic when you become the target of criticism. Every coach has to learn to cope with criticism, but it can be painful, especially when it affects your family. In his book, *Goldwater*, the former United States senator Barry Goldwater addressed this point. He was talking about politics, to be sure, but he could very well have been talking to every coach in America as well:

> You must have the courage to accept considerable criticism, much of it unjusti-fied. You must feel it in your guts and have the courage to accept defeat and continue your goals. Finally, you must believe in yourself, in your principles and in people.

Benjamin Franklin wrote, after being elected to a second term as governor of Pennsylvania:

> Popular favor, not the most constant thing in the world stands by me. . . . A man who holds high office finds himself so often exposed to the danger of disobliging someone in the fulfillment of duty, that the resentment of those whom he has thus offended, being greater than the gratitude of those serviced, it almost always happens that while he is violently attacked, he is feebly defended.

The point here is that people who are satisfied with your work rarely step forward to say so. On the other hand, those who are critical, even though they may be a minority, regularly make themselves and their criticisms heard. Right or wrong, it is the "nature of the beast."

You should also be well aware that coaching is an extremely demanding occupation. It places demands on your time, energy, family life, social life, and physical well-being, and eventually it takes its toll. Rare is the individual who has been a head coach in a high school for more than fifteen years and still has the enthusiasm necessary to do the job well. This is particularly the case with people involved in the "pressure sports," which vary from one part of the country to another but are generally the sports that draw the largest crowds and create the greatest community interest.

Typical Working Day for a Full-Time Teacher

One of the initial realizations that will strike you is how long and exhausting a working day is during the season, especially if you are a head coach. Every day is basically the same, yet you have enough variety to prevent monotony from ever entering your life. The demands on your time will depend greatly on the sport being coached, the number of students involved, whether or not game films are used, the incidence of injury to the athletes, and your desire or willingness to work at the sport over and beyond just practice time. Assuming that you will teach a normal schedule, a workday could look something like this:

7:45-8:00	Hall duty or homeroom
8:00-11:00	Classes
11:00-11:30	Cafeteria duty
11:30-Noon	Lunch
Noon-3:00	Classes
3:00-3:45	Preparation period
4:00-6:00	Practice
6:00-7:00	After-practice incidentals and return home
7:00-8:00	Dinner
8:00-9:00	Phone calls from parents or sportswriters, lesson plans, family and personal business
9:00-11:00	Review of game films or scouting reports

Also to be worked into this schedule are evening meetings with assistant coaches, athletic boards, booster clubs, league members, equipment salespeople, and sportswriters who make it a point to call you at home to get their story for the week rather than attempt to get you out of class at school. Time also has to be set aside for grocery shopping, washing clothes, housecleaning, and other chores. Add to this occasional visits from athletes who have some reason to talk with you at some place other than school, and you have another full day in the life of a full time teacher and coach.

Obviously, a coach who is not a full-time teacher would have a different schedule, but the time factor is still substantial.

The "Pressure Cooker"

If you become truly dedicated to a sport, you become thoroughly involved mentally, physically, and emotionally. Your life can come to resemble a "pressure cooker" because of the stress you create for yourself.

Suppose you accept a position in a school where the athletic teams have not been very successful. Your first goal is to turn them into winners and to create interest in the school and community. At first, each victory is appreciated and enjoyed by the community. But if after a few years you have met the goal, and winning seasons become the rule rather than the exception, the community's attitude will change from appreciation of a win to the expectation of a win. And so it becomes a vicious circle. No matter what the community or part of the country, everyone loves a winner. When fans get a taste of winning, they become addicted to it and expect the team to win all the time, which puts more pressure on you to keep winning. Coaches soon learn that in spite of past accomplishments, one bad season can create pressure. As mentioned earlier, sports fans have notoriously short memories when it comes to winning and losing, which is another reason coaches often feel as though the world of coaching takes place in a pressure cooker, at least during the season.

Emotional tension probably wears out more coaches than anything else. Unless a coach simply doesn't care about a team and what it does, this emotional strain is very real. In most cases it just isn't possible to sit or stand along the sidelines without being totally involved in what happens on the playing field. A doctor once told me that treating a coach during a season was like trying to repair a jet plane in full flight.

Another source of tension is the ever-present element of suspense when coaching high school students. This is related not only to the outcome of the game but also to how the team will perform once the contest begins. Sometimes when a team seems absolutely ready physically and mentally, they collapse and play as though they had never been taught anything. At other times, the athletes don't seem ready, but when the contest begins they catch fire and perform well. The reason for the concern is simple enough. The way a team plays is a direct reflection on you: If the team looks bad, you look bad. And if they look bad too many times, your job might be in jeopardy.

The concern over winning and losing certainly adds to the emotional stress every coach experiences. This occurs in direct proportion to the coach's ambition, the popularity of the sport involved, and the interest of the community toward that sport.

Coaching Salaries

If coaches' salaries were extremely high, it might be easier to live with some of the tensions of the job, but as a rule the salary is low in relation to the demands of the position. To a beginner, the extra pay for coaching will seem like a lot of money, but when spread over twelve months, minus various deductions, this extra allowance is almost insignificant. (Of course, the extra pay for coaching varies with the sport.) For example, an allowance of $3,600 for coaching breaks down to $300 a month. When all deductions are taken out, this means about $180 a month, or $45 a week, in a paycheck. If you work six days a week, that's about $8 a day, which breaks down to as little as $3 per hour or less for some coaches. This added amount might help pay the bills, but it won't alter your style of living very much, and many question whether the compensation is adequate for the time a coach actually spends during a school year. Therefore, if extra compensation is your reason for becoming a coach, you have probably made a bad decision.

Extra pay for extracurricular activities has long been a source of irritation among high school faculties, particularly where coaches are concerned. One group—usually the teachers who are not involved in any extracurricular activities themselves—oppose any extra compensation for additional responsibilities. The members of this group argue that they work after school, too, grading papers and preparing lessons for the next day, and they don't get extra pay for that. So why should a coach get extra pay?

Most of the criticism is directed at coaches simply because if school policy dictates additional pay for after-school activities, the coaches normally receive much more than the band director or yearbook adviser, for example. This fact fuels criticism of the role of athletics in a public school, and it is not unusual for coaches to find themselves being challenged over this point by fellow teachers in the lounge or school cafeteria from time to time. Trying to justify extra compensation to teachers who already have their minds made up is not easy.

Salaries for coaching should be based on a carefully thought-out formula. Here is a sample of factors that could affect coaching salaries:

- Total hours involved after school

- Weekend and vacation time involved

- Number of students involved

- Experience

- Pressure

- Travel supervision

- Indoor or outdoor activity

- Total responsibilities, equipment, funds, facilities

- Risk of injury

A point value should be given to each item, and a dollar allotment per point should determine the salary in a system of this sort.

In some schools the coaching salary is based on a percentage of the teaching salary. Whatever system is used, chances are very good that the money paid to coaches does not adequately compensate them for the work they do.

Coaches' Families

An important aspect of a married coach's daily life is the considerable impact this position has on the coach's family, whether by design or accident (see Chapter 7).

Your spouse gets feedback from a source that you don't—the critic in the stands, who can be quite vicious. Of course, spouses hear compliments, too, not only in the stands but also from parents who write, call, or simply meet them in the local stores. Consequently, it becomes important for your spouse to develop a thick skin in order to survive the sometimes unpleasant world of the grandstand.

People sometimes say things around a coach's spouse that they would never have the courage to say to the coach. As a result, a coach's husband or wife is often aware of things, people, and attitudes that the coach on the sidelines never notices. Therefore, spouses are subjected to a different kind of pressure. Normally, unpleasantness occurs in direct proportion to the numbers on the scoreboard and the won-lost record. Winning seems to be the primary way to curb the vocal abuse in the grandstands.

A coach's children have unique experiences, too. They not only hear good and bad things in the stands, they also hear the same kinds of things from classmates at school. Because one of their parents is a coach and probably well known, the children sometimes share in the special role their father or mother holds in the community. Their friends are happy to associate with the coach's son or daughter and may even be a little envious of them. But when the team ends up on the

short end of a score, particularly in the bigger spectator sports, some of the other students take the opportunity to cut the coach's children down to size by telling them what a lousy coach their mom or dad is. Children can be very nasty and cruel to one another. More than one coach's child has come home from school in tears because of abuse from other children when the team has lost. Of course, when the team is winning, everyone wants to be that child's friend. This is not so strange; the same thing happens to the coach.

One temptation you should avoid is allowing a small son or daughter to dress up like a cheerleader and show off at a game with the school cheerleaders, or allowing a child to show off on the sidelines during a game. This idea might seem cute to you, but it tends to give small children a false impression of their importance, can cause criticism from their classmates and spectators, and can turn these youngsters into "coaching brats." Their showing off during a game can detract from the cheerleaders or from the game, which is unwise. Obviously, a coach's family cannot escape being affected by the coach's position and involvement in athletics. As a result, the family can be drawn together in a closeness that is unshakable. On the other hand, families have been broken up because a wife or husband could not cope with all the aspects of a coach's life.

APPLYING FOR A COACHING POSITION

Coaching can lead to a nomadic existence if you are eager to advance to bigger and better jobs, including those at the college level. Unless they are very lucky, ambitious coaches will probably make up to six moves before finally reaching the position they think they want.

High school coaches who apply for head coaching positions in large school systems frequently find themselves competing with applicants who are currently coaching in colleges. There are several reasons for this situation: college coaches become disillusioned with high-powered collegiate athletics; they dislike recruiting; they want to become a head coach if they have not had this experience; they find the high school salary might be better than college pay; and the athletic program at a large high school might be better than one at a small independent college with limited financial support.

At any rate, under no circumstances should one apply for a specific coaching position until it has officially been declared open. Sometimes coaches hear via the grapevine that a certain coach is thinking about leaving a position, whereupon they immediately contact the superintendent of schools to apply. In most cases the superintendent has no idea of what is going on, and the current coach is put into a delicate situation. This matter is one of professional ethics and should be avoided.

Another situation you should avoid is one in which school board members, booster club members, or school administrators ask whether you would be interested in a head job at their school because they are thinking about firing the current coach. The only catch is that the present coach hasn't been told yet. Clandestine offers like this are to be condemned, yet they do happen. Sometimes these situations become full-fledged emotional issues in a community, and the prospective new coach can suffer because of the secret negotiations that took place. Unfortunately, the old saying about there being honor among thieves does not always apply to some school administrators and members of the coaching profession.

Interviewing

When you apply for a coaching position, the interviewer will be sizing you up to see if you will fit into the particular position available. You should (a) be honest and not try to guess what answers the interviewer wants to hear; (b) have a list of questions of your own to ask about the school and the community; and (c) be aware that seeking a coaching position in a tight job market is an aggressive, time-consuming, costly, and often frustrating experience.

Of course, in many school districts the need for coaches is so desperate that teachers other than physical educators are being hired and assigned coaching responsibilities, with little or no regard to their competencies or interest. As a matter of fact, athletic directors sometimes cannot get any teacher to coach. Teachers cite low pay, long hours, and family reasons for turning down the job. As a result, the first person who volunteers or is coerced gets the position. This often breeds other problems because of the lack of any professional preparation.

Regardless of how attractive a situation might seem, it is a mistake not to ask questions that are important to you personally. The job should be one to which you can adjust without sacrificing personal beliefs about teaching and in which you can be relatively happy. Since your questions reveal a great deal about you, give them a lot of careful thought. You should write down your questions and take them to an interview so you can refer to them from time to time—lest you forget to ask something that really is important to you. The questions you might ask include:

1. How did this opening occur?

2. Is there unrest on the staff because of this vacancy and the way it came about?

3. If the position is head coach, are the assistants currently on the staff being considered for the job?

4. What is the administration's attitude toward the athletic program?

5. Is the administration interested in excellence in the athletic program?

6. How would you describe the students' attitudes toward sports? The community's?

7. Does the head coach have an opportunity to sit in on interviews with prospective assistants, and is the head coach's opinion considered? Who will choose the assistant coaches?

8. Will the head coach be given the opportunity to organize a particular sport in every grade level in which it exists?

9. What is the role of junior high athletics (if any)?

10. What is the relationship between girls' sports teams and boys' teams?

11. How are facilities shared by boys' and girls' interscholastic teams?

12. What are the teaching responsibilities?

13. Do coaches get any release time?

14. What is the school policy concerning attendance at coaching clinics?

15. What type of community is this?

16. Are there educational opportunities nearby for graduate school?

17. What is the housing situation?

18. Are there opportunities for summer employment?

19. Does the school provide fringe benefits?

20. What is discipline like in the school?

21. What do you expect of me?

22. What is the salary scale?

Naturally, not every applicant for a position is necessarily interested in asking these same questions. Your questions will be determined by the circumstances and the position, but a true interview is a reciprocal exercise.

Some of the questions school officials or school board members ask you might be based on problems they have had in their athletic program or on current problems the school is facing. You can learn much about the situation if you listen carefully to the kinds of questions being asked. For example, if several questions focus on discipline, coaches dating students, or enforcing training rules, you can be fairly certain that there was a problem in that area during the previous year. This insight could prompt some specific questions by you later in the interview.

Thoughtful consideration of the questions that might be asked should help you prepare and should certainly help you feel more confident. Going into an interview unprepared is a guaranteed disaster. Some questions you might be asked are:

1. What is your background?

2. Why do you think you would like to coach at this particular school?

3. What is your philosophy of coaching?

4. What is your basic outline for a typical practice session?

5. How do you see athletics in relation to the total school community?

6. What are your ideas on training rules?

7. What are your ideas concerning discipline?

8. What is your attitude toward winning and losing?

9. What kind of offense and defense would you use?

10. How do you see your role in the school and community?

11. Do you believe in cutting youngsters from a team?

12. Are you willing to live in this community?

13. In general, how would you organize this program, seventh grade through twelfth?

14. How do you see the relationship between boys' and girls' athletics?

15. How do you see the relationship between varsity sports and the junior high program?

16. In your opinion, what are the three or four most important criteria for developing a sound program?

17. What would you do if your best athlete violated a rule that called for dismissal from the team?

18. What do you think about another teacher in the school disciplining an athlete by not allowing him or her to compete in a regularly scheduled game?

19. What are your professional goals?

20. Why are you interested in leaving your current position?

21. What would you do if one of your students asked you for a date?

22. Why should we hire you?

As in the case with the list of questions you might ask, this list is not all-inclusive, because the situation will dictate the questions and concerns of the employing officials. The important consideration for you is to be aware of the general line that questions often follow.

Once again, being honest is vitally important. If a school board likes what you say and believe in, they will hire you; if they don't like what you say, you are better off not getting the position, because you would probably be unhappy with it. If you try to guess what an interviewing body wants to hear, you will probably fail in the interview. When people ask for an opinion, you are obliged to give one, but take care not to be dogmatic or indecisive. You have to able to state a belief or an opinion without making it seem like either a declaration or an apology.

If you are serious about becoming a coach, you should take time to put your ideas of coaching in writing, being sure to address some or all of the questions listed above. When you go for an interview and present this written document to the interviewer I guarantee it will make a positive impression that will put you in a special category of top applicants. For example, a document like this might follow an outline similar to the following:

I. A short personal philosophy of coaching

A. organization

B. discipline

C. cutting

D. playing time

E. relationship with parents

F. winning and losing

Putting your thoughts and beliefs in writing is not the easiest thing you will ever do, but the dividends of this exercise will be great—count on it.

And finally, if you really want to learn all about a school and its "inner workings," make it a point to seek out and talk to the head custodian of the school.

POINTS OF DECISION IN YOUR PROFESSIONAL CAREER

Regardless of the kind of coach you are, opportunities throughout your career will create decision points, or crossroads, in your professional life. Sometimes these opportunities will occur by design, but more often they will happen when you least expect them. Most young coaches, eager and enthusiastic for competitive athletics, enter the profession with the idea that they will coach forever. As a result, they frequently fail to consider other possibilities or alternatives in the profession, especially if their current situation is a good one. Most are also unaware that the emotional and physical price

> If you don't know where you are going—any road will get you there.

of coaching is quite different at age 50, for example, than it is at 21. Consequently, when other professional opportunities are offered, they often make decisions hastily, without planning for the future.

It is not easy for most people to look ahead 5, 10, or 20 years and decide what they want to be doing. You need to become an initiator and not a reactor. In other words, you have to have a plan rather than spend your life just reacting to circumstances affecting your personal and professional life. Although it may seem impossible, you should make every effort to consider several possibilities

merely as alternatives for the future, and you should do so as soon as possible. This exercise would provide some sense of direction at the beginning of a coaching career, and your choices can always be reevaluated as time goes on. The important thing about looking ahead and setting goals is that you can begin preparing yourself for several possibilities, so that if an attractive opportunity does come along, you will be ready to take advantage of it. Sometimes opportunities present themselves only once and require a quick decision; tomorrow might be too late.

Circumstances beyond your control might also cause you to arrive at one of these crossroads in an unpleasant way. The decision-making process then becomes more difficult because emotional factors are involved.

Figure 2.2 illustrates the possibilities and alternatives all coaches or prospective coaches should be aware of, beginning as undergraduate students and continuing through the various stages of their working lives. The remainder of this section is an attempt to elaborate on these possibilities and to provide some basis for decisions you might make or consider.

Having completed undergraduate school, you have six possible directions to consider. You could enroll in graduate school, become a graduate assistant coach on the college level, become a head coach in a secondary school, become an assistant coach on the secondary school level, take a position in some related field (such as youth work, athletic equipment sales, sports camps, and recreation centers), or take a position in a totally unrelated field (such as sales, insurance, and management trainee programs, to mention just a few).

Graduate School

You should also be aware that earning a master's degree automatically places you on a higher salary scale in a public school system. This can be a disadvantage when applying for a high school position. Some school administrators are more likely to employ teachers with a bachelor's degree because their salaries are lower than those for teachers with advanced degrees; it is a matter of economics. In addition, earning a master's degree does not necessarily make a person a better teacher or coach. Consequently, one of the poorest reasons for going to graduate school is because you believe you would not be able to find a job otherwise (unless you

> When one door closes, another opens; but we often look so regretfully upon the closed door that we do not see the one which has opened for us.
> —*Alexander Graham Bell* *

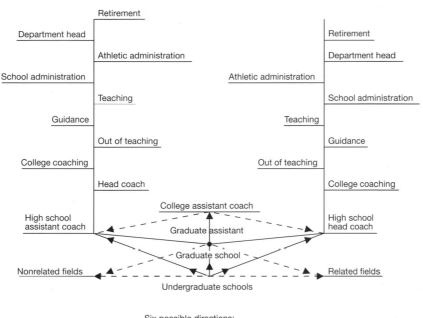

FIGURE 2.2
Possibilities and alternatives for coaching careers.

Six possible directions:

1. High school assistant
2. Graduate school
3. High school head coach
4. Related fields
5. Nonrelated fields
6. Graduate assistant college coach

want to prepare for a different career). All this does is delay job hunting for another year and increase your price tag because of the advanced degree, which can sometimes complicate finding a teaching position.

The main advantage in going directly into graduate school before teaching is that you can complete another year of schooling before being overwhelmed with teaching and coaching responsibilities, or perhaps family responsibilities. The main disadvantage is that the student often lacks perspective on the various courses because actual teaching experience is lacking. The value an inexperienced graduate student receives from coursework is neither as great nor as meaningful as it could be.

Assistant Coach or Head Coach?

At the conclusion of graduate school, you once again have six choices. These are the same choices that existed out of undergraduate school, with one exception: The choice of graduate school is replaced by the possibility of going into college coaching. If you decide not to go directly into graduate school after graduation, the next decision is whether to begin a coaching career as an assistant coach or as a head coach. There is no magic formula to help you make this decision; it really depends on the individual. The chief advantage of becoming an assistant coach first is that the full responsibility for the program is on someone else's shoulders. In this situation, an assistant has an opportunity to learn from someone else while serving a kind of internship. The biggest advantage in starting out as head coach is the opportunity to conduct the program according to your own ideas. Whatever choice you make, in the final analysis it will not necessarily guarantee any advantage or disadvantage to your career.

If you begin a coaching career as an assistant, the next decision is whether to seek a head coaching position. If this is your next objective, the timing is very important. You can be an assistant too long. One of the ironies in applying for a head coaching job is being eliminated from consideration because of a lack of experience and then applying after being an assistant for six or seven years only to be told you are too old. The ideal time to make a move into a head coaching position is generally between three and six years after becoming an assistant.

You might also stay at one location too long and become too comfortable, making a move difficult. This is especially likely to happen if you have children and they have begun attending school. Another consideration is how quickly you can be trapped by finances. Working your way up a salary scale, plus a summer job, makes it much easier to stay put. A move might mean a cut in overall income. It often comes as a surprise to discover that the salary scale in many public schools is higher than it is in many colleges. It is not unusual for an experienced high school coach with a master's degree to be offered an assistant coaching position in a college for several thousand dollars less than the high school salary.

College Coaching

Regardless of whether you become a head coach, the next decision is whether to seek a coaching position on the college level. Contrary to common belief, it is not mandatory to be a high school head coach before making the move into college coaching. Assistant coaches on the high school level can and do become college coaches, usually because someone on the college staff knows them personally and offers them an opportunity. This route into college coaching is the easiest for a high school assistant. The old cliché "It's not what you know but who you know" is true.

Another possibility if you are an assistant is to become a graduate coaching assistant at a college while working toward a master's degree, with the hope that you can make a good enough impression on the head coach to be offered a permanent position. There is always the possibility, too, that a head coach who is impressed will recommend you to a coach in another college if an opening does not exist on his or her staff. If your goal is to be a college coach, this is the best route to follow, particularly if the assistantship is in a prestigious program. This choice usually means that you must resign from a full-time coaching job in a high school, with a consequent cut in pay, which may be a severe one, although temporary. Therefore this commitment is a big one and not necessarily easy to make.

The picture is somewhat different for women coaches. Generally speaking, the need is still greater than the supply of qualified and interested women coaches, as evidenced by the large number of men coaching women's teams. With the concern for women coaching women's intercollegiate athletic teams, there are opportunities available for women who want to become college coaches also. Often, moving to another location is required. If the woman is single, this is usually no obstacle. If she is married, it might present problems. Generally, these problems do not appear to be as great for married male coaches, at least for those whose spouses are not employed outside the home.

If you are a head coach in high school and want to become a college coach, there are certain considerations that do not apply to an assistant coach. The most difficult step for any high school coach is getting that first college job. This means that in most instances you should not be too choosy, and you must be ready to make the move when the opportunity arises. Although a particular job may not be the most attractive one, you should remember that once you are on the college level, it is much easier to move to other college coaching jobs than it is to move from high school to college. The first college position might have to be accepted as a stepping stone to the kind of coaching position really desired. Although it is virtually impossible for a high school assistant to move directly to a head coaching position in a college, it is possible for a high school head coach to do so, and it can and does happen occasionally.

The second consideration specific to you as a high school head coach is the won-lost record. There is little doubt that championship teams attract attention to the coach. This statement seems to imply that a winning team is a coach's ticket to college coaching, but that is not necessarily true. There are thousands of ambitious high school coaches whose teams are winners, and any one of those coaches is probably just as qualified to coach in college as the next one. The deciding factor often is knowing the right people (a head college coach) and being in the right place at the right time.

Oliver Wendell Holmes wasn't necessarily talking about coaches when he made the statement, "Great places make great men," but it is very appropriate. The implication for coaching is that coaches are sometimes successful because of the situation they are in and not necessarily because of their own talent. To an ambitious coach, this idea is extremely important. There are school situations in which the best coach in the nation would have difficulty being a consistent winner, whether because of the size of the school, the attitude of the community and school toward a specific sport or toward sports in general, the strength of the competition within the league, and the kind of community in which the athletes live. For example, if you coach in a relatively small school in an affluent community and have to compete with bigger schools blessed with talented athletes and a philosophy geared solely toward winning, you are going to have difficulty winning consistently. On the other hand, if you coach in the largest school in a league playing a weak schedule, with an abundance of talented athletes and the opportunity to organize the program to provide the greatest opportunities for winning teams, you can win consistently and possibly dominate the league year after year even though you may not have any more coaching ability than the other coaches in the league.

> The swiftest person does not always win the race, nor the strongest man the battle . . . and skillful men are not necessarily famous; but it is all by chance, by happening to be at the right place at the right time.
> —Ecclesiastes 9:11, *The Living Bible*

If the situation is one in which youngsters have many opportunities outside of school to swim and play golf or tennis, coaches of these sports will have an advantage over coaches in situations that don't provide these opportunities. If, as does occur in some communities, children grow up with a football in their hands, coaches can win, and win consistently. Sometimes coaches in these circumstances make the mistake of overestimating themselves by assuming that winning is due to their own ability, and they fail to see and appreciate the importance of the situation and what it is doing for their success in coaching. A great athlete can make a coach look great. Adolf Rupp, the late, famed basketball coach at the University of Kentucky, once said about an all-American basketball player, "God taught that boy how to shoot, and I took the credit."

The eager coach who wants to pave the way to the big time of college coaching with championship seasons must constantly be on the lookout for these great coaching situations. And they are not always found in the most pleasant circumstances. This route is probably the slowest and most difficult one to college coaching. When the dust of the competition finally settles, a great situation will normally produce the great coach—at least in the eyes of the fans and sportswriters. Coaches who accept jobs in impossible situations with the idea of rising to new heights because of their vast knowledge of the sport are overestimating themselves and underestimating the importance of the situation. A bad situation or losing seasons are not always the fault of the former coach.

As a high school coach you must also be aware of the role a principal plays in creating an outstanding coaching situation—or in squelching one. A school principal who believes in excellence in all phases of the school program will do everything possible to help coaches realize their objectives in the athletic program. On the other hand, a principal who is antiathletic can make coaching a constant source of frustration and unpleasantness. A potentially great coach will probably produce only average teams in such adverse circumstances.

Many principals are former coaches. It might seem that they would be willing to boost athletics in any way possible, but that is not always the case. Sometimes these administrators are the most difficult to work for, particularly if they had some success in coaching, even though that success might have been with a single individual who became a state champion. In their minds their coaching success qualifies them as experts in any sport, and they can become a nuisance to a coaching staff. Conversely, if they were not too successful in coaching, they might hesitate to provide the kind of situation that can breed success for others. Also, some principals are biased in favor of a particular sport because they used to coach it. This bias can be good for the coach of that sport but terribly irritating for the other coaches in the athletic program.

There are many ambitious high school coaches who are intelligent, extremely knowledgeable, and fine teachers but who never get the opportunity to coach on the college level. First, they don't know the right people. Second, they never coach in the kind of situation where they could become consistent winners. And third, they become too comfortable where they are and are not willing to initiate a move.

Changing Fields

If a college coaching position is never offered, or if you decide to bypass such an opportunity, one of the next points of decision could be whether to get out of the teaching field. Other opportunities often come to high school coaches—sales positions, jobs in fields related to education, or administrative positions in business. These positions are attractive simply because the financial rewards are potentially much greater than those for a public school teacher. These opportunities seem most appealing in the first few years of teaching, when the coach is discouraged, disillusioned, or discovers that teaching is no longer attractive. Such opportunities are also appealing after six years or so, when the thrill of coaching has worn thin, when teaching is no longer any fun, or when continuing in education becomes impossible for various reasons, including financial ones. This decision to stay or not to stay in teaching often has to be made several times, at different points along a career, and there are probably few teachers who haven't considered the possibility of leaving at one time or another.

Many high school coaches become guidance counselors when they stop coaching. This is a natural progression, since coaches serve unofficially as counselors anyway. Many coaches prepare by including guidance courses in whatever graduate courses they take en route to a master's degree.

Another crossroads would occur if you decide to give up coaching and must decide whether to remain on the faculty as a teacher, either in a classroom or gymnasium. Many people are schoolteachers primarily because that is the only way they can also coach, and when their coaching days are over, the prospect of spending more years as a teacher does not appeal to them. This points up the importance of looking ahead early in your career to determine what the possibilities are and then attempting to determine primary and secondary goals.

The next possibility might be school administration. You can actively seek an administrative position, in which case the decision is easy to make when an opportunity presents itself. But sometimes such a position is offered when you haven't asked for it, and at a time when being a coach is still fun. At this point, the decision becomes more difficult, primarily because you don't know how much you will miss coaching or how much you would enjoy being an assistant principal. There is no question that school administration is the place where the best salary can be made in public school work, but it is also a difficult position, and finances should rarely be the determining factor in such a decision.

Another point of decision to be faced is the possibility of becoming an athletic director or a department head, which might or might not include athletics. Normally this decision is not as difficult as others. However, a stipulation that you must give up coaching to accept the position sometimes complicates things. This is especially problematic if you are relatively young and are thoroughly enjoying coaching. The chief advantage in administering a program is the opportunity to develop a sound, well-rounded program for many boys and girls. To some people this provides much more satisfaction and pleasure than confining their efforts to one sport for just a short part of the school year. If you find this option attractive, you should be aware that a number of universities across the country now offer graduate programs in sport administration.

Four things cannot come back . . .
The spoken word
The sped arrow
The past life and
Neglected opportunity
    —Arabian Proverb

It is possible that you will decide to coach for all of your working years and be fortunate enough to accomplish this goal. It is also possible that all of these opportunities will present themselves at least once before you retire, some more than once, and some not ever. The main point is that you should be aware of all these possibilities, try to anticipate 5, 10, or 15 years ahead, determine your priorities, and begin to prepare for them. In this way, you will not squander opportunities for lack of planning or preparation.

DISCUSSION QUESTIONS

1. Many coaches feel it is important to develop good rapport with various people within the school and community. Who are some of these people, and how should a coach develop that rapport?

2. What is the "power structure" in a community? How can you identify its members? How can you deal with these people?

3. How should a prospective head coach prepare for a job interview?

4. Even if you are successful as a coach, do you feel you could stay in one community too long? Explain your answer.

5. Why do you want to become a coach?

6. Why is the statement "All glory is fleeting" pertinent to the coaching profession? What does it mean?

7. Why should coaches be paid extra salaries when other teachers also work on their courses after school hours?

8. Explain the meaning of "Great situations make great people." Give examples relative to coaching. What does this mean to you in your search for a coaching position?

9. Can you think of any additional questions you would ask at an interview? If so, what are they?

10. What is the main purpose of the section dealing with "Points of Decision in Your Professional Career"?

11. What are some advantages and disadvantages of entering graduate school immediately after undergraduate school?

12. Why should anyone hire you as a coach?

13. What are your goals in the coaching profession?

14. What do you need to keep in mind about trying to please everyone as a coach?

*SPECIAL
RELATIONSHIPS*

Coaches have to build and maintain a number of relationships with a variety of people. That includes
school administrators, the faculty, other coaches, the
athletes themselves, parents, and assistant coaches, to
name but a few.

ADMINISTRATION

The relationship you will have with the administration is unique in a high school
situation, because athletic teams and their accomplishments are so visible to the
community. Most school superintendents would agree that the three most
potentially explosive issues they confront are professional negotiations, new
buildings, and athletic teams—and not necessarily in that order. Because of the
tremendous interest in high school sports, school officials are more likely to be
approached by adults in their community about matters concerning sports teams
and coaches than about any other aspect of the school program.

Without a doubt, the first person coaches need as a friend and supporter is the
high school principal. You should strive to make this person a friend of your
team. Because the principal is responsible for every program in the school, he or
she is in a position to help programs succeed or to suppress them. Without the
support of the principal, your status as head coach, as well as your plans for your
team, is in serious jeopardy. Thus, it becomes extremely important for you to
convince a principal (if necessary) of the value of interscholastic sport, participation, and success. The point is to let the principal know why such values can be
good for the school, that you will help out in any way possible, and that he or she
can count on your support, both in and out of school.

Lines of Communication
You should keep the administration informed about what is happening in the
athletic program so the principal or superintendent will be able to answer
questions or criticisms. An administrator should never have to plead ignorance
concerning the school's athletic program. One possible way to provide information

is for the athletic department to submit annual reports through the athletic director; another is for individual coaches to submit short statements containing their philosophies of coaching and what they hope to accomplish in their particular sports. Still another possibility is for each coach to submit a short report to the principal and superintendent at the end of each season. This report can include (1) a short summary of the program and its growth up to the present; (2) a section on athletes who have graduated and have received scholarships or who have accomplished other noteworthy goals; (3) a section on the coming season; and (4) any actions or procedures that the coach recommends to improve the program and that the administrator has the power to implement.

Such a report will take some time to put together, but it is well worth the effort in helping to establish and maintain a good working relationship with the administrators, and they will appreciate the gesture. It can be embarrassing for a busy administrator when a parent criticizes a coach and the administrator knows so little about what is going on that he or she cannot respond properly.

The lines of communication between coaches and administrators should always be open and should be used constantly, primarily from the direction of the coach to the principal and superintendent. If there is an athletic director, such communication should be one of his or her main responsibilities.

Reciprocal Responsibilities

Normally, obligations and responsibilities in athletic coaching are stated as guidelines for the coach, but the administration also has certain responsibilities to coaches. Countless articles, pamphlets, and books have been written concerning high school athletic coaches and their responsibility to (a) the community, (b) the school, (c) the school administration, (d) the student body, (e) game officials, (f) the boys or girls on the team, and (g) the hometown fans and their attitudes concerning sportsmanship. The implication is that all these responsibilities are the burden of the coach alone. The question arises, however: Should the school administration have any specific obligations toward coaches, and, if so, do they differ from the obligations toward classroom teachers? Many believe that the administration does have a responsibility toward athletic coaches and that the nature of this responsibility is unique.

Because of the very nature of the coaching profession, you will live in an atmosphere entirely different from that of any other teacher in the school. This situation is not inherently good or bad, but it is a fact. You will be subjected to certain pressures that most classroom teachers don't know exist and in all probability will never experience in their entire professional careers. For example, you will feel pressure to win from the "townies," the board of education, the parents, and yourself; pressure to beat a particular rival; pressure as to who will make the team; pressure as to not only who will play in the game but also how much they will play; and, in some instances, pressure from the school administration in various forms and degrees.

Coaches live in a world in which success (winning) is the goal, but they work in a setting where academic and character development of students is supposed to be the primary objective of education. This situation produces a real dilemma: fulfilling a role as a teacher and at the same time doing what is necessary in order to survive as a coach—winning and satisfying the public.

In contrast, classroom teachers exist in the relatively secure environment of their own little domains, where they can isolate themselves and the class from the

world merely by closing the classroom door. Rarely do they have to put a class and their teaching ability on display—and never in front of thousands of spectators once a week to be judged by numbers on a scoreboard as to their competence as a teacher. The classroom teacher might fail twenty or more students in a certain subject, or discover that the majority of a class has failed a weekly test, without fear of criticism or of losing a job. At the same time, one athlete can make a single mistake that loses a game, and the coach will be deluged with stinging criticism that, if allowed to go unchecked, might take a high toll.

Generally, coaches are intense in their dedication to their jobs, and this intensity brings criticism from other members of the faculty. But underlying this intense effort is the knowledge that coaching positions, in far too many instances, depend on the performance of a group of boys or girls playing a game and that coaches will finally be evaluated by the message the scoreboard conveys. Coaches know, too, that if the high numbers are on the wrong side

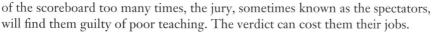

of the scoreboard too many times, the jury, sometimes known as the spectators, will find them guilty of poor teaching. The verdict can cost them their jobs.

To American business people, many of whom sit on boards of education, success is equated with profit. To make money is to be successful; to lose money is to be unsuccessful. Because most businesspeople do not understand education, its ideals and principles, purposes and methods, because they do not comprehend the slow process of personality development in students, they can only understand and judge athletics by applying business criteria to determine what success is. If a business makes money, the board of directors retains the manager; if a company loses money, the board fires the manager and gets another. What effect would a similar situation have on the methods, effort, and attitudes of classroom teachers?

In view of these factors, it seems clear that athletic coaches are in a unique, and too often precarious, position in the school. Because of this position, the school administration has a moral obligation to these people that has not always been recognized or fulfilled. Very simply stated, administrators should be absolutely honest with themselves, the community, and the coaches about what is expected of the people who carry the title "coach."

Sounds simple enough, doesn't it? But coaches are painfully aware that what is said to them in the privacy of a school administrator's office regarding winning and losing is frequently different from what is said to the public by that same administrator. And how many times have coaches heard the painful, well-worn statement, "We don't hire coaches; we hire teachers." Coaches know that in too many cases this is nothing more than lip service given freely while the team is winning. When losses outnumber wins and criticism mounts, coaches suddenly find themselves out on a limb all alone, with their jobs in jeopardy.

Expectations for Coaches

One of the most important solutions to this problem lies in communication between the school and community about what is expected of coaches. Obviously there are many reasons that schools hire the coaches they do, but some reasons in the high-visibility sports are

- To reorganize the athletic program toward a reemphasis of the "major" sports

- To win

- To gain state ranking for the team

- To bring new recognition to the school and community through winning and state ranking

- To work for all-star and all-state recognition for some members of the team

- To satisfy the booster club

- To win championships

- To appease unhappy "grandstand quarterbacks" or power structure in the community

Although serious questions arise about the educational value of these reasons, they are in fact guidelines for filling some coaching positions. But few, if any, boards of education would ever admit to using such guidelines.

Normally, the following criteria are presented to the public. Coaches are expected

- To teach youngsters in and out of the classroom and let the wins and championships take care of themselves

- To keep athletics in proper perspective

- To conduct the best athletic program possible for the student body

- To be classroom teachers first and coaches second

Whatever criteria are used for hiring a coach, the administration has a moral obligation to everyone concerned, and to the coach in particular, to be honest and state publicly what these criteria are and toward what purposes the coach is to work. In fairness to the coach, the time of hiring is not a time for hypocrisy, meaningless philosophical ideals, or diplomatic silence (which allows all the participants to draw their own conclusions); it is instead a time for honesty—a trait that often demands a great deal of courage and that has not always been seen in administrators facing the kinds of criticism that arise over school athletic programs. In other words, if you have been hired to win, you should be told so and should be given every tool needed to accomplish this goal. If the administration is not concerned about championships and won't allow you to organize the kind of program that regularly produces championships, they should say so and then have the courage to back you when the critics ask, "Why aren't we number one?"

Teaching Duties

In most public secondary schools, full-time teachers who also coach are required to teach a full load of regular classes—in math, history, science, or language, as well as physical education—in addition to carrying out their coaching duties. Much to the dismay of school administrators, the effort that coaches put forth in these classes is often a mere fraction of what they put into the sports they coach, and consequently the quality of instruction in the classroom is not always satisfactory.

Certainly there are a number of reasons for this situation, but the chief reason is best summed up by a statement frequently made by coaches: "Look, I can fail a dozen students in my classes and nobody says a word, and I could continue to teach here forever, but if the team I coach fails to win, I've had it."

If a person is both a classroom teacher and a coach and feels that winning games is necessary to keep the coaching job, there is little question as to what will get the greatest emphasis and what will be shortchanged. It is a simple matter of survival. Therefore, if a coach has been hired solely to win, perhaps classroom assignments are not realistic.

On the other hand, if winning were not the primary objective of the administration, and if the community were aware of this and accepted it, many coaches would operate under a different philosophy in their teaching, both in and out of the classroom. If coaches felt certain that the administration was sincere in its stated belief as to the value of athletics in the educational framework of that particular school, that the administration would make every effort to convey this belief to the community, and that it would support the coaches as long as they worked toward this belief, regardless of the scoreboard, the coaches could take their place as a valuable educational asset to any faculty.

The American Alliance of Health, Physical Education, Recreation and Dance has stated that people in athletic administration and coaching need particular competencies in public relations, plus courage to withstand noneducational pressures. This principle is just as appropriate, if not more so, for administrators of a school in regard to the athletic program.

FACULTY

In the eyes of the rest of the faculty, a coach is simply another faculty member and does not have any special status. However, coaches don't always give the impression that this is the case, which can create antagonism with other faculty members. One of the most common points of irritation is the extra salary most school districts pay coaches. Coaches usually receive quite a lot more than faculty

members involved in other kinds of extracurricular activities. Regardless of the reasons and the justification for the difference, there are always some teachers who resent it, and many a debate or argument has taken place over this matter. It seems to classroom teachers that this difference automatically places coaches in a special category, and some teachers are particularly sensitive about what they see as injustice.

The vast amount of publicity sometimes given coaches can also cause bad feelings among teachers. A classroom teacher can be resentful over the fact that he or she is doing an outstanding job of teaching and yet the only publicity in the local newspapers goes to athletics. Classroom teachers sometimes become bitter and assume that very few people, if any, really care about what goes on in the classroom, whereas many people become excited about the condition of a star athlete's bad ankle. And even though a coach might not be responsible for this publicity, some teachers resent it.

One technique coaches use to establish a good working relationship with other faculty members is to check with various teachers periodically to see how athletes are doing in their classes. For example, some coaches send a prepared form to each teacher to inquire about athletes' conduct in class, quality of work, and promptness in handing in assignments. If you try this, just make sure you never interfere with a classroom teacher's method of grading. This can create tremendous problems.

Checking on athletes' schoolwork and conduct lets teachers know that you are ready to help them with a student athlete if necessary. It also alerts teachers to the fact that you are interested in a youngster's classroom performance as well as athletic performance. A form returned by a classroom teacher can also serve as a convenient tool to use in counseling a student when and if the need arises.

While you can be a positive influence on an athlete's conduct in another teacher's classroom, be careful about interfering with that teacher's role. The following piece is a tongue-in-cheek example of the way some faculty members view coaches' interference in the educational process:

Dear Coach Muscleman:

Remembering our discussions of your football men who were having troubles in English, I have decided to ask you, in turn, for help.

We feel that Paul Spindles, one of our most promising scholars, has a chance for a Rhodes scholarship, which would be a great thing for him and for our college. Paul has the academic record for this award, but we find that the aspirant is also required to have other experiences, and ideally should have a good record in athletics. Paul is weak. He tries hard, but he has troubles in athletics. But he does try hard.

We propose that you give some special consideration to Paul as a varsity player, putting him if possible in the backfield of the football team. In this way, we can show a better college record to the committee deciding on the Rhodes scholarships. We realize that Paul will be a problem on the field, but—as you have often said—cooperation between our department and yours is highly desirable, and we do expect Paul to try hard, of course.

During intervals of study we shall coach him as much as we can. His work in the English Club and on the debate team will force him to miss many practices, but we intend to see that he carries an old football around to bounce (or whatever one does with a football) during intervals in this work. We expect Paul to show entire good will in this work for you, and though he will not be able to begin football practice till late in the season he will finish the season with good attendance.

Sincerely,
Benjamin Plotinus
Chairman, English Department

—William Stafford, in *College English*, April 1955

The popularity you as a coach will experience among the student body can also disturb some faculty members. They sometimes view this popularity as a personal threat and resent you because of it. Unfortunately, petty jealousy and envy are not unknown in the teaching profession.

The enthusiasm you bring to your work will disturb some members of the faculty who teach as though they are semiretired and who have long since lost their enthusiasm for teaching. In their eyes, you are rocking the boat. Teachers who are coasting feel threatened by comparison with others who enjoy their jobs and work hard at them. Some teachers work themselves into a comfortable rut and are bothered by anything or anybody that might cause them discomfort in their status quo.

Coaches who choose to ignore faculty meetings or other faculty functions are making a big mistake. Their conspicuous absence helps create the impression that they think they are special people in the school and don't have to bother with minor activities like the rest of the teachers do. Such coaches seem not to care about anything or anybody that doesn't have something to do with athletics. Coaches should attend as many faculty events as possible to avoid this criticism.

Sometimes coaches will be given the use of a new automobile by some local car dealer who happens to be a great fan and who, by the way, doesn't mind the free publicity either. Some coaches consider it a tremendous sign of status or prestige to have their own "command car." They feel their stature is enhanced when they wheel into the parking lot at a coaching clinic with decals on the car announcing that here comes the head coach of a certain sport at "Blank" High School.

Accepting such favors can help create a gap not only between a coach and other faculty members but also between the school's coaches, some of whom coach less privileged sports. This matter deserves careful consideration. Accepting gifts might also be contrary to school policy. Be careful.

I do not mean to imply that all or even any of the touchy situations discussed here should be avoided. But you should be aware that many teachers, rightly or wrongly, are suspicious and critical of coaches and their motives. Some coaches may be oblivious as to how some of their actions will affect their relationships within the school.

It will profit you to work hard to educate your school's faculty about the positive aspects of the athletic program and to conduct yourself in such a way as to show a genuine desire to become an integral member of the faculty, concerned about all facets of school life. You should avoid putting yourself in a special category and isolating yourself in your own little world within the school if you ever expect any understanding and cooperation from the rest of the faculty when problems with athletes arise. A belligerent faculty will be unresponsive in such a situation; as a result, some student might be deprived of an athletic experience through a disciplinary measure by a disgruntled teacher. Causing a student to get caught in the middle of a misunderstanding is inexcusable, but sometimes coaches help cause such things to happen. I hope you won't be one of them.

OTHER COACHES

All coaches have their own hopes and dreams about the sport they coach, and these may not necessarily coincide with the attitudes of the other coaches in the same school. When coaches are aware of these differences and respect them, it is not difficult to have harmony among all the coaches in the athletic department. But when a highly ambitious or self-centered coach turns an athletic department upside down to better his or her own program, regardless of the rest of the teams, conflict will result. Students eventually become aware of such conflict and begin to choose sides, which can cause all kinds of trouble, with often unforeseen ramifications. A strong athletic director can do a lot to prevent this situation from happening, but if the athletic director is weak or unaware, or if there is no director, the problem can quickly get out of hand.

Besides overemphasizing your own sport, another thing you should avoid is pressuring an athlete to give up one sport to concentrate solely on another—usually the one for which you are responsible. This type of influence is grossly unfair to a youngster because high school is a time for students to gain a wide variety of experiences; convincing an athlete to specialize in a single sport cheats that youngster of this opportunity.

What this action boils down to is selfishness on the part of a coach, who wants to make his or her own team stronger with little or no regard for the ultimate impact on the athlete or on other coaches. Such manipulation is certain to cause bad feelings between coaches. Coaches experience enough problems from outside the school; it is ridiculous to create them from within.

Overlapping Seasons

Coaches of various sports need to reach an agreement as to when practice for a new season should begin, to avoid any overlapping with a season already in progress. In many instances this timing is taken care of by state regulation, but rarely are all sports included.

The problem becomes acute when coaches get anxious and begin preseason practice before another season ends. If the season in progress has not been particularly successful, some athletes, particularly substitutes who rarely get a chance to compete, will start thinking about practicing for another sport. The current season is beginning to drag for them, and they are anxious for it to end. They also get concerned because they feel they are falling behind in the upcoming season, since some of their friends are already practicing. This uneasiness can affect their attitude in practice and thus the entire in-season team, including its coach. Obviously, this is not a desirable situation, but it exists all too often simply because coaches forget the effect their actions can have on youngsters and fellow coaches.

Frequently there is overlap in practice time for athletes who participate in successive sport seasons. Some coaches are willing to allow players to begin preseason practice for another sport while finishing the current season. Practice times do not always coincide, so such overlap is a possibility, even though normally it is not good and many coaches do not permit it.

"Minor" Sports

Another situation that can cause problems occurs when a younger, eager coach decides that his or her so-called minor sport is being ignored by students and fans. In a desire to correct this inequity, the coach sometimes conveys his or her sentiments to the team. They too feel they are being neglected, and before long the attitude of the coach and squad is one of "our small, neglected, unwanted team against the world." In an attempt to change the image of this team, the coach is sometimes tempted to sidestep the policies and regulations of the athletic department by going directly to parents with requests and problems.

This "end run" can only lead to more problems eventually and can possibly cause hard feelings that will affect the program for several seasons. The safest procedure for coaches in such circumstances is to go through established channels within the school. If the situation is truly unfair and cannot be changed in the proper way, the coach has four choices: (1) accept it and live with it, (2) continue to try to make changes in the proper way, (3) take the matter to court if it violates laws like Title IX, or (4) leave.

Use of Facilities

Another difficult situation involves the use of the gymnasium during the winter months, when facilities are limited and must be shared by girls' and boys' basketball, wrestling, gymnastics, and volleyball teams, plus intramural teams. School principals and coaches have been tangling with this issue for years, and the problem has become more acute as interscholastic teams have become more numerous.

Many solutions have been tried, such as using the gymnasium for practice in the morning before the beginning of the school day, scheduling girls' practices

right after school and bringing the boys back at night, or vice versa, alternating the use of the gymnasium between girls and boys right after school, or having the one practice after school every day followed immediately by another. Various schools use other solutions, and some have proved satisfactory, but the fact remains that sharing a facility can create a variety of problems. Unless coaches are willing to cooperate, a lot of antagonism occurs. Coaching is difficult enough as it is; fighting over the use of a facility simply complicates things more.

The obvious solution is to build more facilities, which is not always possible. The only fair solution is for the gymnasium to be shared equally among all teams. Most coaches' primary argument against this formula is that they need more practice time. But there is not one shred of scientific evidence showing that a high school team of any kind needs two hours of practice every day of the week to be successful. There is no evidence to suggest that two hours every day is better than an hour and a half every day, or even one hour every day. Coaches tend to be creatures of habit and great copiers or imitators of other coaches, systems, and ideas. Most coaches believe in the two-hour practice only because everyone else does.

A veteran, football coach abandoned twice-a-day practice sessions during the two weeks before the opening of school in favor of one two-hour session each day. His opponents were practicing twice and sometimes three times a day. When the season was over his team had won every game. In the final analysis, the amount of practice time was incidental. His team won mainly because he had more good athletes than anyone else, which is still the number-one priority for a team to be a winning one; time spent in practice hardly runs a close second. Perhaps it is time for coaches to reevaluate their ideas about practice time.

The most important consideration in your relationship with your fellow coaches is to respect what they are attempting to do and to support them whenever and however you can—privately and publicly.

ATHLETES

Without question, the special relationship with athletes is the best part of being a coach. It is also the most important relationship you need to establish. No matter what other attributes you bring to the profession, you will fail without a positive relationship with your athletes. Your two basic considerations are putting the athletes' welfare before anything else and earning their absolute respect.

If your goal is to move on to bigger and better things in coaching, don't spend so much time attempting to further your own career that you neglect to establish great rapport with the youngsters on your team. Athletes are to be taught and led in positive directions. They are not to be used by you or any other coach for personal reasons.

PARENTS

A word to the wise: Make a maximum effort to involve parents in your program by helping them understand what you are trying to accomplish, and why. You will need their cooperation, support, and understanding because they are the people with the greatest investment in a sport—their sons and daughters. Their attitude toward your sport, and their willingness to adjust the family schedule to fit the season, can affect their children's attitude and degree of commitment to the sport. It is your responsibility to create the kind of atmosphere necessary for parents to become supporters of the program and of you. Do not ignore or underestimate this aspect of your responsibilities—it is unavoidable (see Chapter 11).

One factor that upsets families and creates problems is not letting parents know in advance what the hours for practice will be during the week, on Saturdays, and on holidays. A coach can easily forget that there are other things going on in the world besides practice sessions and make a simple change in practice times over a holiday that can affect dozens of people besides team members.

Generally speaking, the concern of most parents is to have their children perform well and participate in all meets or games. As a rule, parents don't usually become unhappy with a coach when their youngster is in the starting lineup. It is when their children are substitutes that parents tend to become frustrated and critical.

Parents' emotional involvement in watching their sons and daughters compete can be total. This is particularly true in individual sports where youngsters win or lose on their own. The parents of high school wrestlers are a perfect example. It is not hard to pick out parents when a match begins. Normally docile mothers can become screaming, fist-waving fanatics, and fathers have suffered heart attacks on occasion.

Parents simply want to see their children excel; they suffer many of the same anxieties a coach does, if not more. If you understand this, it will be easier for you to cope with irate parents. Whether or not a team is winning seldom makes much difference to the parents of a substitute. All they know is that their own "pride and joy" is not in the game.

You already know it is the nature of parents to see their offspring with acute tunnel vision and bias. They are also frequently unable to view their child's athletic ability with any degree of objectivity. This is normal, but you need to understand it in dealing with unhappy parents.

The greatest source of conflict between parents and coaches can be summed up in six little words, "Why doesn't my (son, daughter) play more?" This can also be described as the "every" concept. That is to say, *every* parent would like *every* youngster to play *every* minute of *every* contest, and for the team to win *every* game—obviously an impossibility. One way to deal with this issue of playing time is to tell parents you don't put anyone on the bench. Rather, you put people in a game who deserve to be there.

In some cases parents' concern is selfish; they have a tremendous amount of ego involvement. This is especially the case when a parent never experienced much athletic success and is now trying to accomplish something through a son or daughter. It occurs, too, when parents who were successful athletes relive past days of glory through their youngsters' participation; their child's sitting on the bench becomes a source of embarrassment. Another factor that can contribute to parents' frustration relates to scholarship possibilities. Parents know that college scholarships could save them a significant amount of money over a four-year period, and they also know that bench warmers do not get scholarships.

Parents can become particularly hostile toward a coach when they feel that their child is being treated "unfairly" (sitting on the bench). This "situation" brings to the surface all of the human protective instincts, and parents become quite critical, vocal, and abusive as a result, particularly if convinced that their youngster has not been given a fair chance. Once a parent gets angry with you over what he or she perceive as an injustice, there is a good chance he or she will stay that way as long as you are in that school.

Some parents accumulate individual statistics on their child's performance during a season. There is nothing basically wrong with doing so, unless it affects an athlete's attitude to the point where he or she begins playing the game to pad individual statistics because they have become more important than the success of the team. Selfish players care more about their own accomplishments than the team's.

On the other hand, parents can be strong supporters of you and your program. It all depends on you, your personality, and your willingness to constantly sell the program to parents. It is crucial that they understand what is going on and why. Many of your best friends in a community will turn out to be parents of athletes—not only while the youngsters are in high school, but as long as you live in that community—if you work hard to impress on parents that you care about their children. You need to remember that no one cares more about what happens to athletes than their families.

The following letter was published in the *Pittsburgh Press* some time ago. It is included here as a message to all coaches and prospective coaches, female and male, as a representative concern of most parents regarding their children's participation in athletics:

Dear Coach,

We hardly know each other, and yet very shortly we will have quite a lot in common, namely, our son. Now that your season is about to begin, we are "loaning" you one of the greatest possessions the Good Lord has seen fit to give us—our son, and make no mistake about it, coach, during these next few months he is yours!

To his mother and me he is still a little boy in many respects, but of course we wouldn't dare let him know we felt that way since he thinks he's quite grown up at age 15. To most coaches, he and his buddies are looked upon as young men because they have the backbone to come out for the team and to stick with it. Little boys couldn't do this, only "men" can take it, according to the coaches. But I guess most parents are hesitant to want to see their sons in this light because these youngsters seem to grow up so quickly anyway.

We hope, too, that our boy will not only learn the fundamentals of the game from you but also a respect for authority, the necessity of following rules and the penalty for violating them. He needs to learn that discipline is important to an individual and to a group in order to prevent chaos. He needs to develop an appreciation for hard work and the fact that this is still a good guideline for success in any endeavor. We think he should learn that loyalty is not a bad word and that being loyal to his team, his coach, his school, his family, his church and his country is good and necessary. Through athletics he should develop an understanding of the importance of taking care of his body and not abusing it by using tobacco, alcohol, or drugs. His experiences with you in athletics should also teach him to accept his fellow man for what he is and what he can do rather than the color of his skin or his nationality. No one enjoys losing, but youngsters need to get a taste of it in order for them to learn that the important thing is the necessity of "getting off the floor" and trying again. These are the little things that begin to make men and good citizens out of young boys and I'm convinced that they can be taught through athletics without sacrificing any mechanical aspects of the game.

I realize that every community has its corps of "super-critics" who only have eyes for the scoreboard. But I am suggesting to you, coach, that if you teach "boys" instead of just a "sport," the boys and the parents will rarely, if ever, be numbered among the leather-lunged experts in row X, and your personal scoreboard will record so many young men out of so many boys.

Good luck to you and the team.

Sincerely,

A father and mother

ASSISTANT COACHES

It is vitally important that a head coach be able and willing to make assistants feel that they are an integral part of the total program. Naturally, the larger the staff, the more complicated this process can become, because of the various personalities involved. But the larger the staff, the greater the need to create a feeling of unity.

Every coach on the staff has ambitions, hopes, dreams, and goals. It is important that contributions to the program be recognized publicly by the head coach. The perceptive head coach never misses an opportunity to show appreciation to the assistant coaches for what they are contributing to the overall success of the team. A considerate coach works hard to establish the feeling of "we" and "us" among the staff, including their spouses, since this helps create genuine unity and loyalty, as well as pleasant working relationships. Remember, loyalty is a two-way street.

The following excerpt is from a letter I received from a former student and physical education major whose husband had just finished his first season as an assistant football coach:

> I felt I had to write and say a few words about the coaching course I took last summer at State. I sometimes thought you were going a bit too far when you would describe the intricate ways in which you involved the coaching wives in the workings of the teams. Well, unfortunately, the coaches here are not aware of these finer points, and now, after less than one year of marriage, I have become what is commonly known as a coaching widow. I wasn't too crazy about the great game of football while I was an undergraduate student, but I'm sure I'll hate it for the rest of my life after this.

This is a very sad situation in what should be an extremely exciting life for two fine people.

BAND DIRECTOR

Usually only the football and basketball coaches are involved with the band director. The first realization you must come to is that the pregame band show and the halftime performance mean as much to the band director and band members as the game means to you and your players. There are parents who attend high school games only because their youngsters are in the band. Members of marching bands work extremely hard so they can perform well, and the athletic department should cooperate to see that they get the chance.

If the band needs eight minutes to take the field before game time, the coach should be willing to organize the pregame warm-up so that the team is off the field for that time. At halftime, nothing infuriates a band director more than when a team comes onto the field and runs through one of the band's formations. This behavior is inexcusable and can be avoided very easily, unless the coach sees the band as intruders in a private domain. Such interference is not excusable even if a band is late in getting off the field.

When the proper professional relationship exists, the band director will probably be more willing to arrange for a pep band at bonfires, basketball games, or pep meetings or to have the band form a "funnel" through which a team enters the playing field.

Cooperation is also important when a student would like to be in the band and also participate in athletics. Unfortunately, in some situations a contest develops between coach and band director, neither of whom will compromise, and the student is forced to choose. When this happens, the student is being denied a valuable experience. Students who are involved in several sports should still have the opportunity to play in the band, since bands also have seasons. In the proper atmosphere, a fall season athlete can still participate in concert band, while a wintertime athlete can participate in marching band.

It should be a source of pride when an athlete performs in the band or when a musician participates in athletics. A cooperative spirit is also appreciated by parents, since the student isn't forced to make a choice, possibly giving up music and thereby wasting years of lessons and the cost of an instrument.

In some situations the athletic department gives the music department a part of the gate receipts to recognize its contribution to entertaining the spectators. If the athletic department is solvent enough to do so, this is a wonderful public relations gesture.

A great deal of friction can develop between coaches and the band director unless they are willing to work together and compromise to establish and maintain a harmonious professional relationship. They should be careful not to become so narrow-minded and self-centered that their only concern is their own program, to which they expect everyone else to adjust. If there is a band concert at school, be there!

GUIDANCE COUNSELORS

Coaches often work more closely with guidance personnel than most other faculty members do. Guidance counselors know that coaches are sometimes aware of things about a youngster that no one else is, and this knowledge may be important in helping a student through some difficulty. However, privileged communication must be respected. Therefore, the coach or counselor should exercise good judgment in discussing a particular student when trying to help solve some difficulty or problem.

Coaches and guidance counselors frequently work together when an athlete is being recruited by college coaches. Together they should provide sound enough advice about academics and athletics to enable the student to choose intelligently. Coaches need to make sure that guidance personnel understand NCAA rules regarding athletic eligibility on the college level and the high school's responsibility in order to ensure that athletes meet eligibility requirements for athletic participation on the college level. A coach should never assume that guidance counselors have a clear understanding of these requirements; in fact, it would be safer to assume the opposite (see Chapter 8).

CUSTODIANS

A good relationship with the custodians can be more important to you than to any other teacher in the school, because you will ask more of the custodians than other teachers do. It is important that custodians be treated as important workers in the school and as personal friends, rather than as servants of the teaching staff. When custodians become your friends, there is no limit to the cooperation and assistance they will give over and above the normal requirements of their job.

Custodians can help make your job easier in countless ways through their efforts in keeping fields lined all season, keeping the locker room and offices clean, getting the baseball diamond in condition for a game, keeping the grass mowed, and helping to repair equipment. If custodians don't help you willingly, you can run into great difficulty; be careful not to alienate them through thoughtlessness or in some other way.

SCHOOL SECRETARIES

Unless you are fortunate enough to have your own secretary, you will have to rely a great deal on secretaries in the main office. You should treat these people with professional courtesy just as you would any other co-worker in the school. School secretaries can be of great assistance to you and will be if treated with respect.

MEMBERS OF THE COMMUNITY

There is an old joke that if these three questions were asked of anyone, the answer to all would be yes:

1. Can you drive a car?

2. Can you build a fire?

3. Can you coach a team?

Not only would nearly everyone answer yes to the last question, but most would probably respond affirmatively if asked whether they could do a better job than the current coach. People do not hesitate to question coaches' strategies or handling of the team, sometimes telling them so personally.

Some coaches resent what they interpret to be criticism by people who usually have little or no understanding of what is really going on or who have an ax to grind. Such situations often create antagonism, and handling them requires great patience and diplomacy. The coach who responds to questions from fans with a declaration that "I'm the coach, and I'll run my program however I see fit without any help from you" is probably correct but is not too adept at public relations.

A longtime coaching acquaintance had what seemed to be a good technique for handling most grandstand coaches when they offered free advice. He would hear them out and then say, "You know, that might have possibilities." This seemed to satisfy most critics, and the coach would then go about his business as usual.

MEMBERS OF THE PRESS

Sportswriters can do a great service for high school athletics by publicizing positive stories about games and individuals. Articles emphasizing the good sportsmanship of teams and players can win more solid support for a high school athletic program than any other method.

Coaches have a distinct obligation to be honest with the press. You are using and abusing the press if you issue false injury lists or other statements that are not true solely to psych an opponent; such behavior is unethical and is not fair to the sportswriter, who is also trying hard to do an honorable job. False or misleading information given to a reporter by a coach but printed under the writer's name can make that writer look very foolish.

When sportswriters take the time to cover a high school team, the school can reciprocate by making their job easier. School officials should try to provide parking places at athletic contests for the press and to give reporters working space in the gymnasium, press box, or wherever an event is being held. When reporters do not cover a contest, you should make it a point to send them information. There is no guarantee that it will appear in the paper, and if you want publicity for your team, you might have to send notices time and time again, until a report does appear. Your good public relations gestures will often pay dividends when a friendly press is needed.

Remember that the sportswriter's interest is in writing stories; your main purpose is education. The reporter is concerned primarily with selling newspapers and in most cases has little knowledge of the educational aspects of athletics. It may be, too, that the people reporting the results of various games have little or no background in athletics. In such cases, you or the athletic director should help these people become more knowledgeable about athletics by taking the time to talk sports with them and by inviting them to practices. They should also be encouraged to write about the positive aspects of athletics rather than taking a sensational, negative approach merely to increase the newspaper's circulation.

The press does have a definite obligation to high school athletics. A local reporter does the athletic program a great disservice when he or she becomes a self-appointed expert and concentrates on playing the role of critic. A sportswriter should work closely with the athletic department in publicizing the accomplishments of the teams and individuals rather than assume the role of crusader and expose all the incompetents involved in the high school program. Reporters should also be careful not to print derogatory comments about an opponent, because such articles always have a way of appearing on that team's locker-room bulletin board before the next contest. When such articles offend a team's pride or insult their ability, they only arouse the team to the point of playing a superior game and beating the local team. You should work with reporters to help them understand the kind of publicity high school teams need, as well as the kind that can hurt not only the program but also the boys and girls who participate.

A newspaper reporter who seeks out a disgruntled athlete and publishes the youngster's criticisms of the team, coach, and the school is also doing a great disservice to high school athletics. This kind of writing serves no constructive purpose whatsoever and should be discouraged. In the final analysis, you should take the initiative to create a reciprocal, cooperative working relationship with the press, emphasizing the kind of publicity that is helpful to high school athletics and that is based on fact.

One final point: Be careful. A seemingly innocent "off the cuff" remark by you might not look so good in tomorrow's newspaper.

ATHLETIC EQUIPMENT SALESPERSONS

The business of selling athletic equipment is highly competitive. In communities with several dealers, the competition for school business is particularly rough. When athletic equipment is purchased through bids, the relationship between the coach and sales agent is not too important, but when the coach decides who will get an order, the relationship with the sales agent takes on an entirely different tone.

Generally speaking, there is little difference in the quality of comparable name-brand equipment, and unless you prefer a specific brand, you should order from the dealer who will give you the best price, quality, and service for the school's dollar. If there is no significant difference in price, you will usually order from the sales agent you like best, and who gives the best service.

Salespeople are aware of the influence that personal preference has on buying, and consequently they work to cultivate friendships with the person who spends the money. Sales agents might offer to take you out to dinner or give you gifts of athletic equipment or huge discounts on equipment you buy for personal use.

Sooner or later every coach has to decide whether to accept or reject offers of this nature, in view of the fact that they could be considered bribes and therefore unethical. In spite of this, some coaches not only come to expect such offers from salespeople but actively solicit whatever they can as a condition for placing an order. Not only is this highly unprofessional, it can also be a source of serious trouble. If the school administration discovers that this questionable practice is being followed by one of their coaches and that better prices for similar equipment are being ignored, the coach will be in an untenable situation. If the abuse is great enough, it could cost the coach's job.

Occasionally, equipment companies will have dinner parties and invite many coaches as their guests, not only for dinner but also to see the latest display of equipment. Normally, this is a broad advertising gimmick or public relations gesture that they hope will increase their business; it doesn't carry any commitment for the coaches who attend. Such occasions can be quite pleasant and are not in the same category as personal gifts.

The safest practice is for you to stick to the basic criteria, such as cost, quality, service, and standardization of style and need, of purchasing equipment and to maintain an aboveboard relationship with every salesperson who can supply the quality necessary for the good of the youngsters on the team.

CHEERLEADERS

An important factor for you to carefully consider if you are young and single is the relationship with cheerleaders. To begin with, you might be only a few years older than a high school senior, which hardly places you in the category of a senior citizen in the eyes of an 18-year-old. The fact that you are a coach, young, and possibly single means that everything you say, the way you say it, the way you look at students, and the innocent kidding you do with them can all be interpreted much differently than if a 55-year-old married coach acted the same way.

In short, your conduct has to be professional in all your dealings with any student, especially one of the opposite sex. While a more friendly or intimate interaction can be meaningless for you, it can also be disastrous. It is not unusual for high school students to develop crushes on teachers. So be careful. This is a no-win situation—guaranteed!

CRITICS

> In the battle of life it is not the critic who counts; not the man who points out how the strong man stumbled, or where the doer of a deed could have done better. The credit belongs to the man who is actually in the arena; whose face is marred by dust and sweat and blood; who strives valiantly, who errs and comes short again and again because there is no effort without error and shortcoming; who does actually strive to do the deeds; who knows the great enthusiasms, the great devotion, spends himself in a worthy cause; who at the best knows in the end the triumph of high achievement; and who at the worst, if he fails, at least fails while daring greatly, so that his place shall never be with those cold and timid souls who have tasted neither victory nor defeat.
>
> —*Theodore Roosevelt*

One of the most difficult tasks or requirements for any coach is to learn how to live with critics, grandstand quarterbacks, or downtown coaches. No matter what the size or type of community, you'll have critics, and they are not always just soreheads who are unhappy when a team loses. Even when they win, coaches are criticized by parents who think their youngster should have gotten into the game sooner, whose son or daughter didn't get in at all, or whose offspring was taken out of the game so others could play. Some critics will think the score was too high, and some will think the points should have been piled on even more. Folks will even call up the coach after a football game, for example, to complain because the team came out onto the field while the opponent's alma mater was being played and didn't stop to take their helmets off (how the team was supposed

to recognize another school's song might never be explained). Finally, there are always those who simply complain about the way the team plays.

The point is that people will always find something to pick apart, and the coach who keeps an ear open to everything being said or who tries to satisfy all these "experts" is in trouble. A school administrator once stated that if what we did satisfied 75 percent of the people, we were doing a fantastic job. The following story illustrates the folly of attempting to satisfy critics:

> There was an old man, a boy, and a donkey. They were going to town, and it was decided that the boy should ride. As they went along they passed some people who exclaimed that it was a shame for the boy to ride and the old man to walk. The man and boy decided that maybe the critics were right so they changed positions. Later they passed some more people who then exclaimed that it was a real shame for that man to make such a small boy walk. The two decided that maybe they both should walk. Soon they passed some people who exclaimed that it was stupidity to walk when they had a donkey to ride. The man and the boy decided maybe the critics were right, so they decided that they both should ride. They soon passed other people who exclaimed that it was a shame to put such a load on a poor little animal. The old man and the boy decided that maybe the critics were right, so they decided to carry the donkey. As they crossed a bridge they lost their grip on the animal, and it fell into the river and drowned. The moral of the story is that if you try to please everyone you will finally lose your ass.

Just remember, there is no way that you will ever be able to satisfy all of the people all of the time, so don't try. Decide what you think is best for your team and have the courage to conduct your program accordingly.

It should be obvious by now that being a coach involves much more than merely teaching youngsters to play a game. Like every profession, coaching includes some aspects that we could do without. One thing is certain: You will never be bored.

DISCUSSION QUESTIONS

1. What are some typical problems that develop between coaches and administrators?

2. Discuss several things a coach could do to gain the support of parents and fans.

3. What are some of the problems that can occur between coaches and other faculty? with other coaches?

4. Should athletes be permitted to begin practice in another sport before the current season ends? Why?

5. Discuss the "every" concept.

6. Should parents be permitted to attend practice sessions? Why?

7. How can a coach make the principal a supporter of athletics? Why is this important?

8. It has been said that friends come and go, but enemies multiply. If this is true, what are the implications for coaches?

9. Why do problems arise between coaches over sharing a facility?

10. Do you agree that coaches should not date students in their schools? Why?

11. Who has the final responsibility for the athletic program in a secondary school?

12. What is the greatest source of conflict between parents and coaches?

13. If one of your students asked you for a date, how would you handle the situation?

4

DESIRABLE QUALITIES OF A COACH

Whatever principles you believe to be correct, they will no doubt be cumulative, having developed over time as a composite from all the coaches you have played for, from what you have learned and observed as an assistant, from ideas gathered at coaching clinics, and from experience in the profession. It is important that you use a great deal of discretion and critically evaluate all that you see and hear from other coaches when determining what is best for you in a particular situation. Techniques and methods that have proved successful to one coach might prove disastrous to another, because of circumstances and personalities. So if you are a beginning coach, be careful in attempting to pattern yourself after a famous "name coach" or in trying to imitate this person. To emulate a great coach is one thing; to imitate the same coach might be a very big mistake.

For example, a highly successful coach was once described as an ingenious architect, efficient contractor, and relentless boss. He was also a tyrant, father, protector, Moses figure—and a winning coach. Another big-time coach was once referred to as the cruelest coach in football, and in terms of victories, one of the most successful. A long-time Big Ten coach was known to take off his watch, throw it on the ground, and smash it by jumping on it or to tear his cap to shreds when things went wrong at practice—and his teams won consistently. On the other hand, there are coaches who run low-key practices, who don't scream at their athletes, who don't act like wild people during an athletic event, who are fairly calm—and their teams win, too.

The point is that there is no single right or best way to coach, and you should not look at another coach's won-lost record and then imitate his or her coaching ways because you believe they will bring success. It is dangerous for high school coaches to pattern themselves after winning big-time coaches when the name coaches' techniques are foreign to their own personalities. Your own views of teaching, your personality, and your circumstances should determine how you will conduct yourself.

> Always do what is right. This will gratify some people and astonish the rest.
> —*Mark Twain*

As you establish your philosophy of coaching, consider the following points. These items tend to be of the greatest interest to those who employ coaches, on the high school level at least, and as such are frequently part of the interview process. You should therefore clarify in your own mind how you feel about:

1. The role of athletics in an educational institution

2. The purpose of athletics

3. The justification for the existence of athletics

4. The concern of winning and losing

5. Your responsibilities as a coach

6. Your goals as a coach

7. The relationship between you and the athletes

8. Discipline

9. The issue of playing time for each athlete

10. The abuse of steroids and other drugs

11. Player conduct in school and during athletic events

12. The lessons you expect to teach youngsters through sport, over and above the skills of the game

13. Your relationship to parents

This list is not exhaustive, but it should give you a good starting point.

The remainder of this chapter is devoted to an in-depth examination of the various qualities desirable in a coach, beginning with transparent realism.

TRANSPARENT REALISM

Frequently, coaches attempt to project an image based on preconceived notions of how they think youngsters view coaches. For example, some coaches deliberately attempt to exhibit specific qualities, such as toughness, aggressiveness, and manliness or femininity, depending on the image they want to create for the athletes. Consequently, athletes often don't really get to know their coaches and leave school with a distorted view of what they were really like. Over the years, a lot of coaches have conducted their professional lives in this manner. Doing so really isn't necessary and might hinder some coaches from accomplishing goals they had set for the team.

One of the qualities you should develop is *transparent realism*. That is, instead of pretending to be something you are not, you should allow your human qualities to show. These qualities include such things as empathy for individual athletes, concern, anger, sorrow, and tenderness if need be, as well as toughness and aggressiveness. If you are angry, be angry. If something funny happens at practice, laugh at it. In other words, be yourself. To be effective as a teacher in

the broadest sense of the word, you should let the athletes see you as a human being. Some coaches think that letting their human qualities show is a real threat to the long-established image of toughness in a coach. This concern about image is more a matter of insecurity than sound educational practice.

ABILITY TO ORGANIZE

The ability to organize is a vital trait if you expect to be successful. First, you must be able to organize your own thoughts and ideas to determine the direction and goals for the overall program. Then you must be able to organize the coaching staff so they will be aware of your objectives and will function efficiently to accomplish them. You must be able to organize the program to make it the kind that gives every athlete an opportunity to demonstrate individual ability, one that will be enjoyable, and one that will be a worthwhile educational experience for each participant.

The ability to organize becomes increasingly more important as the size of a coaching staff increases and as the number of people on the team grows. Without this ability on your part, a tremendous amount of time will be wasted, everyone will be confused, discontent will grow within the coaching staff or on the team itself, and the team will not be consistently successful.

In spite of the demand for organization of preseason, in-season, and postseason activities and plans, you must also remain flexible. Plans are intended to serve as guidelines, and they should be changed whenever the situation necessitates it. Be careful not to become so rigid in organizing a program that you will not or cannot change. Flexibility is one of the criteria for growth, not only in your ideas and goals but in a program as well.

The planning that has proved successful for a season or several seasons should never be looked on as a panacea for all time, because people change, and certainly the situation changes in high school athletics year after year. Colleges can plan a program and then recruit people to fit the plans, but a high school coach in the typical situation cannot. Therefore, you need to maintain flexibility in your thinking and planning.

ABILITY TO MOTIVATE

One of the biggest challenges you will face is motivating people. This is not always an easy task, and of course the larger the team, the more difficult it becomes. If everyone responded to a single motivational approach the same way, there would be no problem, but this simply is not the case. Motivating people will always be an important part of coaching. Therefore this is a personal skill that deserves a lot of attention.

Learning

It has been said that motivation is the key to learning. When youngsters are ready to learn, both physically and mentally, and want to learn, they will learn, but not before. Therefore the primary task for coaches in motivating athletes is to make them want to learn how to become better athletes, better competitors, a better team, and winners. It is important to remember that you cannot make athletes commit to whatever it is you are trying to get them to do unless they see value in it and buy into the plan or goals. This is the crucial element.

The question is, do athletes ever have to be motivated by coaches? The answer is an emphatic yes, and this holds true for practices as well as for games. There are as many reasons for this as there are personalities in athletics. Perhaps one of the primary reasons on every level of competition is the frame of mind that coaches refer to as the "comfort zone." The comfort zone is the natural tendency of athletes or coaches to be so happy with attaining a certain level of achievement that they fail to strive to improve. The Japanese have a word, *shoribyo* (victory disease), for this attitude. The implication is that when people get used to a certain level of success over a period of time, they have a natural tendency to become complacent, followed by failure to plan and prepare thoroughly for the next contest. There is danger in both aspects.

Norman Vincent Peale, in *The Positive Principle Today*, said that there is a deep tendency in human nature for us to become precisely what we imagine or picture ourselves to be—we ourselves determine either self-limitation or unlimited growth potential. If this is true, it is up to coaches to motivate youngsters in such a way that they develop a burning desire to become as good as they can possibly be.

Mike Ditka, professional football coach, said: "The most important thing in any person being motivated is that person. The individual must want to achieve the ultimate she/he can with the talent they have. And they must be relentless in the pursuit of excellence—to be the best."

The best kind of motivation, without question, is self-motivation. Some youngsters who participate in high school athletics have a high degree of self-motivation, while others have little or none. The highly motivated athletes are seen by coaches as real competitors. Normally these people are the easiest to coach because they come "ready to play." These people are self-starters, and they make coaching pure pleasure.

For a high school coach to consistently find teams made up totally of highly self-motivated boys or girls is extremely rare. Thus your ability to motivate, to make a group of young people want to work to excel and to reach their maximum potential, will be tested. This is true for practices, and particularly in the preseason, when the first game seems so far away. One of the best ways to encourage the team is for you, the coach, to be the most enthusiastic person there. Enthusiasm is contagious.

Generally speaking, athletes have two basic motives: *in order to* or *because of.* For example, they can be motivated to act *in order to* make the team, break a record, win, earn a scholarship, or make their parents proud. They can also be motivated *because of* peer pressure, anger, pride, and tradition, to mention a few. You as a coach have to discover which factors are important to your players and then use those factors as motivation.

One of the methods you can use to discover what these factors are is through the use of goal setting. If you can learn what goals individuals have set for themselves and the team, you can use them as motivation to assist individuals to accomplish some or all of those stated goals, dreams, or hopes.

Challenges

If we agree that motivation is the key to learning, is there a key to motivation in sport? The answer is yes, and the key is challenge. If a youngster is a competitor, challenge can be extremely effective as a motivational tool. However, it is important that challenges be realistic, or they become meaningless. Since not everyone responds to motivation the same way, coaches have to know their athletes as individuals so the proper motivation can be applied. Coaches must also be sensitive and have a feel for the personality of a team as well as the individuals on it. President Dwight D. Eisenhower once said, "You can measure people by the way they respond to challenge." Experienced coaches know this is so.

Many coaches believe that when all factors are fairly equal, the teams or individuals who win are those with the highest motivation and the best mental preparation.

When coaches are able to instill a burning desire to succeed in a group of athletes, that team will be a difficult one to compete with and, although it might get beaten, it never loses. In other words, if they come up short on the scoreboard, it is because their opponent was better and not because they themselves played a poor and uninspired game. Everyone wants to win, but it is the individuals who don't want to lose who are the most successful. Many coaches believe that the goal of motivation in sport is to develop players who are competitive and who play to win.

Some will argue this point and insist that the goal of motivation is to instill a desire for excellence. Some also believe that playing to win can hinder excellence because in playing to win the only thing that matters is the score—never mind how the points come, just as long as we have more than the opponent at the end of the contest. On the other hand, many coaches believe that winning is excellence and that you cannot have one without the other. Ultimately the answer comes down to each coach's own philosophy of sport, including the importance he or she places on winning.

Competitiveness

There is the belief, too, that the basic purpose of motivation is to make youngsters competitive. Competitiveness in this context is defined as the desire to succeed in "the game," to show superiority over an opponent.

However you view the purpose of motivation, one fundamental fact overrides all else, and that is that youngsters bring different degrees of competitiveness to sports. Much depends on their past environment, both familial and social.

If boys or girls grow up in an environment where competitiveness is rewarded, they are more likely to respond to motivation than youngsters who come from an environment where competitiveness is minimized. Coaches obviously need to know the individuals on the team and their backgrounds.

Motivational Methods

Motivating people to consistent levels of readiness is a fascinating and difficult process. The basic problem is that there is no one best or right way that fits all people all the time. As a result, coaches constantly strive to discover effective ways to accomplish this task. There are as many ways to motivate athletes as

there are coaches. Most coaches would admit that they have tried them all at one time or another. To further complicate matters, the method that worked in firing up a group today might not work tomorrow, next week, or next year. People change, circumstances change, moods change, and the personalities of teams change. To beginning coaches this becomes an exercise of trial and error.

In their desire to become motivators of athletes, some coaches become "gimmick" coaches, relying a great deal on inspirational slogans, music, signs in the locker room, and various awards throughout the season. Their belief is that these gimmicks will excite the athletes, fire them up, and help get them into the proper frame of mind for competition.

There is nothing wrong with this approach, but too much of anything can become counterproductive, and so it is with gimmicks. The real danger in this approach to motivation is that coaches can get so wrapped up in gimmicks that they neglect to teach youngsters how to play the game.

Noise or complete silence, inspirational talks, humor, and pleas or threats to motivate a team are other possibilities. Waiting until just before a competition to inspire athletes with an emotional speech is usually a waste of time, because such inspiration is short-lived. Attacking the team's or individual's ego or pride can sometimes be effective. The coach's personality is the key, moreso in this situation than in one in which gimmicks are used extensively.

The slightest amount of motivation will affect performance to some degree, but an attempt to increase motivation excessively may actually result in poorer performance. Increasing evidence shows that it might be a mistake to key athletes up before competition. In fact, it might be better to calm them down so they can relax and perform better. Getting athletes too high can hinder athletic performance. Anyone who has participated in sport and didn't perform well because of being too "tight" can appreciate this concept. The problem is to determine how much and what kind of motivation it takes to get people to perform their best.

Readiness and Timing

Another factor influencing attempts to get every athlete on the team to perform maximally is the possibility that different athletes are on different parts of the performance curve at the same time (see Figure 4.1). As a result, athletes are at varying degrees of readiness at any given time. This situation causes a high degree of anxiety for coaches, because it is so difficult to tell whether athletes are mentally ready to play their best. This is particularly true with high school athletes because they have so many other things on their minds, but it is also a concern among college and professional teams. As a result, a coach in a typical high school cannot always be sure what a team will do once they take the field or court, and this uncertainty can be very disturbing.

The timing involved in motivation is also crucial. The right thing said at the wrong time can cause an adverse reaction. Too much motivation too soon can leave an athlete or team exhausted before the competition begins. Generally, the

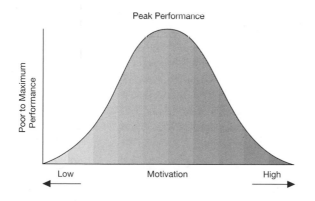

Figure 4.1
The performance curve.

best technique is to begin preparing athletes mentally several days or more before the contest and to build to a peak when the competition is about to begin.

Playing on the emotions of an individual athlete or group of athletes is a delicate technique, since there is such a fine line between too little motivation and too much, too soon, or too late. One of the cautions to be considered in attempting to get athletes psyched up for an athletic contest is to try to avoid the peaks and valleys of emotional readiness.

Tom Landry, former coach of the Dallas Cowboys, said in *The Game Makers*, "Emotion can cover up a lot of inadequacies, but in the end it also gets in the way of performance. An emotional team cannot stay that way consistently over a full season or even a few games." Individual athletes cannot survive an entire season at the peak of emotional arousal either. Somewhere along the line there will be a letdown, and when that occurs performance suffers. Many experienced coaches have learned this the hard way.

Frequently, when a team gets sky-high for a really big contest—win, lose, or draw—the athletes are drained emotionally and as a consequence might not play well for one or more contests afterward. If this is the last contest of the season, obviously there is no problem. But during the season it can be a pretty stiff price to pay for getting all those competitive juices flowing for a single contest.

The trick is to keep the athletes consistently on the high side of the scale, with infrequent attempts to reach the peak of emotional readiness (see Figure 4.2). As some coaches have put it, you can only go to the well so often before it runs dry. Often, when a team fails to perform well it is because of this motivational factor rather than of how well they were taught the mechanics of the game.

The ability to consistently motivate people to do their best might be one of the most important qualities a coach can have. A former manager of the Los Angeles Dodgers had this to say: "Never gloat on the peaks and never stay in the valleys."

Coaches often become so involved in the organization and mechanical aspects of sport that they neglect the personality of the team and begin to take motivation for granted because they themselves are highly motivated. You should make every effort to develop and perfect the ability to motivate youngsters throughout your coaching career.

Figure 4.2
Coaching is truly an exciting occupation, involving the whole gamut of emotions from super highs to heartbreak.

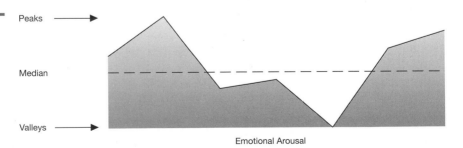

Peaks

Median

Valleys

Emotional Arousal

DEDICATION

Dedication is another important quality of a coach—dedication to doing the best possible job all year, to becoming a better coach, and to making the sport the best it can be for the youngsters who participate. You also need to have a great desire to be the best and to do whatever preparation is necessary to reach this goal. If you do not have this kind of dedication, you will probably never advance beyond the level of mediocrity as a coach. Dedication to the profession is a must if you hope to be an effective teacher/coach.

> If you want to move people,
> It has to be toward a vision that's positive for them,
> That taps important values,
> That gets them something they desire,
> And it has to be presented in a compelling way
> That they feel inspired to follow.
> —Martin Luther King, Jr., *"I Have a Dream"*

WILLINGNESS TO MAKE HARD CHOICES/DECISIONS

When you are faced with a difficult problem it matters not how much input and advice you get from your staff or anyone else. The final decision is yours, simply because you are the head coach. If you are lacking decisiveness, discipline will suffer and so will the athletes' respect for you. You have to have the backbone to stand tall and do what you believe to be the best for individuals and the team.

When coming to a final decision, it will prove helpful to remember these steps:

1. Identify the problem. The problem is not always clear or obvious and might require some probing on your part.

2. Determine immediate goals. Don't be in a hurry.

3. List possible alternatives.

4. Make a final decision.

5. Consider possible repercussions.

ABILITY TO DISCIPLINE

The need to be a firm disciplinarian is an integral part of teaching. In this context *discipline* is defined as control. Youngsters need guidelines, and they need to know the limits of their conduct. There is nothing wrong with telling young people what they can or cannot do, or with teaching them how to respond to an authority figure. In spite of a desire for individuality and "doing your own thing" in today's society, there is and always will be a need for discipline to guarantee some form of order. Young people still need to learn to follow rules and to discover what the consequences are of breaking rules. Today it might be rules of the game, but tomorrow it will be the rules for living in society as an adult.

There is no concrete proof that the discipline a player experiences in athletics will necessarily carry over into any other walk of life—only teachers' belief that it does, and their occasional firsthand experience when they can see that it does. In the book *Plain Speaking*, President Harry S. Truman remarked, "We were taught that punishment always followed transgression—I was punished and it hurt, but I tried never to do whatever it was again." This is not a bad philosophy of discipline, even in the 2000s. The important point is that if there are rules there must be a penalty for violating them, and whatever penalty is to be paid, it has to hurt. This in no way implies physical punishment for an athlete; but hurt nonetheless. For example, it hurts an athlete to be benched; it hurts a starter not to start; it hurts a first-team player to be demoted to the second team; and it hurts a competitor to be kept out of competition. Without the threat of some kind of penalty, rules are virtually useless.

> Being punished isn't enjoyable
> While it is happening—it hurts.
> But afterwards we can see the result,
> A quiet growth in grace and character.
> —Hebrews 12:10, *The Living Bible*

The keys to maintaining discipline are firmness, fairness, and consistency. Whatever rules are made must be reasonable, must have a purpose, and must be understood by everyone concerned. To eliminate a lot of problems and misunderstandings, many coaches have written rules for athletes and see to it that parents also get a copy. To make a greater impact on athletes and their parents, coaches sometimes have both parties sign forms attesting to the fact that they have read the rules, understand them, and agree to abide by them or face disciplinary action.

There are four main approaches to rules and disciplinary action.

The first is to allow members of the team to write the rules along with possible penalties. If you use this method, don't be surprised to find the athletes' rules tougher than those you would write.

Two is to write down both each rule and the penalty to be paid if the rule is broken. This approach certainly makes things clear, but it also takes away options. It means that anyone who violates the rule will pay the same penalty—if not, you are not being consistent, and problems will arise. Another difficulty with this method is that a fine youngster with an excellent attitude who makes a one-time thoughtless mistake must be penalized the same as a chronic troublemaker. Some coaches cannot accept this notion.

The third approach is to list the rules and several alternative penalties for each. This gives you some options and prevents you from being trapped in a corner.

The fourth approach is simply to list the rules without stating any penalties. This gives you all the latitude in the world, because each case can be handled on its own merit, taking into account the individual, the violation, and any extenuating circumstances. It also means that a violation by more than one player might be dealt with in more than one way. The most important thing with this approach is that you have a reason for whatever you do, and follow through on the consequences.

ABILITY TO IDENTIFY GOALS

If you are to be an effective teacher, you need to identify goals for yourself and the program. Establishing specific objectives is a basic principle of teaching, and when made clear they provide direction for all facets of the activity, including the way you perform within the framework. Out of necessity, some goals will have to be accomplished immediately, while others will be medium range, and still others will

> One of the greatest qualities of successful leaders is vision.
> —*Father Hesburgh, former President of Notre Dame*

be long range. These goals should be self-directed as well as team directed. (Goal setting is discussed in greater detail in Chapter 10.)

It usually takes several years to accomplish all your goals, and some may never be reached. It is therefore important to be patient with yourself, the athletes, the program, and the administrators of the school. Your timetable, along with your objectives, might have to be reevaluated and readjusted several times. You might have overestimated your own abilities, you might have misjudged the capabilities of the athletes, or your goals might change as you become more experienced and begin to mature in the profession. The mismatch between goals and reality is normal, and you should not be so impatient that you become discouraged if things move more slowly than planned.

An administration's effect on the program often requires a great deal of patience also. Administrators are sometimes slow to help bring about all the changes coaches desire in order to upgrade their programs, but you must keep working toward your objectives anyway. If you feel frustrated in reaching specific goals because it appears that the administration is stifling and will continue to stifle the growth of a program, consider moving to another coaching position.

The quality of salesmanship is closely related to this point. Unless you are given carte blanche in organizing a specific program for a high school—an unusual situation—meeting some of your goals will depend a great deal on salesmanship.

If your predecessor had a different philosophy toward coaching and different goals for the program, the goals you establish for the team and ways in which you hope to attain them will be affected.

ABILITY TO RECOGNIZE ATHLETIC TALENT

It has been said that rarer than ability is the ability to recognize ability. Therefore, evaluating players and choosing the team become primary concerns for all coaches. The ability to recognize talent is a quality that should be developed to its fullest. There is much more to spotting talent than meets the eye, and this ability should not be taken lightly.

Skills alone do not indicate a player's true talent, nor will a player's physical makeup, speed, strength, or relation to someone who was a great athlete. Physi-

cal skills are not difficult to recognize, and in some individual sports like tennis, track and field, or swimming, the stopwatch, the height of the crossbar, or a challenge match usually determines who will participate. The greatest difficulty in evaluating players is to try to determine how each athlete will perform in the game or contest. You must identify as quickly as possible who the "gamers" are. These are athletes who, regardless of their skill, size, speed, or whatever, simply get the job done. A gamer cannot always be determined before a season begins or without seeing the youngsters in game competition.

Drills will not serve this function in every case, although they frequently indicate certain qualities you look for in an athlete. But suppose that in a contact game like football, you match two boys in a drill that demands a lot of aggressiveness. Although one of the boys might be naturally timid, he will stand and fight rather than be embarrassed in front of his teammates. However, when the same boy practices with a whole team, he may not compete well because all eyes are not on him, and he may lose himself in the crowd, which is his preferred mode of behavior. Thus, all other things being equal, the best way to evaluate a player's overall ability is through game participation.

There is no way to predetermine what is in the heart of athletes about game-time competition—their actions in the game itself will reveal this. Consequently, you should organize practices like game situations as soon as possible and use preseason scrimmages or meets to find out who the competitors are.

ABILITY TO USE AVAILABLE TALENT

Along with the ability to evaluate personnel, the ability to improvise with the talent on hand is also important in achieving a successful season. It is a rare situation when a high school team has no weaknesses or shortcomings in personnel. Whereas a college coach can recruit athletes to fit a particular system, a high school coach must make a system fit the talent on hand, and the mix of talent changes year by year. Thus, it is an obvious waste of time for any coach to keep saying, "If we had stronger athletes, faster athletes, more athletes," and so on. Instead, all your thoughts have to be directed toward improving what is available, doing a great job of teaching, devising strategy that will give your athletes the greatest chance of competing well, placing various athletes in different positions if necessary, and finally, camouflaging whatever weaknesses still exist in order to make it difficult for an opponent to detect them.

Do not let what you cannot do interfere with what you can do. Good coaches will take what talent there is and do the best possible job they can with it. They won't spend time in the futility of looking at a squad and saying, "If only we had this or that." It is also futile for you to try to fit athletes into a particular system that does not match their abilities instead of adjusting the system to fit the talent.

> Your desire to win must be infectious, so overriding that there is an osmosis process at work where that desire is keenly felt by the players.
> —*Woody Hayes*

DESIRE TO WIN

Instilling a burning desire to play to win is a basic obligation of coaching—and, like enthusiasm, it is contagious. There is absolutely nothing wrong or evil in teaching young people to play to win and to excel, providing this is always done within the rules and spirit of the game. It is only when rules, written and unwritten, are violated that this notion is corrupted.

Another important consideration is that your athletes learn that although playing to win is essential, a game is not an all-or-nothing experience. That is, a team or player that fails to win must not feel like a failure. There are lessons to be learned in both winning and losing, and it is your job to see that the lessons are learned. The biggest lesson in losing is that the sun will rise again tomorrow. A game is, after all, still a game.

> In a race, everyone runs but only one person gets first prize. So run your race to win. To win the contest you must deny yourselves many things that would keep you from doing your best—so I run straight to the goal with purpose in every step. I fight to win.
> —*I Corinthians 9:24, The Living Bible*

There is a danger in the play-to-win attitude, of course, and that is the temptation to win at any cost—by breaking rules, using and abusing athletes, abusing officials, or using unethical tactics to gain an advantage over an opponent. The desire to win does not excuse any of these acts, and they have no place in high school athletics.

Poor conduct on the part of coaches is often justified on the grounds that they hate to lose. This rationalization is pure nonsense and causes a great deal of malpractice in high school athletic programs. In some situations the game ceases to be a game, becoming instead an ego-satisfying experience for the coach. This danger must be avoided at all times.

DISLIKE OF MEDIOCRITY

Coaches must also have an intense dislike for mediocrity in anything that concerns the program in any way. You must develop in athletes the attitude that whatever is done has to be done the *right* way—your way—and anything less than that will not be satisfactory. There is a right and wrong way to do the right thing, but there is no right way to do the wrong thing. There are a lot of ways to accomplish a certain task in any sport, but the athletes have to understand that when all factors are taken into account—personnel, ability, speed, and so on—there is one best way for this group to get the job done and that it is important that everyone do it this way. Mediocrity breeds mediocrity. Abraham Lincoln once remarked that an individual cannot help being born average, but no one has to stay that way.

In athletics, typical high school youngsters will not drive themselves to rise very far above mediocrity unless they have a high degree of self-motivation. So you must insist that each individual strive to become the best that he or she can. To create or tolerate an atmosphere in which youngsters learn that mediocrity is acceptable in sport or life would be a flagrant abdication of your responsibility as a teacher.

The German philosopher Goethe said that if you treat people as they are, they will stay as they are, but if you treat them as if they were what they could be, they will become what they ought to be. You need to encourage your athletes to always strive to go higher and to understand that within themselves they can be greater than they think.

> If you can't be a pine on the top of the hill,
> Be a scrub in the valley—but be
> The best little scrub by the side of the hill;
> Be a bush if you can't be a tree.
> If you can't be a bush, be a bit of the grass,
> Some highway happier make;
> If you can't be a muskie, then just be a bass—
> But the liveliest bass in the lake!
> We can't all be captains, we've got to be crew,
> There's something for all of us here,
> There's big work to do, and there's lesser to do,
> And the task we must do is the near,
> If you can't be a highway, then just be a trail,
> If you can't be the sun, be a star;
> It isn't by size that you win or you fail—
> Be the best of whatever you are!
> —Douglas Malloch

One way to avoid mediocrity is to insist on precision in everything affecting the team. The first step in precision is punctuality. Tardiness on the part of athletes or coaches should not be tolerated. Some coaches deliberately set odd times for meetings or for a bus to leave for a game. For example, to make people more aware of punctuality, you could set a meeting for 8:13 rather than 8:00 or 8:15, and then start the meeting at the set time. Precision is also important in the way the athletes and coaches dress for practice, because they are members of a team, and as a team they will succeed together or fail together. You should also insist on precision in practicing or teaching the techniques that will be used in a game.

The greatest benefit to be achieved through your dislike of mediocrity is teaching people to be thorough and to pay attention to detail. No matter what the sport is, the movements involved and the plays executed are all made up of many small details. If details are ignored, the final product will suffer. Youngsters are impatient to play the game and do not like to work on details or fundamentals, but coaches cannot afford to take shortcuts. Attention to detail is the

foundation on which consistently strong teams are built. If you take care of the little things, the big things will take care of themselves.

ABILITY TO REASON

Another quality you should develop is to have well thought-out reasons for everything you do in coaching. You should carefully consider every decision, with all its ramifications, before you act. You need to look at all phases of the program as well as at your personal philosophy and ask yourself, "Why are we doing this?" or "Why do I believe this?" Such questioning forces you to evaluate everything you believe and do in coaching.

Time is always a factor in coaching a team. Unless you can come up with a reason for doing specific things, you should eliminate them to avoid wasting time, which very few teams can afford to do. If you cannot justify or explain all the things you do in coaching, in your own mind at least, you shouldn't be doing them. A good mind is constantly under revision when it comes to organizing athletic programs.

There are times when your methods, techniques, and beliefs will be questioned by adults in the community or by the school administrators. In such

> When the players are not performing as well as I think they are capable of, I explode. But what I'm telling them is that I'm mad because I know you can do better—you can do more.
>
> We do not let a player get away with a mistake without forcefully accenting that mistake.
>
> —Woody Hayes

situations you will experience great difficulty if you have not carefully thought out precisely why you conduct the program or certain aspects of it the way you do. This doesn't mean that you have to explain everything you do to every critic in the stands, but you should be able to. You should not do things in athletics simply because someone else does. If a school superintendent asks you why you do things in a certain way, you should be able to answer the question clearly and intelligently.

Whether or not anyone outside of the coaching staff agrees with your reasons is not of prime importance at any given moment. What is important is that you can justify what has taken or is taking place.

INTEREST IN INDIVIDUALS

You should also cultivate an intense and continuing interest in the overall development of each individual you coach or have coached. It is too easy to forget what is happening to youngsters after a season is over, when they are not directly involved with you every day. When you do forget, you lend credence to the critics who insist that coaches care about people only during the season, and then only because the players are doing a job, but once the season ends the coaches cannot be bothered anymore. If you truly care about people you should never allow yourself to fit this stereotype.

The athletes have to know that you care about each person on the team as an individual rather than as a piece of equipment simply to be used. They must also know clearly that everything you do, everything you ask, expect, or demand of them is for one reason and one reason only and that is to help each of them realize their full potential as an athlete and as a human being. Once you establish this mind-set, you can begin putting a team together.

A genuine concern for athletes should carry over into all phases of a youngster's school career and should continue after high school days are over. This means that while students are in school, you are concerned about their academic achievements, conduct, problems, concerns, and successes. It means that you are willing to help, if need be, in guiding a youngster to decide about college or choose a profession. It means you are ready and willing to offer assistance in time of difficulty, as in serious illness or death of an athlete's parent. Your presence can serve as solace and strength for a young person when support is greatly needed.

There will be times when athletes earn the lead in a school play or participate in a band concert. You should feel great pleasure in seeing them excel in something other than sports and be willing to share in this experience by attending such functions. It means a great deal to youngsters that someone other than members of their family—someone who is important to them and is special in their eyes—has taken the time to watch them perform in something other than a game.

Occasionally you will be blessed with athletes who go on to college and are skillful enough to participate in college athletics. Make an effort to attend at least one of their games during a season. It means a lot to athletes when their former high school coach comes to campus to watch their team compete, and it also lets athletes know that you are still interested in their achievements even though they have graduated from high school.

The ultimate in satisfaction, for a coach who cares, occurs years after an athlete has left high school and has become successful in whatever field he or she has chosen to pursue. Long after the games have been played, this is what really counts. This is the time when a coach is permitted the luxury of thinking that the experiences someone had as a member of a particular team might have helped that person become what he or she is as an adult, and as a citizen of the community. There is little research to substantiate this, but coaches do receive enough feedback from former athletes to believe in their hearts that some of the lessons they attempted to teach through the discipline of athletics have made enough of a difference in the lives of their students to make their hard work all worthwhile.

RESPECT

The next quality you should strive for is respect. You cannot demand, dictate, or purchase respect—it must be earned. Generally speaking, you earn the respect of students by how you treat them, the kind of person you are, and what you stand for. Beginning teachers often confuse respect with popularity, but there is a big difference. It is possible for you to be liked as a person but not to command respect. On the other hand, you might not be very popular among students yet have their respect.

Some coaches, in their desire for students to like them, often go easy on discipline and try to establish a friendly "one-of-the-gang" type of image. The biggest difficulty with this approach is that once you cross that invisible line between student and teacher by trying to be a buddy, your role as a professional person is compromised in the eyes of students, colleagues, and the community. Discipline can become a serious problem, which will eventually cause a great deal of resentment on the part of some of the athletes. In the final analysis, the desire to be a pal to players on the team will prove to be a big mistake—a friend, yes—a pal, never. It just doesn't work.

The teacher who is fair, who maintains discipline, who lets the students know what is expected from them and what they can expect in return, and who maintains the line between student and teacher so that the students are always aware that the teacher is their teacher—rather than a buddy with backslapping or first-name familiarity—will be on the way to earning respect from his or her students. Once this feeling develops, the teaching-learning process is enhanced greatly.

You should conduct yourself in such a way that respect comes not only from the members of a team you coach but also from the student body, faculty, school administrators, and people in the community. If you are eager to fulfill all responsibilities of the position and to be an effective teacher and leader, it is mandatory that you work hard to earn and keep the respect of all who know you.

Because of the nature of the position, you are constantly in the public eye. When you are respected for what you are, what you do, and what you believe in, your job becomes much easier. This is especially the case when the team has a bad year in the eyes of the community (the team loses more than it wins). The critics will have their say as usual, but they will be less of a threat to a coach who

is highly respected as a teacher of young boys or girls than to another kind of coach. People tend to be tolerant of those they know and respect and to be particularly critical of those they don't.

ENTHUSIASM

Enthusiasm is a necessary quality for any coach, but especially a head coach, since a team is normally a reflection of the head coach. And because enthusiasm is contagious, it follows that it should emanate from the coaches. This is especially important during preseason practice sessions, when monotony and boredom become a reality. The enthusiasm of the head coach and its effect on the rest of the staff and athletes help make practice less of a chore and more fun.

Enthusiasm is also important to a coach personally. It is this trait that helps create the desire and willingness to spend long hours working during a season, to attend coaching clinics, and to make a continuing effort to learn more about coaching, year after year. Without this quality, coaching is no longer any fun and it is time to give up the job.

WILLINGNESS TO WORK

Another quality of a good coach is the willingness to work hard and to put in long hours when necessary. When the school day ends, a big part of your day is just beginning, and the end of practice does not necessarily mean the end of the working day. Because all the members of a coaching staff usually have teaching responsibilities, staff meetings will have to be held in the evenings or on weekends. You might also have videotapes to review, practice plans to develop, phone calls to make, phone calls to answer, and injured athletes to care for or take home, to mention just a few possibilities.

In many situations, coaching a particular sport has become a year-round occupation rather than a seasonal one. This prolongation of the season usually occurs because the coach feels it is necessary in order to compete well against the teams on next year's schedule. There might be league and state rules that prohibit off-season coaching, but many related activities can be done legally. For example, there are physical conditioning programs to oversee, clinics to attend, notebooks to revise, videotapes to review, and staff meetings to hold for reviewing the season just passed and making plans for the one to come. In high school, all of this must usually be done on your own time, because your daily teaching schedule will not normally provide time for these tasks.

Even though coaching does take a lot of work, you should be careful not to create work for yourself just for the sake of working. There comes a time when this extra work reaches a point of diminishing returns, and you should develop the ability to recognize how much is too much. A weary coach or weary staff will not be effective. In the final analysis, the key to a successful team is still good athletes, and all the meetings in the world will not change this fact. Your most important consideration here is efficiency, not the amount of time spent in planning.

KNOWLEDGE OF THE SPORT

Knowledge of the sport is particularly critical for a head coach. An assistant coach can be effective by being knowledgeable about a particular phase of a sport, but it is mandatory that a head coach have a thorough knowledge of all phases of the sport in order to organize and supervise the program properly and efficiently. The head coach is, in effect, the master teacher and therefore must develop a great knowledge of all the intricacies of the sport. Competing in a particular sport provides the basic knowledge on which can be built additional knowledge gained through study and experience.

Additional ways to increase your knowledge include attending clinics, reading coaching books, watching videotapes, talking with other coaches, visiting college coaches, and coaching at summer camps.

UNDERSTANDING BOYS AND GIRLS

Because your professional career will rise or fall on your ability to teach youngsters, it becomes imperative that you prepare yourself in every way possible to understand what makes teenagers tick. To motivate and teach them, you have to understand and appreciate their concerns, problems, anxieties, interests, physical capabilities, and mental characteristics. Since so many physiological and psychological changes occur in each individual during the teenage years, you should realize that most youngsters have many concerns in addition to athletics.

Remember that to most of these young people, a game is a game and not the beginning and end of the world. There are too many other things clamoring for their attention, even though a person like you sees the same game from an entirely different point of view. Unless you are aware of this vast difference in outlook, you might assume that the players don't really care because they seem to get over the disappointment of a loss so quickly. Before too much time has passed, they are talking about other things. You might feel a lot of frustration and disappointment unless you remember that a game is only a game to the youngsters on the team.

> If a "man" does not keep pace with his companions,
> perhaps it is because he hears a different drummer.
> Let him step to the music he hears,
> However measured or far away.
> —Henry David Thoreau, *Walden*

Another false assumption you can make, and that can create misunderstanding, is the belief that youngsters come out for a sport and stay on the team because they love it—just as you love the sport. Nothing might be further from the truth. There are many reasons why young people go out for athletic teams. Included among them are social pressure, getting to wear the uniform, and pressure from parents, as well as love of the game.

Social Pressure

Pressure might come from a girlfriend, a boyfriend, or a group of friends. Peer pressure is one of the strongest influences on teenagers. Not only might this influence their decision to try out for a team, but it also sometimes dictates which sport.

The Uniform

Some youngsters stay on a team just for the opportunity to be seen wearing a game uniform. They enjoy the pregame warm-up because they get a chance to show off a bit, but by the time the game begins, they have been satisfied. They have had their moment of glory, and they really don't care to play in the game.

These people sit on the end of the bench, and when you turn around to look for a substitute, they quickly look in the other direction, hoping you won't notice them.

Pressure from Mom or Dad

One of the saddest reasons for students to be on a team is because their parents want them to be. In such cases the youngster is usually unhappy and probably hates every minute of practice. If you are unaware of this possibility, you might add to the youngster's misery by "getting on" this player because he or she isn't doing a good job in practice. Youngsters in a sport that is highly aggressive with body contact might suffer a great deal of inner torment because the situation is so disagreeable and unpleasant. There might also be an element of fear.

Boys and girls who go out for a sport because their mother or father expects it should be pitied for the unhappiness being forced on them. If you become aware of this and feel strongly that a student would be much better off if he or she weren't part of the team, you should consider talking to the parents to try to make them aware of what they are forcing their child to do. On the surface, this might sound very easy, but in reality it can be quite difficult. Some parents will refuse to listen because they don't believe what you are saying or they don't want to hear what you are saying. Either the parents were athletes and they want their children to be athletes too, or they weren't and are trying to live this experience through a son or daughter. The high cost of a college education coupled  with greater opportunities to win athletic scholarships has created additional parental pressure. Whatever the case, it takes a great deal of tact and diplomacy to deal with parents like this, and even with the greatest tact, you might fail.

Another possibility to consider is cutting the student from the team. By doing so you can take a player out of an unhappy situation and still not destroy his or her relationship with the parents; after all, the player didn't quit the team—you cut him or her. If, in your judgment, this is the best course of action for the youngster's mental and physical well-being, you should be willing to do it in spite of criticism from the frustrated parents—and it will come.

Love of the Game

There are still people who go out for teams because they enjoy the sport and love to compete, and these people are in the majority. In spite of all the criticism aimed at sport in our modern society, hundreds of thousands of youngsters across the country participate because they love a sport and everything that goes with it. You simply need to recognize that not everyone on the team feels this way.

Ego Involvement

Ego involvement is also a big factor in being a member of the school team. There is evidence to suggest that without it students will not play—or if they do, they won't really work hard. You should attempt to identify this factor in each athlete, and then use it to get each athlete to do the best job possible to help the team succeed.

It may also be that ego involvement on the part of a coach is what keeps men and women in the coaching profession.

Athletic Scholarships

Some students participate on teams because there is the promise of a scholarship, and with it the opportunity to go to college. For some, this might appear to be the only way they will ever have to get a college education, and with escalating costs this factor provides tremendous motivation for many athletes—and their parents.

KNOWING WHAT MAKES THE DIFFERENCE BETWEEN WINNING AND LOSING

As any athlete or coach knows, both controllable and uncontrollable factors affect the outcome of any athletic contest. Generally speaking, the six factors that follow are among the most important to consider. You will notice that five of these factors can be controlled by you, and not by circumstances or an opponent.

Superior Personnel

The prime prerequisite for winning is to have great athletes on your team. No team has ever won consistently without them, regardless of the ability or intelligence of the coach. Sam Rutigliano, former coach of the Cleveland Browns, said, "Good coaches with bad players get beat by dummies with good players." In the book *Bear*, Coach Bryant of Alabama is quoted as saying, "You can't make chicken salad without the chicken. You have to have winners and you have to be able to recognize them." Beginning coaches who have been blessed with outstanding athletes and who start a coaching career by winning sometimes fail to appreciate the contribution of the highly skilled youngsters, and they assume that the wins occur because they themselves are extraordinary. In situations like this it is easy for coaches to overestimate themselves, thereby minimizing the value of great athletes. Contrast this with coaches who believe that winning is 90 percent outstanding athletes and 10 percent coaching.

Superior Conditioning

Regardless of the ability of the athletes, it is your responsibility to make sure that each individual is in the proper physical condition to play the game. Tired athletes are more prone to injury than those who are still fresh. Fatigue makes cowards of us all, and the harder you work, the harder it is to surrender. So one of your goals should be to condition a team so well that they are as strong physically at the end of the contest as they are at the begin- ning. Often the outcome of an athletic event is determined at the end, and the team in better physical condition has a greater chance of winning at that point.

Fewer Mistakes

Military people know that a battle is a succession of mis- takes and that the side that blunders less emerges victori- ous. And so it is in sport. Athletic contests are basically games of mistakes. Normally the team or individual that makes the fewest mistakes has the greatest chance of win- ning. The mistakes a team or individual makes in competi- tion usually occur in direct proportion to the quality of instruction, frame of mind, discipline, attention to detail, thoroughness of preparation, and physical condition. Mis- takes are inevitable when youngsters are swept up in the excitement of a highly competitive situation. Your job, then, is to prepare the team well enough so that mistakes are kept to a minimum. The perfect game has probably never been played, although that should be the goal of every athlete and coach in every competition.

Superior Mental Attitude

When people of similar ability compete, the difference in winning or losing usually depends on being mentally ready. In high school competition, where talented athletes come in cycles and a league is fairly balanced, the coach who has the ability to prepare players mentally will have teams that are consistently at the top of the standings.

A great baseball player illustrated this superior mental attitude when he said, "If you have better people than us, you'll win; if we have better people than you, we'll win. If we're even, we'll win." That is confidence.

Superior Teaching

The importance of a coach's teaching ability was discussed earlier. There is, however, one other phase of teaching to be considered, and that is not to talk too much in the practice area. Most of the talking should be done in group meetings or team meetings, so that you can take advantage of all possible practice time at

Positive Thinking

If you think you are beaten,
   you are

If you think you dare not,
   you don't

If you'd like to win, but you think you can't

It's almost a cinch that you won't.

If you think you'll lose, you're lost,
   For out in the world we find

Success begins with a fellow's will,
   It's all in the state of the mind.

If you think you're outclassed,
   You are.

You've got to think high to rise,

You've got to be sure of yourself before
   You can ever win a prize,

Life's battle doesn't always go
   To the swifter or faster man,

But sooner or later the man who wins

Is the man who thinks he can.

   —*Author Unknown*

the site. Remember—the key is not how much you know, but how well you can communicate what you know to the athletes. This is what matters. Great coaches are, without exception, great teachers.

Superior Placement of Personnel

Whatever the situation, the level of competition, or the sport, there are always only five, nine, or eleven best athletes, depending on how many are needed on the first team. One of the first priorities of a new season is to determine who the best athletes are, and then make whatever position changes are necessary to put these people into the starting lineup.

It is ridiculous to have a fine athlete on the bench when a change of this player's or someone else's position could put her or him into the contest. Not only is it critical to put the best people into the competition, it is also crucial to put the best people in the right position. You should never hesitate to place athletes in different positions if you think it is the right thing to do. Even though an athlete should be willing to make a move, your ability to sell the youngster on its value both to the player and the team will do much to smooth the transition. Being blessed with fine athletes is one thing, but using them properly is quite another.

ABILITY TO FOSTER PRIDE

One of the goals you will want to strive for is to develop pride and tradition if it doesn't already exist in the team you coach. Team pride carries over to the individuals who make up the team. When athletes are proud of their team and its accomplishments, being a member of the team becomes highly desirable and creates an atmosphere in which it is pleasant to coach. Pride can be used as motivation for the team, and athletes in this case become more susceptible to the methods you feel are necessary to prepare the group to compete.

Pride and tradition cannot be purchased or borrowed or established by edict; they must be inherited or developed over time. Development can come about through various means, such as outfitting a team in sharp uniforms, instilling discipline, developing excellent facilities, maintaining the locker room in top condition, encouraging hard work, or offering first-class treatment during a season. But the primary means is through success (winning). Once pride and tradition are established, they become self-perpetuating, provided the team continues to experience more success than failure. A winning tradition not only solves a lot of problems but also prevents many problems from ever arising. Obviously, inheriting tradition and pride can make a coach's job much easier.

Teams that have established this characteristic consistently dominate, unless they experience a down cycle—an absence of great athletes or an unusual number of injuries during the season. Championship teams and championship athletes have always had great pride in their accomplishments and as a result struggle fiercely to maintain the pride they feel for themselves and the team. Pride provides the motivation necessary for athletes or teams to come from the brink of defeat to victory. Tradition and pride sometimes take years to establish, but once they are a reality, their value to a team is immeasurable.

PROPER USE OF LANGUAGE

The apparent ease with which many people—youngsters and adults, men and women—resort to cursing in normal conversation and especially in athletics is a matter to address in your own mind before meeting your team for the first time. You must decide whether swearing is acceptable from your athletes, your coaches, and yourself, and be prepared to justify your decision if necessary. If you choose to accept this kind of language or use it yourself because you believe it will make for better rapport with the athletes—don't. It is a mistake for any teacher to get down on a level with students. Your basic responsibility is to bring students up to a higher level in every area over which you can have influence, including the proper use of language. In actuality, every teacher in every school is a language teacher—or should be.

Unfortunately, far too many coaches believe that it is necessary to swear at athletes because they think it shows toughness. For the most part, swearing only demonstrates ignorance of the language. All teachers should have enough command of language to express themselves clearly, without abusing a youngster with curse words. Cursing does absolutely nothing to enhance you as a positive role model. It is degrading both to the user and to those at whom it is directed. Cursing at youngsters does not make a male coach more of a man, and it certainly doesn't do anything for a woman's feminine image.

Regardless of how you feel about swearing, our society has developed the belief and expectation that teachers simply do not curse at their students in the teaching process. The fact that you teach on a playing field rather than in a classroom does not alter this idea one iota. There is not one shred of evidence to prove that cursing players helps them learn quicker, better, or more. Nor is there any evidence to substantiate the belief that it makes any individual tougher or a better athlete. Therefore, cursing by coaches and athletes should be unacceptable.

If you believe that cursing will add to your stature as a model for your athletes to emulate, you are wrong. Resorting to language of the gutter also demonstrates an undesirable quality for a coach—"phony tough."

A lot of youngsters live with parents who do not curse them, so they will resent a teacher who does. You can destroy a great deal of respect a player might otherwise have for you by resorting to swearing. There might be some truth to the idea that swearing is a strong way to show a weak mind.

The following tongue-in-cheek list should help as you consider the effect cursing has on students, including your own image as an educated person.

Fourteen Reasons Why I Swear
1. It is the mark of being a real gentleman or lady.
2. It is an example of self-control.
3. It pleases my family so much.
4. It is a sign of refinement and culture.
5. It shows how well educated I am.
6. It demonstrates my command of the language.
7. It sets a good example for youngsters.
8. It shows how tough I am.
9. It makes me a better teacher.
10. It makes people respect me.
11. It adds dignity to my role as a coach.
12. It demonstrates how much respect I have for you.
13. It will make you a better athlete.
14. It will help us win.

MORAL STANDARDS

Traditionally, coaches are expected to have high moral standards. This quality is important for any adult who is a teacher of young people, but it is especially critical for an athletic coach. The special role a coach fulfills in the lives of impressionable youngsters, and the fact that coaches do teach by personal example, requires a life guided by high moral standards. You should take great care to avoid being a hypocrite in the eyes of the athletes: Do not advocate one set of values while practicing the opposite. Hypocrisy will destroy your credibility and will eventually impair your effectiveness as a teacher, model, and leader of boys and girls.

There seem to be few absolutes concerning moral standards today. So you need to determine in your own mind what you believe is morally correct for yourself and the youngsters you teach. If your standards are not acceptable to administrators of a particular school, it would be better for everyone concerned if you taught somewhere else. Administrators have been given the responsibility of running the schools and employing the kind of teachers they believe will provide the best possible education for all the students. If a coach's moral standards do not fit the expectations school administrators have for their teachers, it is their duty to dismiss this person or not hire him or her in the first place.

HONESTY

Honesty is another desirable quality you should demonstrate at all times, and one that should be insisted on from everyone in sport.

An experiment was conducted several years ago using several hundred high school girls and boys to test the hypothesis that youngsters involved in interscholastic sport are more honest in situations calling for honesty than students who are not athletes. The assumption was made that honesty is learned better through participation in athletics than in everyday life. This assumption was proved false. In short, if honesty is to be learned in athletics, it must be deliberately taught by you, the coach, as situations arise that demand an honest reaction.

> This above all: To thine own self be true.
> And it must follow as the night the day,
> Thou canst not then be false to any man.
> —Shakespeare, *Hamlet*

Coaching provides unlimited opportunities to teach honesty. It also provides unlimited opportunities to teach youngsters how to be dishonest and how to cheat. In fact it is probably easier to teach the latter. It is possible that sport teaches little or nothing that is good unless you make a deliberate attempt to teach the athletes more than the skills of the game. "More" includes honesty, and it cannot be learned by accident. It must be taught and demonstrated through your example: by how you deal with the players, their parents, the officials, and the opposing coaches; how you observe the rules of the game; and how you set your strategy for playing the game. Through these situations you can teach honesty or, conversely, dishonesty.

It is one thing to agree on the importance of being honest and to subscribe to the idea of fair play, but this lip service can be tested when winning a crucial game is concerned. To the coach who has a great deal of integrity, this situation would not make any difference, and ideally all coaches, leaders of young men and women, should demonstrate a high level of integrity at all times. In sport there can be no justification for dishonesty, but because human beings are what they are, dishonesty is often called something else. Some coaches will do almost anything to win, and then they rationalize their behavior by claiming that their tactics were good strategy. Such tactics can involve bending the rules, outright breaking of rules, or doing something to upset or outsmart an athlete on the other side. No high school game should ever be this important.

Honesty is still the best policy.

DIGNITY

The dignity with which you conduct yourself will be noticed by all who know you, not only in game situations but during school hours, at league meetings, and in the life of the community. Maintaining dignity becomes difficult at times, such as immediately after a disappointing performance by a team or in the face of criticism from grandstand quarterbacks, both of which situations are inevitable in coaching. It can be embarrassing to lose your cool and then read your comments in the local newspaper the next day.

A coach's loss of self-control during a game or contest is painfully apparent to everyone present. This is particularly true in sports such as wrestling, volleyball, and basketball, where the crowd is close to the action and a coach can lose control in the wild excitement of the contest and the mob spirit it generates. The sight of an educated adult stomping, screaming, throwing things, abusing athletes or officials, and having a temper tantrum on the sidelines certainly does little for the dignity of the individual or of the profession. No one likes to lose, but not everyone behaves like a spoiled child when it happens.

Classroom teachers rarely lose control and scream at the class, break furniture, smash something, and put on a real show of anger because a class didn't do well on a test. Contrast this with the actions of some coaches on the sidelines when things aren't going well; the difference is incredible. There are many reasons for this difference, but one of the strongest is the degree of ego involvement. Classroom teachers are in their own little world of four walls and a closed door, while the coaches have their students on display every week, sometimes in front of thousands of people. If the team loses, it is because the coach is incompetent, say the fans. Consequently, maintaining self-control during and after the excitement of a highly competitive contest is not always easy.

> Last, but by no means least, courage—moral courage, the courage of one's convictions, the courage to see things through . . . it's the age old struggle—one struggle—the roar of the crowd on the one side, and the voice of your conscience on the other.
>
> —*General Douglas MacArthur*

COURAGE OF YOUR CONVICTIONS

Courage of your convictions—what a wonderful trait for every person to cultivate and live by, especially coaches. To gain this courage, you first have to do some thorough introspection to determine what you believe in, and why. You must then have the courage to stand up for your beliefs, no matter what. Because if you don't stand for something, you'll stand for anything. When you begin to compromise your beliefs, you are finished.

This quality is important in every phase of a sport, and if your convictions are not compatible with the situation, you have three choices: You can compromise to satisfy the situation, you can begin to look for another job, or you can compare what is taking place with what you believe in, to see whether you are being unwise, unreasonable, stubborn, or unwilling to change because your ego will not permit admitting to being wrong.

If you are to be a true teacher and leader of young people, you will eventually have to take a position on some issue that will require the courage to stand up and be counted. Not everyone has this courage, but it is an important ingredient in a coach's image. Some coaches give a lot of lip service to this kind of courage but are nowhere to be found when the time comes to be counted.

In an age when beliefs and convictions are constantly being challenged, you have to use good judgment in clarifying your principles and then be willing to defend them when the need arises. And if you coach for any period of time, the need will eventually arise at some time in your career from the team, assistant coaches, administration, parents, or critics.

> I do the very best I know how. If the end brings me out all right, what is said against me won't amount to anything. If the end brings me out wrong, ten angels swearing I was right would make no difference.
> —Abraham Lincoln

In the book *Chalk Dust on My Shoulder*, the author tells of a situation in a high school where an English teacher's job was in jeopardy because of some unfounded gossip in the community. The classroom teachers' association voted unanimously to back the teacher. Later, one of the coaches came to this teacher and informed her that he had voted to back her, but if it came to a showdown with the board of education, he would not take a stand because he feared the board would be unhappy with him and he would lose his job. This is a perfect example of an individual coach who obviously did not have the courage of his convictions.

The result of living and working with people who lack this kind of courage is illustrated by the following, paraphrased from a quote stressing the importance of speaking up for others:

> When they came after the football coach, I didn't speak up because I wasn't a football coach. They came after the band director and I didn't speak up because I wasn't a band director. Then they came after the history teacher and I didn't speak up because I wasn't a history teacher. Then they came after the principal and I didn't speak up because I wasn't a principal. Then they came for me and by that time there was no one left to speak for me.

What I am really talking about here is "gut check" time. In other words, when your convictions are challenged, will you have the courage to stand up and do what you believe in your heart to be correct, or will you fold?

> The hottest fires in hell are reserved for those who in time of moral crises maintain their neutrality.
> —Dante, *The Divine Comedy*

ETHICAL STANDARDS

Another challenge you will frequently face concerns ethical standards (see Chapter 1). Ethics in sport have been discussed, argued, legislated, and written about ever since sport was first developed, and they are still of great concern. If your standards are high, it sometimes takes a great deal of courage to maintain them, particularly when opposing coaches use unethical methods to win.

> To know what is right, and not to do it is the worst cowardice.
> —*Confucius*

Coaches will deliberately break rules and then rationalize their behavior by saying that their opponents all do it, so they must break the same rules in order to compete. No matter what the rationale, breaking rules is unethical and serves as a poor example to all the athletes involved. You should be strong enough so that no game is worth winning if you have to become unethical to do it. If you do not believe this, you simply teach youngsters that cheating can be justified if someone else is cheating, too.

GOOD JUDGMENT

Good judgment, which is the standard guideline for every decision you will ever make, develops through experience and maturity. One caution here is to avoid making snap decisions in anger or issuing ultimatums to a person, especially in front of the team. Such actions create a confrontation—something you should always try to prevent. Good judgment can do a lot toward solving potentially upsetting problems, as well as preventing some from ever happening.

CONSISTENCY

Consistency in enforcing rules, in discipline, in teaching techniques, in expectations of the team, and in dealing with individual members of a team is important. Consistency throughout the program helps prevent confusion, misunderstanding, and doubt from permeating the program. It also eliminates moral problems by showing the athletes that there are no favorites on the team.

One of the things young people rebel against is inconsistency from adults, especially when it comes to discipline. They see a great deal of inconsistency in the way rules are enforced; consequently, they test or challenge rules all the time to see how far they can go and what they can get away with. When a team knows what it can expect from you, confusion and frustration will not interfere with the players' attempt to accomplish their goals.

FAIRNESS

Being fair and impartial requires treating all members of a team alike when it comes to determining who will play. You should make every effort to ensure that everyone trying out for the team has an opportunity to show how well he or she can play the game; do not predetermine who can perform well and who cannot.

One of the mistakes you can make is to base assumptions about an athlete on what an older brother or sister accomplished previously. Such prejudgment is unfair not only to the youngster but to other members of the team, and it should be avoided at all costs. When a season is over, you should be able to honestly say that everyone on the team had a fair chance to prove his or her ability, so that any criticism that you were unfair and did not give somebody a chance cannot be justified.

Human nature being what it is, complete impartiality is extremely difficult to practice. Personalities vary, and there will be people on a team that you like more than others, but you should take great care to avoid the impression that certain athletes are teacher's pets. Fairness is a prime expectation parents and athletes hold for coaches.

IMAGINATION

Even though coaches are notorious copiers of other coaches' ideas, there is still a great deal of opportunity for imagination in coaching. Sometimes the coaches who exhibit the greatest imagination are those having a losing season. Nothing seems to be working for them, so they use a lot of imagination to try to come up with some idea they haven't tried or even heard about before, to give the team the extra edge it needs to get into the win column.

Coaches who are consistent winners have less of a tendency to call on imagination, because whatever they are doing is proving successful and they are therefore hesitant to change anything. Some high school coaches always look to the successful college teams and copy them as much as possible rather than take a chance and use their own imagination for their own unique situation.

An imaginative coach generally runs a program in which monotony and boredom seldom exist. High school coaches sometimes sell themselves short when they reject an idea they have come up with because it didn't come from some big-name college coach. Being a high school coach does not place limits on creativity and imagination.

SENSE OF HUMOR

Everyone enjoys seeing or hearing something funny, and many funny things occur in sport. When they do, you shouldn't be rigid and try to squelch them.

Humor at the right time can do a lot toward lessening tension, creating a good feeling with a group, and letting a team know that you, too, can laugh.

Practices and meetings should never be so serious and businesslike that the opportunity for occasional good humor is eliminated. After all, the sport is a game, and playing on a team should be fun. A good coach remembers this fact. When the opportunity presents itself, you should be the source of the fun. Well timed and well directed, humor can be a valuable tool in helping create the pleasant atmosphere that should surround any high school athletic team. Incidentally, don't hesitate to laugh at yourself once in a while. Let the players see that you don't always take yourself too seriously.

HAVING A PLAN FOR EVERYTHING

Before a season begins, you should develop a plan for everything that could possibly happen during the season—a plan for when the team wins, loses, or ties; a plan for discipline; a plan for competing in bad weather; a plan for adjusting to injury to key personnel; and so on. The point is to plan so thoroughly that the team or staff will rarely be surprised or unprepared for whatever happens.

> We have met the enemy
> and he is us.
> —*Pogo*

Of all the desirable qualities of coaches described in this chapter, the four most important ones in terms of winning consistently (assuming a fair share of good athletes) are, in order:

- The ability to organize

- The ability to establish discipline in all factors of your program

- The ability to evaluate players

- The ability to motivate youngsters

And three things we all need to survive in this world are:

- A funny bone

- A wishbone

- A backbone

DISCUSSION QUESTIONS

1. What is the best or right way to coach? Explain.

2. How can a coach earn respect?

3. How important is winning to you? Discuss.

4. What are the real reasons some youngsters go out for an athletic team? What implications does this have for you?

5. Why do some coaches win more consistently than others?

6. What does it mean to have "courage of your convictions"?

7. Everyone wants to win—it's the individuals who don't want to lose who are the most successful. Explain.

8. "Show me a good loser, and I'll show you a loser." What is your reaction to this statement?

9. "To know what is right and not do it is the worst cowardice." What does this mean to you?

10. Should a coach's lifestyle be a concern to parents and players in regard to his or her position as coach? Support your point of view.

11. Is an intense desire to win a legitimate quality of a good coach?

12. How can challenge be used in motivation?

13. Discuss the concept of peaks and valleys in regard to athletic performance.

14. What are some ways you can think of to motivate athletes?

15. What are some of the cautions and concerns coaches should keep in mind when they attempt to motivate athletes?

16. Define *transparent realism*. Of what importance is it?

17. What does it mean to say that we can measure people by the way they respond to challenge?

18. Discuss the concepts of discipline and punishment and their relationship to each other.

19. What is your definition of a winner?

20. Discuss the difference between imitating and emulating another coach.

21. Define *comfort zone*. What are the implications for the team and coaches?

22. Explain the ramifications of *shoribyo*.

23. "Thru this life we travel thousands of miles / Once and forever." What does this mean to you, and what relevance does it have for students under your supervision?

5

THE ROLES OF A HEAD COACH

There is a natural tendency for new coaches to assume that most of their time and effort during a sport season will be spent in actually coaching a team. Consequently, novice coaches tend to concentrate on learning all they can about the mechanics of a particular sport. After all, that's what coaching is all about, isn't it?

In actuality, nothing could be further from the truth. If coaching were merely a matter of teaching youngsters the fundamentals of a particular sport, the job would be relatively simple. But this is a unique occupation that makes many demands above and beyond teaching players physical skills. Consequently, a head coach is called on to fulfill many roles. The degree of involvement in the numerous roles varies with coaches, the sport, the number of athletes involved, circumstances, and the basic philosophy of the coach.

> Teachers affect eternity—
> they can never tell where
> their influence stops.
> —*Henry Adams*

Some of these roles are filled constantly, with little or no awareness on the coach's part. Others include tasks that need to be dealt with only periodically. Sometimes, depending on the circumstances (possibly unpleasant ones), filling just one of the many roles might demand an excessive amount of time.

The point is that when you become a head coach you will be required, by the position, to fill many different roles in carrying out your responsibilities, whether you want to or not. These roles are inescapable and therefore cannot be delegated or ignored. These kinds of expectations often take more time than coaching the team and can take some of the pleasure away from coaching.

> Those who want to leave an impression for one year should plant corn.
> Those who want to leave an impression for ten years should plant a tree.
> Those who want to leave an impression for 100 years should educate a human being.
> —*Ancient Chinese Proverb*

This chapter is intended to alert you to some of these roles and your part in them.

I don't think there is much difference between a teacher and a coach. They have to prepare people; urge and motivate them. They have to teach skill and knowledge involved and then test them. Teachers have a great deal of influence on people in what they say, the way they act, the way they present their material and the role model they present. They must be themselves, must have values, must incite and be honest. They have to get people to want to do things and yet understand that each is an individual. They have to respect their individuality and respect what they want to get out of a course or athletics.

—*Joe Paterno*

TEACHER

First and foremost, a coach must be a good teacher, in every sense of the word. Just as there are teachers of math, art, language, shop, and music, there are teachers of athletics. The late Bart Giamatti, president of Yale and Commissioner of Baseball, emphasized the point that coaches are just teachers with a different sort of classroom. But not everyone views coaches this way.

As mentioned in an earlier chapter, prospective coaches frequently hear comments during an interview to the effect that a school hires teachers first and coaches second. You should carefully consider the implications in this statement in order to develop a response that will help school administrators understand how you see your role as an effective teacher in their school system.

As a teacher of athletics, you must, of course, be completely knowledgeable about the sport you are to coach. Youngsters are alert and perceptive; if you don't know what you are doing, they won't be fooled for long. Then your credibility will be gone, along with their confidence in you. The best way to learn a sport

and prepare yourself to become a coach is to participate in the sport you intend to coach. Certainly there are exceptions, but as a general rule this is true. Unfortunately, sometimes public school administrators will, out of desperation, assign someone who has had little or no background in a certain sport, or in any sport, to coach a team. This not only puts the coach in an extremely difficult spot but is also unfair to the members of the team. This situation could have legal ramifications as well. Consequently, head coaches and athletic directors should make every effort possible to prevent this sort of assignment.

You can develop your understanding, knowledge, and competence through actual coaching experience, study, and clinics. Classes are important, but there is no substitute for experience. You can gain experience through attending various practice sessions on campus, coaching intramural teams, serving as a part-time coach in the local schools or community, and volunteering your services at your home high school during vacations. Another extremely good opportunity is to get involved in coaching while student teaching—whether or not it is required.

There are two general ways in which you affect the way your athletes learn: through indirect and direct teaching. Whereas indirect teaching involves nonverbal communication, direct teaching is largely verbal.

Indirect Teaching

Nonverbal teaching can be further broken down into two elements: image and example. In athletics, especially, it may be that the most important lessons and the ones most readily absorbed by students will be taught by the image you present. Image can be explained with the old adage: "Coach, what you are speaks so loudly that I cannot hear what you are saying." Students' image of a teacher is often formed during the initial meeting and is affected by your appearance and how you walk, stand, or talk, to mention just a few elements. Whether their impressions of you ever change will depend on how they observe you over time. You hope that whatever image they perceive is accurate and one you would like them to have.

I'd rather see a lesson
Than to hear one any day,
I'd rather you'd walk with me
Than to merely show the way.
The eye's a better teacher
And more willing than the ear,
And counsel is confusing
But examples always clear.
The best of all the teachers
Are the ones who live the creed.
To see good put in action
Is what everybody needs.
I soon can learn to do it
If you let me see it done.
I can see your hand in action
But your tongue too fast may run.
And the counsel you are giving
May be very fine and true,
But I'd rather get my lesson
By observing what you do!
    —*Author Unknown*

Beginning coaches especially are not always aware of the importance of image and the impact it can have on others. So the image they project develops without design. Sometimes it is a real shock for a coach to discover how the athletes, student body, parents, and other adults in the community see him or her. You will definitely be at the center of attention, and very little of what you do or the way in which you do it will go unnoticed. This includes behavior in school, during practice, during a game, and in everyday life in the community. Like it or not, this goes with the territory.

It is a matter of fact that even when nothing is being said between teacher and student, another kind of communication is taking place. Your facial expressions, gestures, or body movement—showing anger, frustration, acceptance, empathy, disapproval, or pleasure—can and do affect members of a team or

You tell on yourself by the friends you seek
By the very manner in which you speak
By the way you employ your leisure time
By the way you make of dollar and dime.
You tell what you are by the things you wear
By the spirit in which your burdens bear
By the kind of things at which you laugh
By the records you play on your phonograph.

You tell what you are by the way you walk
By the things of which you delight to talk
By the manner in which you bear defeat
By so simple a thing as how you eat.

By the books you choose from a well filled shelf
In these ways and more you tell on yourself.
So there is really no particle of sense
In an effort to keep up false pretense
    You tell on yourself.
        —Author Unknown

students in a classroom. Youngsters learn at an early age to interpret this type of communication.

Pupils assume that nonverbal cues are more revealing of your actual feelings and thoughts than words are. So when a contradiction arises between your verbal and nonverbal behavior, students will assume that the nonverbal message is more valid. What you say makes little difference if students perceive a different message from your facial expression, tone of voice, or gestures. Body language is an important factor in communication, and if you are not aware of what your posture and gestures say, you could be sending messages that you have no conscious intention of sending.

The significant difference between image and example is that although the image you project normally occurs by chance, the example you set should be planned and deliberately based on how you want the athletes to see you. This means that the first thing you have to do as coach is take a good look in the mirror and decide exactly what kind of example you want to set for your athletes. You should then live that example every day.

The processes of identification and modeling are of some concern to women in athletics when they note the relatively large number of men coaching women's teams; they are concerned with role modeling for these young women, or its

No written work or verbal plea
can teach young hearts what
they should be—not all the books
on all the shelves, but what the
teachers are themselves.
        —Author Unknown

absence if the coach is a man. If you accept the fact that teaching by example is legitimate and that role modeling is a large part of the process, you will agree that women should be coaching women. This call for female coaches has nothing to do with the technical aspects of coaching but concerns the infinite lessons athletes can learn from the example of their coaches.

One of the things you must guard against is acting in a way that makes you appear to be hypocritical in the eyes of the athletes. An example would be stressing the importance of following rules and then going

In learning to be civilized human beings, the process of identification and modeling is of tremendous importance, with parents the foremost, but by no means the only models. School age brings teachers as secondary sources of modeling . . .
        —Sherwyn Woods, in Quest

to great lengths to show the team how to bend them. This lesson can also be taught by coaches who study the rules carefully to see how far they can bend them to their advantage and then justify doing so by claiming that it is good strategy. Whether or not this behavior is in the spirit of the game makes no difference to such coaches.

Another example of hypocrisy is coaches who smoke in front of athletes while telling them that they shouldn't smoke because it is harmful to their health. Or coaches who tell a team that they drink but the athletes shouldn't; because the coach is an adult, drinking is okay. The tradition of an adult (coach) telling youngsters to "do what I say, not what I do" is hypocrisy at its worst, and this kind of example surely has an adverse effect on the respect and admiration athletes and many parents develop for coaches.

> Business managers responding to a survey reported that athletic coaches, in particular high school football coaches, were important influences on their lives. They were seen as models and teachers of fairness and sportsmanship. They were also remembered for the values and skills demanded by team membership with which they imbued their students.
>
> —Barbara Ley Toffler, *Tough Choices, Managers Talk Ethics*

Direct Teaching

The second way that students will learn from you is through direct teaching: lecture, explanation, and demonstration. A common mistake among inexperienced teachers is to assume that this method is not only the best but also the only way to teach. This is not always true. Not only is this technique the most widely used, but it is probably the most abused, in that teachers frequently talk too much and become uncomfortable if they aren't saying something at all times while they are in front of a group. Verbal communication is of course important, but it can lose its effectiveness when used unnecessarily, es-

pecially during a practice session. In other words, say a little and have the players do a lot, and be careful not to cause "paralysis by analysis."

Unfortunately, verbal communication suffers tremendous abuse in our society. Many people have trouble getting to the point when they speak. Many have a hard time putting their thoughts into words so that everyone clearly understands what they are trying to say. Some people also have a tendency to saturate

I know you believe you
understand what you think
I said, but I am not sure
you realize that what you
heard is not what I meant.
—*Author Unknown*

speech with words that are difficult to understand in order to impress listeners. Doing so only results in confusion or misunderstanding.

Mental Practice

Because the proper execution of skills is vital, the typical practice session is mainly devoted to perfecting skills. But no matter how carefully practices are organized and how well the athletes are taught, some will never play up to their potential, or they will "choke" in a contest. When this occurs chances are very good that such problems could be mental rather than physical.

A player's frame of mind is recognized by many experts as an integral part of coaching and an integral part of sport. Coaches thus need to teach players how to use mental imagery (also called eidetic imagery), biofeedback, or psychocybernetics as a tool to see themselves performing a skill successfully. Research has shown that mental rehearsal can reduce anxiety and dramatically improve athletic performance. This technique could be compared to daydreaming, but with a specific purpose.

One highly successful professional golfer improved his game to championship level partly because he spent time each day visualizing success. He said that to be successful in anything, a person has to dream of being successful. In preparing for a tournament he would play his last practice round and then go back to his room and think about the course for about an hour and a half, trying to visualize all the possible conditions he might face and the shots he would hit in each situation. He said that if he then won the championship, it would not be a shock to him because he had already won it in his mind ten thousand times.

To learn a new maneuver in gymnastics, a serious gymnast has to train many hours each day and repeat the trick hundreds of times. A highly successful gymnastics coach, who believed mental rehearsal to be far more important than wearing down the body, required his gymnasts to describe their routines in writing, including key points on which to focus. After putting the descriptions in writing, the athletes were to shut their eyes and see themselves doing the routines correctly and successfully. This process enabled the athletes to cut their repetitions drastically and still accomplish their tasks.

The underlying assumption in this approach is that athletes can punish their bodies all day long and gain nothing if their minds are not cooperating. If this technique is to be successful, the following principles need to be observed:

- The mental picture athletes have of themselves sets the boundaries for what they can or cannot do. Repeated failure or success too easily gained can damage the ego and directly affect a youngster's self-image. Because an athlete's self-regard is a precondition for achievement of his or her goals, it should be a primary focus in teaching.

- By improving a player's self-image, you will improve ability and performance.

- The mind does not always know the difference between the real and the imagined. Both the real experience and the vividly imagined can be stored in an athlete's memory bank. As far as the mind is concerned, practice is practice, and the results of real or imagined practice will be similar.

- Each individual has an inborn instinct to succeed. Cybernetics suggests that the mind is really a guidance mechanism. It directs the body toward the goal an individual sets. Therefore, athletes need to set clear-cut goals and develop positive habits of thinking in order to use this guidance mechanism to achieve success.

All athletes in every sport can improve their performance through mental practice. Here are four ways to utilize this process:

1. *Think positively*. Athletes who believe in themselves are already on their way to being successful. Instead of worrying about their shortcomings or weaknesses, they focus on their strengths and picture themselves at their best.

2. *Strengthen weaknesses*. Athletes must picture the skill in their minds and then visualize completing that skill successfully. They then mentally replay the scene over and over again— almost as if watching a motion picture of themselves in action, always performing successfully.

3. *Concentrate totally*. This should be done somewhere that is peaceful and quiet. Again, the players need to visualize themselves being successful.

4. *Practice diligently*. Change will not come without effort; it takes hard work every day. Athletes should be encouraged to use their mind's eye to focus on some particular task they will be called on to do in certain situations during a contest. They should always see themselves as being successful; then, when this situation arises in the event, they will react instantly because in their minds they have been there a thousand times before.

Clearly, mental as well as physical practice is a key consideration in helping athletes reach their maximum potential. Based on the evidence available, it would seem prudent for you to include and set aside time for mental practice in conjunction with physical practice for specific skills.

DISCIPLINARIAN

Without discipline there can be no teaching or learning. Unfortunately, most people associate punishment with the word *discipline*. In our context, the term refers to the ability to convince youngsters of the value of precise attention to detail, dependability, and punctuality; the standards of personal conduct in practice, during the game, and in school; and, of course, the reasons for following rules. In the history of sport, no team has ever been consistently successful over a period of years without a high degree of discipline. This is an absolute. The winningest coaches are always among the strictest disciplinarians in coaching. If you are going to be in charge, then be in charge.

No person has ever been hurt by growing up with discipline used wisely and fairly, but many young people have suffered because of a lack of discipline. To discipline youngsters is to love them. Today, this aspect of coaching is more difficult than ever, since the fashionable attitude is for everyone to be left alone to do their own thing. Added to what some people describe as the "me generation" is the concern for interfering with personal rights. People ask, "Do coaches have the right to discipline athletes?" In the minds of some people in today's society, the answer is not clear. But make no mistake about it; much of what you do with a team ties in with discipline and the need to run an orderly program. You have to be "king of the hill" yet temper your demands with understanding and good judgment.

The way in which you establish discipline depends on many factors, but primarily it depends on your personality and the situation in which you work. In most communities, parents expect teachers to enforce certain measures of discipline, since most adults recognize the benefit for their children. Sometimes parents will ask for your help in instilling some discipline in a son or daughter because they haven't been able to do the job themselves. Even though youngsters themselves won't admit it, they want and need an authority figure, and if you don't provide one for athletes, they may well feel cheated and lose respect for you.

SALESPERSON

The role of salesperson is important to you because the attitude of modern-day high school students toward athletics seems to have changed. In many communities (not all), too many things compete for a youngster's attention. With access to automobiles and motorcycles, a pocket full of money, and a variety of activities to choose from, young people may not put participation in sport at the top of their priorities. You have to sell the program to students in such a way that they aspire to become a part of the team. You must sell to the parents to help them understand all the purposes of the program and to get their support. And finally you must be a sales agent to the whole community to create a better understanding of the role of athletics in a high school.

This aspect of coaching is also important when you fill a job that has just been vacated. Initially, everything you do and say will be compared to the ways of the previous coach. So it is important that you sell your ideas and goals to those concerned as quickly as possible to obtain needed cooperation before too much valuable time passes.

This role can be a difficult one to fill for coaches of teams that don't have great crowd appeal or the attention of the community; a lot of people just don't care about the "other" sports. This means that some coaches have to work harder than others at filling this role.

PUBLIC RELATIONS EXPERT

Since you are or will be in the public eye more than most faculty members, you have a great opportunity for public relations, both in and out of the community. If you are interested in all phases of the school community, you can provide good public relations not only for the athletic program but for other school programs as well. An open house for parents or members of a team, or perhaps a meet-the-team night for everyone in the community greatly enhances public relations for the school and athletic department. Your ability to interact well with the public will be tested periodically when adults in the community become vocal in their criticism of you, the team, or individuals on the team.

The demands of this role are in direct proportion to the visibility of the sport you coach, which varies somewhat from community to community. Obviously, if your team competes in front of 10,000 spectators regularly and my team draws crowds of 150 per event, your concern with this role might be greater than mine.

Regardless of the visibility factor, every coach will find the time spent in this area to be worthwhile, especially for the athletes who see themselves as unappreciated in a school athletic program—and their parents. This will require a lot of initiative on your part—just like everything else in coaching.

Good public relations also develop when you take time to participate in community functions that might or might not be school related. Every coach, by the nature of the position, is a full-time public relations person for the school, seven days a week, twelve months a year. If this situation bothers you, remember that it comes with the territory.

GUIDANCE COUNSELOR

It is common for youngsters to look to their coach for advice or guidance with a problem or concern. Often athletes are faced with a problem they feel they cannot discuss with their parents or the guidance counselor in the school, and because of the special rapport that develops between coaches and athletes they turn to you, their coach. This can occur during a school day or at almost any other time, and it is not unusual for athletes to call or come to your home late at night when they feel they need help.

One of the principles of guidance is to let the student seeking guidance do most of the talking. You should try to help him or her see both sides of the problem and to recognize all the possible solutions or courses of action. The student can then decide what needs to be done. In guidance, the teacher gives help and advice but should not tell the youngster what to do.

Another consideration is that of privileged communication. You might be told something in strictest confidence because a boy or girl has faith and trust in you and doesn't know whom else to turn to. Just be careful not to get yourself boxed into a corner by promising a youngster that you won't tell anyone what he

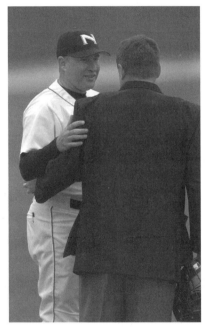

or she is about to say to you. Your ego might be stroked because you are the one person the student feels he or she can confide in, but beware. Getting caught between a troubled student and a set of parents is a no-win situation for you.

Sometimes a student doesn't really need advice but simply someone who will listen. In spite of the busy schedule coaches live each day, no youngster should be turned away in this situation. In all of an athlete's career, this particular moment could be one of the most important to a troubled boy or girl, and you should never underestimate the importance of your role. Students never interrupt a teacher's work—they are your reason for existing. Remember this.

DIPLOMAT

Coaches must be diplomatic in their relations with parents and others in the community. It is inevitable that spectators will question tactics, the use of personnel, and the performance of the team. Sometimes people raise questions in a highly antagonistic way. For example, you might walk into a local shop and before the door is closed hear someone say in a loud, belligerent voice, "Why did so-and-so play in the last game? The kid is lousy." Your first reaction will probably be one of fury, but on second thought you might consider that there are better ways to combat ignorance than with a sledgehammer. Although it is not always easy, it is possible to answer such critics positively and still maintain a certain degree of dignity. Don't get down in the gutter with a nasty critic.

Sometimes it is much more difficult to be diplomatic with parents. It is particularly difficult when a youngster rarely gets into a game because he or she doesn't really have the heart for it. You know that the primary reason this youngster stays on the team is because Dad or Mom wants it. Your first impulse might be simply to face these parents and tell them their child isn't playing because he or she doesn't really like to compete. It may be that in certain situations this would be your best course of action. But you should also consider that being painfully blunt simply to stifle personal criticism could destroy a boy or girl in the parents' eyes. If this is the case, you need to look for other ways, less painful to all concerned, to answer these parents. You might elect to remain silent and take the criticism personally, or you might say, "You are right. I'll give this some consideration," and then do what you think best anyway. The most important concern in this problem is what happens to the youngster. Your actions should be dictated by this concern.

The following anecdote provides a good description of diplomacy. An office boy noticed two women at lunch with the boss. Later in the day he asked, "Who were those women I saw you with?" The boss replied that one of them was the most beautiful actress in the world and the other was his wife. The youngster said, "Which one was the actress?" The boss took out a ten-dollar bill and gave it to the lad. "What's this for?" asked the boy. "Nothing," replied the boss. "I just want you to remember when you get to be president that I once gave you money."

ORGANIZER

As noted in Chapter 4, the ability to organize well is critical for any coach in any sport. There are three phases of organization. The first applies to the head coach, and the others apply to the coaching staff and team. All are discussed thoroughly in subsequent chapters. Suffice it to say here that the ability to organize is a trait of all successful coaches.

DETECTIVE

Although "detective work" is not one of the pleasant roles associated with coaching, it can sometimes become a necessity. Situations such as stealing in the locker room, rumors of an athlete or athletes being involved in rules violations, or a principal's reporting a suspicion or accusation regarding someone on your team will require you to get to the bottom of the situation at once.

Although dealing with such problems is difficult and unpleasant, in most instances you cannot simply walk away. The way you handle such problems depends a lot on your personality and rapport with the athletes, the degree of mutual respect between you and the athletes, and the circumstances. A great deal of good judgment is required on your part.

PSYCHOLOGIST

One of your greatest concerns will be to try to understand the personality of a team as well as the personalities of the team members so that you can motivate them to perform to the best of their ability. The days of the highly emotional, gimmick-laden locker-room pep talks are over. Youngsters today are perceptive enough to see through gimmicks, and appealing to their emotions too often is risky. As we saw in Chapter 4, a team can reach an emotional peak just so many times in a season before it falls flat. The method then becomes meaningless. This does not mean that there is no room for occasional inspirational talks throughout the season, but to rely solely on them to get athletes up to play each game is a mistake.

Beginning coaches learn how to handle this important aspect of coaching through the trial and error of experience. The important thing to remember is the need to establish good rapport with the athletes and to determine as quickly as possible just what makes each of them tick. Then you can determine the best possible approach to that team. Be careful about doing something that is foreign to your nature; such actions generally will be ineffective and adversely affect the team. Be yourself.

This facet of coaching is also critical where individual athletes are concerned. The key word is *understanding*, and the faster you can determine how to reach each youngster, the sooner you can help them realize whatever potential they have. A common mistake of most beginning coaches, especially of team sports, is to assume that everyone on a team can be dealt with in the same way. This is not true. Each individual is different, and a shotgun approach to motivating a group of athletes is not the best way of achieving the desired results—peak performance and winning.

Researchers have identified certain personality traits that create high degrees of anxiety among athletes—traits that indicate which athletes can and should take a good scolding and which athletes cannot, and traits that indicate which athletes need to be left alone or praised. It may be that these researchers are simply reinforcing what successful coaches have been aware of for a long time but haven't taken the time to contemplate. At any rate, there is some convincing evidence that dealing with individuals according to their personality is the crucial element in determining the success or failure of many athletes. How the athletes react to you and whether they will finish a season or quit the team depend on individual traits. This role will always be a challenge for coaches.

JUDGE AND JURY

Regardless of the number of coaches on a staff, the head coach alone serves as judge and jury. Many situations throughout a sports season require hard decisions by the head coach, who has the final responsibility for everything concerning the team and staff. When questions are asked, the head coach is accountable and is the one who has to come up with the answers.

In every situation, assistant coaches can only advise and offer opinions. This is most evident in potentially troublesome or controversial situations such as disciplining an athlete, dismissing an athlete from the team, issuing policy statements, deciding on whether a student will be allowed to come out for a team because of previous difficulties in or out of the school, and deciding cases when no school policy exists. When the chips are down, the head coach has to cast the deciding vote, as always. This role cannot be delegated. Good judgment, based on experience or plain common sense, is the key.

This role can become unpleasant on occasion, but it cannot be ignored. A head coach needs to have the courage and the backbone to act in the face of possible criticism. It is therefore vitally important to formulate a personal philosophy of coaching and athletics on which to base important decisions.

LEADER

There are three kinds of leaders:
1. Rowboat—a leader who goes only where pulled.
2. Sailboat—a leader who goes in the direction the wind blows.
3. Motorboat—a leader who determines a direction and plows ahead to reach a goal.

Which of these three "boats" best describes you and your leadership ability? How do you think your colleagues would rate you?

You need to establish leadership in three primary areas: the team, the staff, and the faculty. You have many obvious ways to exhibit leadership in the first two areas—by image, example, dedication, personality, knowledge, courage of convictions, integrity, dignity, and loyalty. Although most coaches are well aware of these and of the importance of filling the leadership role, many may forget or ignore the role's importance within the faculty.

One criticism frequently leveled at coaches is that they live in their own world, with little regard for anything or anyone else, or with little concern for the school as a whole. In some situations this is no doubt a legitimate criticism; in others it may not be justified. However, when coaches become so involved in a sport that they make little or no effort to show interest in other facets of the school community, the assumption is that they just don't care.

> Leadership is not so much leading as having the people led accept you. You know how you do that? You've got to win the hearts of the people that you lead. The personality of the individual has to do it.
> —*Vince Lombardi*

You should not allow yourself to acquire this kind of image. If the rest of the faculty realize that you do care about something other than sports, they will be more likely to cooperate with the athletic department when necessary. Teachers will be more willing to help athletes who are having difficulty, and you will have much more pleasant working relationships with various departments in the school. You should do your best to eliminate the idea that coaches set themselves apart from the common folk (teachers) because they occupy a privileged position in the school.

You can use your leadership ability by attending teachers' meetings, by serving on teachers' committees such as those involved in negotiations on salary and professional rights and responsibilities, and by serving as head of some of these committees when time permits. Some of these activities might be short-term obligations that can be completed in the off-season. Accepting these kinds of responsibilities can add to your stature among faculty members; it will make you feel closer to the school, will contribute to the good of the school, and will help prevent criticism of athletics by faculty members who might otherwise resent your isolation from the rest of school life.

> Another description of "dynamic leadership" is:
> When in doubt—ponder.
> When in trouble—delegate.
> When you don't know—mumble.

Attendance at band concerts and plays is something else you should consider as a gesture of genuine interest in other programs within the school. Doing so also makes a positive impression on athletes who are participating in these events. You will find it helpful to see these young people in a light other than that of the locker room or playing field, and the better you know them, the easier it is to understand them.

MOTHER FIGURE/FATHER FIGURE

Your role as mother figure or father figure varies according to the age of the athletes and the school situation. As might be expected, boys and girls who come from homes with only one parent, from an orphanage, or from homes with uncaring parents probably have the greatest need for a parental relationship and frequently look to a coach to fill it. They need someone to talk to, they often need someone other than a parent to listen to them, and they sometimes simply need adult advice from someone in addition to or other than a member of their family.

You will soon discover that this need also exists among students from affluent communities and homes. Young people sometimes need a relationship in addition to what they have at home or because they don't have such a relationship at home. With the breaking down of the structure of families in our society, a teacher who really cares may be the most influential person in a youngster's life.

Just be careful—don't get too close and cross that invisible line between teacher and student, especially if you are coaching a team of a gender opposite from yours.

DICTATOR

The word *dictator* has many connotations, most of them uncomplimentary. We use it in the sense of a benevolent dictator—one who cares about the program, the team, and the people involved but nevertheless finds that there are times when a decision must be made without time for discussion. A benevolent dictator makes such decisions according to what is best for everyone concerned. Since the head coach is the individual in charge, the head coach's word has to be final—always.

When coaches on a staff disagree about some issue concerning the team, the head coach must make a decision that everyone will be expected to abide by. In other words, if there are four assistant coaches on a staff, the head coach always carries five votes. This is not to say that the democratic procedure has no place in coaching, but coaches and athletes also need to learn that in the excitement of competition some circumstances demand that they react instantly and without question to decisions and instructions from the head coach. This is no time to have a committee meeting. A good leader tolerates uncertainty only up to a point.

POLITICIAN

Regardless of the provocation, you should make every effort to avoid antagonizing people, particularly the parents of boys and girls who are members of a team. A good politician learns how to do this very quickly. Perhaps this role goes hand-in-hand with diplomacy.

The political role comes into play most often when you deal with critics in the community. Ideally, they wouldn't exist, or at the least we could ignore them and simply coach the team. But in reality, they cannot be ignored, nor should they be. If left unchecked, these critics sometimes grow like a cancer and can create serious problems for you. The coach who is a good politician can do a great deal toward preventing critics from getting out of hand, avoiding a confrontation, or worse.

Good politicians and good coaches also know that the time to make friends and firmly establish themselves is when the team is winning and at the top. When the tide turns—and cycles do occur in high school programs—you and the program will need every friend you can find. If you didn't line up friends when the team was riding the winning crest, you surely won't do it when the team is losing. Winston Churchill once said that the most important qualification for a politician is the ability to predict what will happen tomorrow, next week, next month, or next year—and be able to explain afterward why it did not happen. Could he have also been talking to coaches who end up on the wrong side of the season's won-lost record?

ACTOR

In the movie *Patton* the general reprimanded his staff because a job needed to be done, and he was not satisfied with the progress being made. After the group left, Patton's aide turned to him and said, "You really didn't mean all that, did you, General?" Patton simply replied, "No, but they don't know that." The point is that he was acting out a role to get a job done. In this respect, you too will find it necessary to act out certain parts when the situation requires it.

Sometimes you will have to play a role that is foreign to your personality, such as scolding an individual or team, or remaining calm even though you feel like exploding at an individual, your staff, or the entire team. The pitfall is appearing phony. This will destroy what you are trying to do, because youngsters are not fooled for long by insincerity. If you believe in what you are doing and recognize that the situation calls for a role to be played, you will find that doing so can be an effective tool in accomplishing your goal.

The perceptive coach seldom fails to recognize when such situations arise. They cannot always be anticipated, but with experience and common sense you will be able to make a quick judgment about the proper response. The ultimate actor is the coach who, while being driven out of town by an irate community, makes it look as if he or she is leading a parade.

FUND-RAISER

Rarely do coaches feel they have enough funds to purchase the kind of equipment they would really like to have in the amount they think necessary. As a result, coaches often dream up fund–raising projects to supplement their approved budgets. Candy, cookie, and hoagie sales are just a few examples. These campaigns might take place in school, in the community, or both. Some coaches, however, object strongly to such fund-raising. They feel that it downgrades what they perceive as an important program in the school and that hustling money should not be part of coaching. Coaches of the so-called minor sports are particularly sensitive about this, especially if coaches of basketball and football or other high-visibility sports don't have to raise money.

Some school districts strictly prohibit such fund-raising campaigns as they can create public relations problems in a community already financially burdened with supporting the schools. You should always check with the school administration before attempting to raise funds on your own, to avoid learning after the fact that you are violating school policy.

CHIEF EXECUTIVE

Every head coach assumes the role of chief executive along with the position. Someone has to be in charge. Someone has to provide direction for an entire program, which might include not only the varsity and varsity coaches but all the other teams and coaches in a particular sport down into the elementary level. Depending on the situation, this could constitute a fairly large organization, in which everyone involved would be looking to you, the head coach, for decisions and direction. The failure to recognize your obligation in filling your role could result in chaos, with everybody going off in different directions. It therefore becomes critical that you determine in your own mind precisely where you want your program to go before you attempt to guide others.

EQUIPMENT MANAGER

Rarely does a high school employ someone whose sole job is to take care of athletic equipment. As a result, the ultimate responsibility for purchasing, issuing, policing, collecting, and taking inventory of equipment falls on the head coach. For coaches of some sports, golf for example, this may not amount to much, but for a football coach this job can become monumental.

Equipment problems can occur every day of the season and become a real nuisance. You will have to invest a great deal of thought, planning, and organization in this role. One way to deal with it, except for the final inventory, is to assign this duty to an assistant coach. If you have no assistants, a competent student manager might be able to handle at least some of the daily equipment problems, but in the end you will be accountable.

TRAINER

Because they feel they can't afford it, far too many high schools fail to provide the athletic department with a certified trainer, or even medical supervision during practices. As a result, the responsibility falls directly on the coach. It thus becomes absolutely essential that you prepare yourself by learning as much as you can about first aid, prevention and treatment of athletic injuries, taping techniques, and CPR.

Another serious concern is treating injuries where bleeding is present since life-threatening diseases can be transmitted through blood. Advice from the medical profession on proper treatment in such situations is critical.

Rules requiring or suggesting medical supervision at athletic events are violated repeatedly and are rarely observed at practices. You become responsible by default. The ability of school administrators in many states to hire part-time coaches, many of whom have not been professionally trained, has increased concern in this area. Not only is the health and welfare of your athletes a major concern, but so is legal liability, which you cannot afford to ignore.

This is not an area to be taken lightly. If you are coaching now, or about to begin, make certain that you are prepared to deal with this crucial role.

CITIZEN OF THE COMMUNITY

There are basically three kinds of citizens: those who live *in* the community, those who live *off* the community, and those who live *for* the community.

The coach who merely lives in the community is one who doesn't care about what goes on in the community and therefore makes no contribution toward making it a better place to live.

The coach who lives off the community is someone whose interest is primarily selfish. This coach is concerned only with using the community for personal gain—that is, moving on to a better job, getting special deals from the merchants in town, and accepting what the community can do for him or her.

The coach who lives for the community has a genuine desire to be a part of the community and to contribute in any way possible. This often means serving the parent-teacher organization in some capacity, working as a member of a service club, participating in the work of a civic group, helping organize the neighborhood Fourth of July parade, or volunteering time to the cancer crusade, heart drive, and so on.

Regardless of your personal goals and ambitions, you could be missing some of the pleasures of being a coach and occupying that special role in a community if you don't take the opportunity to become a part of it. No matter how short your stay may be before a better position comes along, you could feel a tremendous inner satisfaction if you thought that a community was just a little better place in which to live, for a moment anyway, because you worked to help make it that way. Don't confuse this satisfaction with conceit; this good feeling comes with the knowledge that you have made a contribution to something or somebody just because you wanted to.

Sometime when you're feeling important
Sometimes when your ego's in bloom
Sometime when you take it for granted
You're the best qualified in the room.
Sometime when you feel that your going
Would leave an unfillable hole
Just follow these simple instructions
And see how it humbles your soul.
Take a bucket and fill it with water
Put your hand in it up to the wrist,
Pull it out and the hole that's remaining
Is the measure of how you'll be missed.
You may splash all you please when you enter
You may stir up the water galore
But stop and you'll find in a minute
That it looks just the same as before.
The moral of this quaint example
Is do just the best that you can.
Be proud of yourself, but remember
There is no indispensable man.
   —Author Unknown

CITIZEN OF THE SCHOOL

Some coaches isolate themselves in their sports, to the exclusion of other school activities. As I've mentioned previously, such nonparticipation tends to bring criticism from other faculty members, who assume that coaches don't care for anything in the school that doesn't pertain to their team. Some faculty members resent these types of coaches for not fulfilling all the obligations of a teacher. The responsibilities of being a teacher do not begin and end with teaching classes or coaching a team. You will quickly discover that many other duties and obligations are involved in teaching, and everyone is expected to share in them as much as possible, including coaches.

Many coaches use the excuse that they don't have time. The argument gets no sympathy from fellow faculty members, because coaches are usually paid extra for coaching. While other teachers spend time after school at committee meetings without pay, the coach is spending time at practice with pay, and this can become a touchy point.

In light of this situation, you ought to make a genuine effort to be a part of the school, and to participate in social functions with the faculty. Letting the teachers get to know you can help eliminate any suspicion they might have that all coaches see themselves as privileged characters and have little regard for anything or anyone outside the athletic department. Besides, you could become friends with some pretty fine people.

DISCUSSION QUESTIONS

1. How can a coach be himself or herself and still fill the roles discussed in this chapter?

2. "What you are speaks so loudly that I cannot hear what you are saying." Discuss this statement and the image you plan to present as a high school coach.

3. What is the difference between image and example?

4. What does the term *coach* signify to you?

5. Give some examples of ways in which a coach can be a citizen of a community.

6. Should coaches live in the community where they teach? Why?

7. What kind of image do you want high school athletes to have of you?

8. How would you describe nonverbal communication? Give some examples.

9. Why do coaches need to understand the concept of nonverbal communication?

10. What does it mean when a team or athlete is described as "disciplined"?

11. Why are role models necessary for athletes?

12. Interpret this statement: "To discipline youngsters is to love them."

13. Interpret this statement: "A skillful leader is one who does what he can, with what he has, where he is."

14. Do you believe coaches really teach by example and image?

15. You never have to meet the general of an army: if you meet his troops, you know him. How can this be applied to athletics? What are the implications for coaches and athletes?

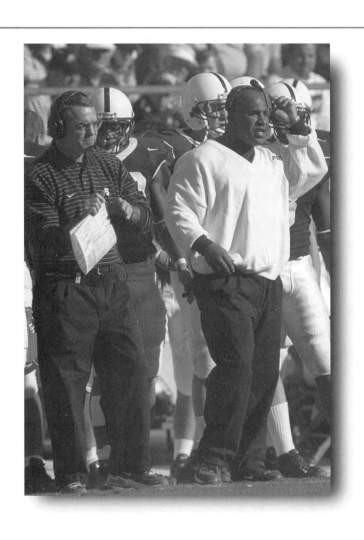

6

THE ASSISTANT COACH

One of the early decisions you might be faced with in your professional career is whether to begin as a head coach or as an assistant. Much of this book deals with head coaching responsibilities, but this chapter is devoted primarily to the special role of being an assistant. However, the material that follows is important to head coaches as well as to assistants in that it provides a clearer understanding and appreciation of this unique position. The information in this chapter should also be helpful in creating the kind of atmosphere that will allow assistant coaches to make positive contributions to a program and be relatively happy in the process.

> There is a vast difference between making a suggestion and making a decision.

Here are some points you should be aware of before we start:

- Head coaches on the high school level do not always have a voice in the hiring of assistant coaches.

- Not all assistant coaches assigned by the superintendent of schools are necessarily qualified for the position.

- Many assistant coaches, particularly those who are new, do not understand their role.

- In many states it is permissible to hire people to coach who are not full-time teachers and who have no professional preparation as coaches.

- Head coaches might not find the same high degree of commitment to the program on the part of assistants as they have themselves.

- Many head coaches do not know how, or are unwilling, to effectively use assistant coaches.

- It is a primary responsibility of a head coach to make clear to assistant coaches their responsibilities and duties to prevent any misunderstandings after they accept the position or once the season begins.

PHILOSOPHICAL DIFFERENCES

Being an assistant coach, or associate coach, can be a rewarding and satisfying experience in which you can experience the excitement and fun of coaching while growing professionally. The job can also be frustrating, stifling, and, therefore, unhappy. The determining factor usually is the head coach and that coach's personal philosophy of coaching, which includes views on the role of assistant coaches. Thus, it becomes extremely important for a head coach and a prospective assistant to clarify their beliefs about coaching to each other during an interview or at some other time before making a final decision about the job.

> I beg you, do not be unchangeable. Do not believe that you alone can be right.
> —Sophocles

Sometimes beginning coaches, in their eagerness to land a job, forget to investigate this aspect of the position. If a prospective assistant's point of view is drastically divergent from the head coach's, it would probably be a mistake for these people to coach together, because the assistant would feel frustrated and discontented. At the same time, the head coach would be unhappy with an assistant who disagrees philosophically with the basic foundation of the program. Neither love of a sport nor the love of coaching will compensate for basic philosophical differences.

A simple example of differing philosophies would be a case in which one coach believes in teaching with an "iron hand"—screaming at youngsters, cursing at them, and doing whatever is necessary to win, including bending the rules—when the other coach believes in just the opposite approach. In this situation, someone is going to be unhappy.

If you find yourself seriously at odds with the head coach during the interview process, be careful not to accept the job anyway because you are impressed by the reputation of the school or of the head coach. By the same token, a head coach in this situation should be wary of hiring an assistant simply because of the prospect's reputation as a player. Friction will be inevitable, unless the head coach thinks the assistant's beliefs can be altered enough so that they are fairly compatible with the coaching situation. Although it is wise to enter the profession with certain ideas, ideals, and principles, it is also important for assistants to keep an open mind and to be receptive to new ideas and thoughts. Dogmatic, uncompromising individuals can be disruptive factors within a coaching staff, and this can cause a lot of problems.

> Yon Cassius has a lean and hungry look;
> He thinks too much; Such men are dangerous.
> —William Shakespeare, *Julius Caesar*

You should not take this to mean that an assistant coach should never disagree with the head coach. Not only will they disagree, but they should and must, if the program is to grow and improve; but all disagreements should center primarily on the mechanical aspects of the game.

Philosophically, all the coaches on a staff should believe basically in the same things if they are to maintain a degree of harmony and unity, both of which are important to the staff's effectiveness. Unlike Shakespeare's Julius Caesar, the head coach should never look suspiciously on assistant coaches who question ideas.

APPLYING FOR THE JOB

Before interviewing for a position as an assistant coach, it would be great to know all the questions that were going to be asked. But of course, this is impossible. However, you can anticipate some of the possibilities as you prepare for an interview. Here are some typical questions that you might be asked:

1. Why do you want to be an assistant coach here?

2. What are your goals in the profession?

3. What is your idea of a great assistant coach?

4. What do you want to do in the off-season? (Continue to work with the athletes in weight training, coach another sport, or rest?)

5. Would you object to working with our athletes in some way during the summer? (A lot of programs also work out at 6:00 or 6:30 in the morning now.)

6. What can you do for this program?

7. How can you justify in your own mind the time required by coaching?

8. What do you think are your best qualities and strengths?

9. Are you willing to attend coaching clinics on nonschool days?

10. How do you see the role of assistant coach?

11. Define loyalty from an assistant coach's point of view.

12. What is your philosophy of coaching?

13. What is your attitude toward winning and losing?

14. Why should we hire you at this school?

Every interview should be a reciprocal exercise. That is to say, the person being interviewed should also have an opportunity to ask questions of the interviewer. There is no single best set of questions for every prospective coach in every situation. Obviously, every individual has his or her own concerns about a job; therefore, you need to devise your own questions about the position.

The questions you ask will reveal a lot about you to an interviewer. As a result, you should give your questions a great deal of thought before the interview. Write them down and take them with you so you don't forget any of them.

Even though no two situations are exactly alike, here are a number of questions that should apply to most situations.

1. How did this opening occur?
2. If I fill this position, will it create any hard feelings because someone already on the staff wants the job?
3. Who will have the final say about who is hired—head coach, principal, athletic director, or superintendent?
4. What is the head coach's philosophy of coaching?
5. What is the head coach's attitude toward winning and losing?
6. What are the head coach's future goals and plans?
7. What would my role be during practice?
8. What would my role be during games, meets, matches?
9. What would my role be during the off-season (summer, mornings, etc.)?
10. How does the head coach feel about athletes participating in other sports during the year?
11. How does the head coach feel about a weight training program?
12. If I took the job, would I be able to coach any other sports?
13. What are my chances of advancing on this staff?
14. How does the head coach see the relationship between head coach and assistants?
15. Do assistant coaches have opportunities to attend coaching clinics?
16. Do assistant coaches have an opportunity to contribute to the program? How?
17. How many people come out for the team?
18. What kind of attitude do these youngsters have toward this sport?
19. Describe a typical week of practice.
20. Describe a typical week out of season.
21. Describe a typical week during the summer.
22. Does the administration support this sport?
23. Docs the community support this sport?
24. How much pressure is there from the administration or community to win?

25. Do we have a chance to win in this league?

26. What is the salary?

Considerations in Choosing Assistants

When given the opportunity to select assistant coaches, a head coach should consider the words of Machiavelli (1469–1527). This outstanding statesman of the Italian Renaissance wrote in *The Prince*, his classic treatise on the use of power: "The first opinion that is formed of a ruler's [head coach's?] intelligence is based on the quality of 'men' he has around him." In coaching, this means simply that head coaches should try to surround themselves with assistants who are smarter, more eager, harder workers, and better coaches than they are, and then be willing to delegate responsibility to take advantage of these qualities. In this way everyone benefits, and chances of having a happy and productive staff are greatly enhanced.

Another consideration for a head coach in choosing an assistant is not to make a choice based on an applicant's athletic accomplishments, awards, and honors alone. Success as an athlete does not guarantee success as a coach. It never has and never will. No doubt having an all-American on a coaching staff would impress members of a team and add prestige to the program, but the ultimate concern still has to be how well the person can teach. An outstanding performer sometimes has more difficulty in teaching average boys and girls than a former "occasional" player does, because a star cannot appreciate the problems of being average. The benchwarmer, or someone who had to struggle to accomplish anything in athletics, might tend to have more empathy and patience for young athletes. This is a generalization, but it is something to think about, especially if the coaching position is in junior high school, where a high level of athletic performance is not the norm.

The Head Coach's Involvement in the Interview Process

Even though head coaches should, when given the chance, be discriminating in selecting assistants, and young coaches should be discriminating when accepting a position, philosophical differences between a head coach and the assistants can arise after they begin to work together. Too many school administrators never give a head coach an opportunity to interview prospective assistants; they are simply assigned. In such cases, the coaches never meet until after the position has been filled. The erroneous assumption made by administrators is that all coaches think alike, and since they have a particular sport in common, they will get along famously. Of course, that's not always the case.

If you find yourself as head coach in a situation where administrators customarily do the hiring, try as hard as you can to convince them that they should involve you in the interview process. They have to understand that you are not trying to override their authority; rather, you are interested in assisting in the process for the good of everyone concerned—especially the athletes. If friction develops on a staff, the youngsters will pay the stiffest price because the program will probably go downhill. This is not fair to any group of athletes.

The Assistant Coach's Responsibilities

Being an assistant can be rewarding if you and the head coach agree, generally at least, on what you both consider to be a sound philosophy of coaching a high school team. Also, it is absolutely crucial for the head coach to clarify the exact responsibilities for you and every other assistant. There must be no doubt or confusion over the role any assistant coach is to fill if the staff is to be efficient and do a good job of teaching. Many head coaches have an "assistant coaches' duties" manual. This manual lays out everything from coaching responsibilities to any extra administrative duties each coach has within the program. If the head coach believes in delegating responsibilities, assistant coaches should be able to contribute significantly to the team and be recognized for it.

The head coach should also allow assistant coaches to be creative. They probably have many good ideas that should be considered. Such consideration usually gives the assistant great satisfaction and motivation, as well as creating good feelings throughout the staff. It also creates an atmosphere of unity, since, instead of a situation in which the head coach does everything and assistants simply put in time, everyone is closely involved in preparing the team. Such a "we" and "us" proposition usually helps solidify a coaching staff.

Assistant Coach or Head Coach? Pros and Cons

There are two schools of thought concerning the advantages or disadvantages of a first-year coach's becoming an assistant rather than a head coach. Some believe that a coach's first job should definitely be as an assistant. In their view, the new coach is, in effect, serving an internship while making a contribution; he or she is really learning what coaching is all about. Without the pressures associated with being head coach, the assistant is free to learn through actual coaching experience and by observation.

Another consideration is that a person who wishes to be an effective leader must first learn how to be led. Thus, by experiencing the role of an assistant, a coach will gain greater insight into how to establish the most effective working relationship between a head coach and a staff. Another advantage is that an assistant can and should benefit from the experience of the head coach. There is little question in the minds of experienced teachers that during the first year the teacher probably learns more than the students; it isn't until the second or third year that a teacher really begins to become effective. This is a generalization, to be sure, and naturally there are exceptions.

On the other hand, some believe that beginning coaches should make every attempt to start out as a head coach. In this way they can try out their own ideas and learn by trial and error. In addition, an idealistic young man or woman can begin coaching without being influenced by a head coach who might have become cynical, lazy, or unethical after prolonged involvement with high school athletics. The question of which way to start is something you must decide before accepting that first coaching job.

DESIRABLE QUALITIES OF AN ASSISTANT COACH

It is no secret that an assistant coach has far less responsibility than a head coach, but the position requires more than teaching skills. You should give careful consideration to the several very desirable characteristics and qualities every good assistant coach should have.

Loyalty

Of all the desirable qualities of an assistant coach, loyalty ranks highest. Without it, any other quality is of little or no value. Loyalty applies to others on the coaching staff, the head coach, the team, and the school. Even though it is a top priority for all assistant coaches, loyalty should be reciprocal. That is to say, not only does an assistant demonstrate loyalty, the head coach should offer the same in return.

You would be a rare individual indeed if you always agreed with everything the head coach did or thought about in coaching a particular team. Actually, disagreement is healthy as long as you are open and honest with the head coach, as long as disagreements end once a staff meeting is over, and, most important, as long as *in public, you support the head coach completely.*

When the time comes for the head coach to make final decisions, the assistant coaches must support those decisions—even if they disagree with them. If an assistant ever gets to the point where he or she cannot do so, it is time to look for a new job. Always remember that it is the head coach's program and ultimately all the accountability falls back on that position.

> *Loyalty*
>
> If you work for someone, in heaven's name work for him; speak well of him and stand by the institution he represents . . . remember—an ounce of loyalty is worth a pound of cleverness . . . if you must growl, condemn, and eternally find fault, why, resign your position and when you are on the outside, damn to your heart's content . . . but as long as you are a part of the institution, do not condemn it—if you do, the first high wind that comes along will blow you away, and probably you will never know why.
>
> —*Elbert Hubbard*

The worst mistake you could ever make as an assistant coach is to undercut, criticize, or bad-mouth the head coach or program somewhere other than at a staff meeting or to the head coach's face. Making this mistake can create a

potentially explosive situation that could tear a staff or team apart. The organization of a staff should be such that coaches can and will disagree strongly at a staff meeting, but when they leave, everyone walks out united toward whatever was finally agreed on by consensus or by edict. This is the way the best decisions are finally made—by the give-and-take of dissent and agreement. The important thing is that if you as an assistant haven't been able to sell an idea, you must be willing to accept the decision of the head coach and work as hard as possible to make it succeed. This is not always easy, but it is what loyalty is all about for an assistant coach. Everyone can be part of the process, but ultimately one person must make the final decision.

Teacher and Technician

As stated earlier, every coach must be a good teacher, but the teaching job of an assistant might involve only six to a dozen athletes, depending on the size of the staff and the sport. Thus, it is imperative that you have a thorough knowledge of the techniques of the game. Many times the teaching done by an assistant coach is a great deal more specific than that required of the head coach. One advantage of starting out as an assistant is that you can concentrate on just a few aspects of teaching the game, rather than having the overall responsibility of presenting the "big picture" to a large group.

Knowledge of the Sport

The greater your knowledge, the more valuable you become, and the greater your contribution to the whole program. Playing experience must be supplemented by a thorough study of the sport, methods of teaching, and areas related to teaching. This particular process never ends for coaches who desire to improve and grow in their profession. You have to stay abreast of the latest ideas and techniques to keep pace with opposing coaches and the sport itself.

Unfortunately, not everyone who has been appointed as an assistant coach has had playing experience in a specific sport or, for that matter, in any sport. On the other hand, some might have participated in athletics but might lack professional preparation in coaching. For whatever reason, school administrators have appointed and will continue to appoint people with or without these credentials.

In such cases, a head coach has no choice but to teach the assistants what to teach and how to teach. These people can become effective coaches in time and can make valuable contributions to the youngsters in the program. Unfortunately for many coaches, such orientation becomes an annual exercise when assistants leave the program after one season, only to be replaced by similarly unqualified people.

Enthusiasm

Genuine, spontaneous enthusiasm is contagious. It is an important criterion for teaching athletic skills, especially in preseason practices when boredom easily sets in. An excited, enthusiastic teacher can take some of the dreariness out of a practice session and evoke great response from youngsters. Enthusiasm for coaching is especially important, because when you begin to lose enthusiasm for the job, the parade will quickly pass you by. There are also days when your enthusiasm is not there. On these days it is important to conduct practice with "mock enthusiasm." Your athletes need to feel and see enthusiasm from the coach. Real or not, make sure it is there.

Initiative

It is not difficult to show initiative if you are genuinely enthusiastic about being a coach and about possibly becoming a head coach. If this is your situation, you will constantly look for things to do to improve the program or to improve a particular phase or aspect of a program. You will also be concerned with doing whatever is necessary to become a better coach, not only for the present but with an eye toward your own future in the profession. You do all of this without instruction from the head coach and because you are dedicated to doing everything possible to contribute to the success of the team. Your attitude relieves some of the burden that the head coach carries all season long.

Coaches with initiative generally make great contributions in many ways, because they make things happen. If you ever fill a position with the expectation of doing only what the head coach says, you are not fulfilling all the requirements of the position and should do some soul-searching to see whether coaching is really for you.

Good assistant coaches anticipate what needs to be done and then get it done before being directed to do so.

Dependability

Dependability is important in any teacher, but particularly in a teacher of athletics. When a head coach asks an assistant to perform certain tasks, to assume certain responsibilities, or to accomplish specific goals, he or she should have little doubt that the request will be filled, and promptly. You should perform your duties in such a way that the head coach does not have to spend valuable time double-checking to see whether the job is done. The head coach should be able to have complete confidence in your dependability, not only because it is expected but also because you have earned it.

Sound Philosophy

Regardless of whether you decide to seek a position as head coach or assistant coach, it is imperative that you begin formulating a sound philosophy of coaching early in your professional preparation. Your early beliefs will be influenced by your own high school coaches, college coaches, playing experience, and professional courses. You should take advantage of every opportunity to test your ideas on others in order to help clarify your thinking and to adopt other sound ideas. The college classroom is the ideal setting for this exercise.

It is highly unlikely that a philosophy of coaching formulated in college will stay unchanged after you actually begin coaching. This is neither good nor bad, but every coach needs to constantly reevaluate personal beliefs about coaching, and be willing to grow. Such reevaluation should be based on lessons learned through experience.

Clarifying your beliefs while still a student will help prepare you for job interviews. On the basis of these beliefs you should be able to answer questions more confidently and to ask intelligent questions specific to a particular position. You should take time to put your beliefs in writing. This is not only an excellent way to clarify your thinking but also an excellent way to force yourself to think through your reasoning.

Desire to Be a Head Coach

A head coach should encourage assistants to advance. This policy probably sounds strange, because it means that a head coach will lose members of the staff periodically. But the advantages of doing so far outweigh the disadvantages.

When assistant coaches have no desire to be a head coach, or if they lose this desire, their professional growth becomes limited. People in this situation often perform as though they were semiretired; they tend to do only what the head coach tells them to do and little else. Such coaches show little initiative and enthusiasm and are generally uninspired in their teaching, which severely limits their effectiveness and contribution to the team. The only motivation for such coaches is usually the extra money they get paid for coaching or the chance to identify with an athletic team—neither of which justifies their position on a coaching staff.

On the other hand, those who have great desire to become a head coach operate with an entirely different attitude. What they are really doing on the staff is preparing themselves to be head coaches. Consequently, they study, question, suggest, advise, argue, debate, try new and different techniques and ideas, and constantly evaluate what is taking place in the program. Throughout this process, and because of it, their contributions to the program are limitless. When all the coaches on the staff have this desire, an air of electricity surrounds the group, and the members of the team benefit from genuine, unbridled, enthusiastic teaching.

Even though this goal is a positive one, there are two important cautions to keep in mind. First, don't be in too much of a hurry; and second, in your ambitious desire, do not take aim at your head coach's job. This is not only unethical but dangerous, because it can create all kinds of dissent within a staff, as well as on a team if youngsters begin to pick sides. If you are not careful and allow yourself to fall into this trap, you could pay a severe price.

At the same time, you should know that some head coaches discourage assistants from leaving by hinting at early retirement as head coach, implying that an assistant could move up. You would be wise to carefully assess such a situation and set a timetable to see whether the head job does, in fact, open at the school. If it does not, begin an active search for a head job elsewhere. It can be frustrating to hang on for years while the head coach dangles the bait of retirement in front of you. In too many cases, when the head coach finally does retire, a new head coach is brought in over a long-time assistant because the board wants a younger person or someone who has had head coaching experience.

Playing Experience

To repeat an earlier point, of all the lessons in professional preparation, playing experience is the greatest single factor in preparing to become a coach. But keep in mind that such experience is no guarantee for success in coaching. Game time is not the critical issue; being on the squad is. Experiencing, both physically and mentally, what you will teach provides a much sounder basis for coaching than any textbook or any lecture. Some people become good high school coaches in a sport in which they did not participate, but this is an exception rather than the rule, and often there are other contributing circumstances.

Even though not everyone is big enough, fast enough, or good enough to make a team in a large university, it is still possible to be a part of the team as a manager, statistician, trainer, or walk-on in order to learn more about a sport. Another possibility for a nonteam member is to get permission from head coaches to attend some of their practice sessions. In this way you can learn a great deal by observing and listening.

Willingness to Attend Clinics

A good way to continue to learn about the latest ideas in whatever sport you are coaching is to attend clinics. Naturally, there is a limit to the number of clinics you can or should attend, so you should choose them with specific purposes in mind. Assistant coaches who are dedicated to the profession should take advantage of this opportunity; the semiretired type of assistant will probably have to be required to attend.

A clinic may not cause you to change your thinking, but every clinic should encourage you to do some self-evaluation, and this is good. You will either change your thinking or reinforce what you already believe. If you are a young assistant coach, you can learn what other coaches are doing in similar programs. You can then compare their ideas to your own and apply them to your situation. The greater your understanding of the different methods of successful coaching, the better a teacher you should become.

It is also possible for high school coaches to get "private clinics" by visiting with a college coaching staff. College coaches are concerned about developing good relationships with high school coaches—primarily for recruiting purposes. Most of these people are willing to spend time with high school coaches if the high school people take the initiative to call and ask. The time spent visiting and observing college coaches can sometimes be of much greater value than a typical clinic. If you ever decide to visit a college coach, just make sure to call ahead so you can be fit into the coach's busy schedule; normally you will find coaches to be receptive to your request. By the way, this is also a good way to meet some pretty nice people as well.

A word of advice: Be careful not to be lured to clinics by programs featuring athletes and coaches of professional teams. Most of them are entertaining but have little to offer to a high school coach. The experiences of these professionals have little significance for anyone involved in high school or junior high school athletic programs, since professional sport is a world of its own, and what takes place there is, in many ways, not appropriate for teenage athletes.

Many times a clinic composed only of high school coaches is the most meaningful to other high school coaches. They talk the same language, understand the same problems, and live in the same kinds of circumstances. Consequently, what they say is relevant to any other high school coach.

Clinics serve another purpose, too. They provide great opportunities for meeting coaches from different areas and learning about coaching vacancies. There is no way of knowing when some chance meeting with another coach will pave the way to another job.

Rapport with Athletes

Establishing positive rapport with students is crucial to any teacher, and it is an absolute must for coaches. Without good rapport there are limits to the athletes' acceptance of you and what you are attempting to teach, regardless of how sound your techniques are. Again, this requirement emphasizes the importance of a teacher's concern for the players rather than for the mechanics of teaching. Rapport means that the players respect you, respect what you know, and respect what you are attempting to teach.

You will have a great opportunity that a head coach does not have, solely because of the nature of each position. Someone has to be the boss, the ramrod, the driver, and the pusher, and in practically all cases this is the head coach. Obviously, these roles create an image for a head coach that prevents having the close working relationship with every member of the team that an assistant can establish. You will be primarily concerned with teaching an assigned group, establishing rapport with them, and getting them to want to do the best they can. If yours is a typical coaching staff, the number of athletes you will be responsible for could be very small, so the athletes often identify with you more readily than with the head coach. An assistant coach really should zero in on the players, for it is through them that you derive your satisfaction throughout the season. Ultimately, of course, the team's accomplishments are a source of satisfaction too, but satisfaction comes from the players first.

On some occasions the head coach will find it necessary to scold or discipline athletes, who may get so discouraged that it affects their performance. In this situation an assistant has to back the head coach but should also try to boost players' morale and provide whatever kind of encouragement is necessary to get them back in the proper frame of mind. Special efforts like this do a great deal to enhance rapport between an assistant coach and athletes.

Ability to Serve as Liaison Between Players and Head Coach

Because of the special rapport that should be deliberately cultivated by assistant coaches, they also serve as a liaison between players and the head coach. The head coach needs to be constantly aware of the feelings of the players, their concerns, their morale, any grumbling that might be going on, unhappiness on the team, athletes who think they are not being treated fairly, and how the team is reacting to certain things the head coach says or does.

Not many boys or girls will go to a head coach and volunteer this kind of information, or be perfectly frank when asked. The perceptive coach usually is aware of these situations when they exist, but not always, especially with a large squad. At the same time, the coaching staff might decide that, because of certain circumstances, the head coach should do or say certain things to the team to create or cause specific reactions. Assistant coaches can find out easily whether or not a planned move has had the desired effect on the team.

It is possible, too, for assistant coaches to serve as a liaison when they themselves see something the head coach is doing that is having a negative effect on an individual or a team. The atmosphere within the coaching staff should be such that you can speak freely without causing any resentment between the head coach and yourself.

Willingness to Work

Even though the final responsibility for an athletic team rests with the head coach, a good assistant is more than willing to carry a fair share of the load before, during, and after the season. Coaching is a lot of work, and you should never adopt an attitude of sitting still and doing nothing until the head coach has everything organized for the season. This is what semiretired assistant coaches do. Good assistants never do it, and if they had to, they would probably feel very frustrated and useless because they weren't making more of a contribution.

Willingness to work means attending clinics, usually on Saturdays; attending evening meetings after a long day at school; meeting with the head coach in the summer or during vacations to plan for the coming season; scouting; and doing what the head coach believes is necessary for a good program for the students. If you cannot fulfill this role without resenting it, in fairness to the other coaches and the members of the team, you should give up coaching, at least in this particular situation. However, if you are a part-time coach, you might not be able or willing to do some of these things, and the head coach should understand your situation.

Willingness to Contribute Ideas

The head coach should encourage the sharing of ideas among coaches on the staff. If assistant coaches have come from different colleges or other coaching staffs, they have all been exposed to different ideas and techniques. Sharing them can make the program better and serve as in-service training for everyone concerned.

Brainstorming sessions in the off-season provide a good setting. In brainstorming, people throw out ideas, no matter how wild they might seem, and allow everyone else to react to them. Frequently these ideas trigger other ideas or possibilities in someone else's mind, and changes in the program can follow as a result. Industry has been using this technique for years among company personnel. Brainstorming is an exercise in reaping benefits from the abrasive effect of one sharp mind on another.

The opportunity to present an idea and have it become a part of the team is a tremendous morale builder for assistant coaches. If assistants are high-caliber people, they should not only present their own ideas but also add their thoughts to the ideas of others to help make the team a better one.

Motivation

The ability to motivate youngsters does not rest solely with the head coach. Assistant coaches also have a responsibility to motivate those players for whom they are directly responsible. Therefore, you should have a good knowledge of each of these youngsters and a thorough understanding of motivational techniques and concepts.

In addition, you will need to practice self-motivation, particularly if things are not going well and the head coach is "down." This feeling can be contagious, but you must not allow it to affect you or the players you are responsible for.

Flexibility

Flexibility is far more necessary for an assistant coach than for a head coach, simply because it is the assistant who must adjust to the head coach. This means you should be willing to be flexible in your philosophy of coaching and athletics, willing to move as opportunities present themselves, and willing to consider and change ideas.

The ability and willingness to do what is necessary to become a good assistant coach is to be admired. It is not always easy, but it is a learning experience that can be valuable to you now and in the future.

DISCUSSION QUESTIONS

1. The opinion of a head coach's intelligence is based on the quality of the people around him or her. Explain.

2. There is a vast difference between making a suggestion and making a decision. What are the implications of this difference for assistant coaches?

3. What questions would you ask of the head coach, principal, athletic director, or superintendent of schools when interviewing for an assistant coaching position?

4. How would you deal with a critic of the head coach if you yourself were not totally supportive of an idea of the head coach's?

5. If you were a head coach, what questions would you ask a prospective assistant?

6. Give some examples of the ways assistant coaches can serve as a liaison between the players and head coach.

7. List some reasons why hard feelings develop between a head coach and an assistant.

8. If you had several offers to become an assistant coach, what factors would affect your final decision?

9. What do you believe would or could be the most frustrating part of being an assistant coach? How would you deal with this?

10. How can loyalty become a problem for an assistant coach?

7

Whether you are married or single, the nature of the coaching profession will have a significant impact on your personal life. Thorough discussion of this facet of the coaching profession tends to be overlooked in the professional preparation of young men and women interested in becoming coaches. This chapter is not meant to be a philosophical presentation of the ideal life experienced by coaches, families, and friends; rather, it is grounded solely in reality. Do not be too quick to judge the material that follows. What may seem unreasonable to you in a classroom setting could mean quite something else when you are actually in the field.

The material in this chapter is a general overview of coaches' families and of the single coach on the high school level. Because so many factors affect a coach's personal life, it would be impossible to cover every conceivable possibility. In addition, the perspective from which you digest this chapter will most certainly influence your interpretation of and reaction to it.

The information presented here has been gathered over a number of years and comes from many people associated with coaching—both married and single. What follows are frank and honest reactions, feelings, and perceptions, and although they won't be common to everyone, you will experience some of them in the future. The purpose here is simply to make you aware.

A COMPARISON OF MALE AND FEMALE MARRIED COACHES

It makes little difference whether or not married coaches want their spouses to become involved in their jobs, because there is simply no way to avoid it completely. Regardless of personal desires, coaches and their families soon discover that the job does come home in several ways. Depending on the sport and the interest of the community in that sport, the job affects the home through (a) telephone calls (some anonymous) from parents, fans, students, or athletes; (b) athletes dropping by either for a friendly visit or because of a problem; (c) family members hearing critics or grandstand coaches during an athletic event;

141

(d) publicity about the coach and the team in the news media; (e) incidental contact with parents of the athletes in various places in the community; (f) late hours; (g) Saturday contests; (h) coaching meetings, possibly in the coach's home; and (i) the coach's frame of mind during the season, especially if the team is not doing well.

Depending on the circumstances, some of these factors might not be of any real concern with a particular sport. But the most difficult aspect to control is your frame of mind during the season, which depends, of course, on your degree of commitment to coaching.

For some, coaching is not only a profession but an obsession; for others, coaching is merely something to be tolerated because it provides some extra pay.

It is not too difficult to understand why people become obsessed with coaching when we consider that it is (a) a chosen career; (b) a means of livelihood; (c) a possible step to better jobs; (d) a matter, sometimes, of great ego involvement; and (e) a direct reflection of a coach's ability to teach.

It is rare to find individuals who can completely disassociate themselves mentally from coaching once they leave the locker room for the day. The excitement, problems, happiness, anguish, and plans usually go home with the coach either consciously or subconsciously. At any rate, the family will be aware of these inner feelings and be affected by them.

A coach's children cannot escape involvement if they are of school age. They will be the envy of many in their peer group and will often be told how lucky they are. Others will not hesitate to tell them what a terrible coach their mother or father is and will blame their parent when the team loses. A coach's children learn some lessons of life early, but when they feel they are a part of what is going on in the planning for the season and individual games, they wouldn't trade places with any other boy or girl in town.

Because there is no way a coach's family can be completely insulated against critics, it might be wise to include the family in the inner circle of the team's operation. Doing so can help the family face whatever they come up against in the stands, in the town, at school, or at home. Your family will be less likely to resent your preoccupation with the season or the time spent in preparation for each game if they feel they are a part of what is occurring. Usually it is when family members feel excluded or left out that they become less tolerant of your commitment to the team and season.

Coaches commonly make the mistake of assuming that everyone around them, including their family, shares their boundless enthusiasm for the sport they are coaching. Of course, this is not always the case. Making this assumption can cause serious problems in a marriage. If you are just entering the profession and plan to get married, do not assume your spouse will automatically become a perfect, understanding partner just because he or she is married to a coach. Unless this person has a tremendous interest in sports or has grown up in a coaching family, he or she has no idea of what kind of life awaits. To avoid problems later on, you must make every effort to explain what coaching is all about, especially the demands it will make on your time, thought, and energy, before you get married. You owe it to your future spouse and to yourself. One easy way to do this is to have your future husband or wife read this book, or at least this chapter. (You can decide whether or not to give them a written test!)

The noncoaching member of the family will need to be willing to adjust almost daily to the merry-go-round life every coaching family experiences. Your spouse will have to learn how to deal with criticism and to live with the various moods you go through during the course of a season, ranging from the exhilaration of a great win to despair over an unexpected loss. If the husband is a head coach, the wife will often be expected to help and encourage the families of the assistant coaches to become involved in the excitement of the season. If she elects to take this role, she can be

especially helpful to these families in their adjustment to a new community. The prospective husband of a head coach should be prepared to become similarly involved. In short, it takes a special person to be a coach's husband or wife. Coaches fortunate enough to have this kind of spouse should count their blessings.

This aspect of coaching is one not often considered but is an area that should not be taken lightly. An unhappy spouse in this demanding profession can have an adverse effect on your career and of course can result in more serious problems in the marriage.

THE MARRIED FEMALE COACH

Years ago, it was the wives of male coaches who had to make many adjustments at home for husbands who were coaching athletic teams. Basically this is still the case, since the number of married men coaches is greater than the number of married women coaches. But a growing number of men now find themselves making adjustments at home because their wives are coaches.

Frequently, part of a husband's attitude toward a coaching wife and the time she spends with the team stems from his belief that he is the main breadwinner of the family and must work. Such men do not expect their wife to support the family forever, and as a result, they think her involvement in coaching and all its ramifications and effects on the marriage are simply not necessary. So when problems occur, or when the wife is unhappy with some part of her coaching, her husband is likely to say, "Why don't you just quit coaching?" In the husband's mind the aggravation just isn't worth it; the economic impact would be minimal (for a high school coach), and besides "It's only a game" and really not too important.

Obviously, this attitude can create a great deal of friction if the wife is committed to coaching and striving for excellence in the profession. A husband who is a physical educator or a coach is likely to have a far different attitude from one who is neither and who might never have participated in sport.

When the husband is not in physical education or coaching, his wife might feel professional loneliness. Her husband might not care very much about the team because his own job presents problems that seem far more important to him than his wife's concern over a 16-year-old girl having trouble shooting foul shots, for example.

Life for a married female coach is demanding. Not only must she work all day, coach after school, and take her team on lengthy trips, she must also share the joint responsibility of the house with her husband, and possibly the care of children. Someone has to cook, wash and iron clothes, clean the house, and shop for groceries, all of which should be shared. Without a great deal of support and help from her husband, the coach's mental, emotional, and physical costs can be high.

According to a survey of men whose wives were coaches on the secondary school level, their biggest concerns were:

- The demands on her time

- Late dinners for both

- Her emotions, anxiety, frustration, depression, and anguish as affected by her job

- Too little time spent together during the course of a season

When asked what advice they would give any young man planning on marrying a coach, they said:

- Be aware of the amount of time she will be spending with the team.

- Become involved in her sport and share her interest in it.

- Be understanding, patient, and supportive.

- Realize that she will be tired and irritable when she gets home.

- Spend time together whenever possible.

- Establish an open and honest relationship before you get married.

Their advice to a female coach intending to get married was:

- Make sure your husband-to-be understands the amount of time your job as a coach will require away from him at clinics, practices, games, banquets, coaches' meetings, tournaments, and league meetings.

- Help him become interested and involved in some way.

- Never let coaching become more important than your marriage.

The single common item running through these concerns is clearly the time factor. There simply is no escaping it for any coach.

Certainly it is possible for a woman to be a wife and a coach. Yes, there are problems, but with a lot of cooperation and understanding they can be handled. What I am suggesting is that it is important, before marriage, for clear, frank communication regarding the fact that the woman does intend to coach, that coaching is important to her, and that there are some ramifications that need to be understood. If the man is unwilling to accept the job's obligations before marriage, it is doubtful that his attitude will improve after the wedding. Finally, it should not be necessary for a woman who wants to be a coach to choose between that career and marriage.

THE MARRIED MALE COACH

Certainly not every woman sees her role in being married to a coach the same way. There are those who choose to have as little to do with their husbands' jobs as possible; there are those who are somewhat involved; and there are those who choose to become as involved as they possibly can. Whatever decision is made should be acceptable to both parties and with any luck will not become a problem in the marriage.

The following paragraphs are a transcript of a presentation Ralph's wife gave to a group of prospective coaches (male and female) on campus. Although she was speaking from a wife's perspective, much of this material is also pertinent to husbands of coaches. What follows clearly reflects her decision to be an important part of our high school coaching family.

A Wife's Perspective

At first I didn't know what I could say to you regarding the life of a coach's wife. Then I sat down and began thinking about some of the experiences we've had and the things we did as a high school football and baseball family. I discovered that there really is a lot involved in being married to a coach, particularly one who is coaching a sport with several assistants and a good number of athletes.

As new men joined our staff, they and their wives were guests in our home soon after they arrived in town. Often these young men were newly married and reporting to their first coaching position. We would sit and talk in general about what they could expect to happen in their young lives within the next few years as they began to grow in the coaching profession. This talk always seemed to mean a lot to them, because they were not really aware of many of the ways coaching would influence their lives.

Perhaps you wonder why it is important that the woman in the family be aware of or understand what it means to be a coach's wife. Well, she should understand what kind of life she is getting into, and the young man must point this out to her very early before they decide to get married. She must realize very early what will be expected of her, or it will be a shock as time goes on. She has to understand that coaching is going to demand a great deal of her husband's time

and thoughts, and there will be lots of times when she is going to feel second in line of importance to her husband's team. For a young bride this can come as a real disappointment. She must understand that to her husband, coaching is not just a little boys' game. Instead, the team's performance is a reflection of his ability to teach and is displayed in front of thousands of people several times over a season, on the field, in the gymnasium, in the pool, or wherever the contest takes place. To him it is more than a game—it is his chosen profession.

Basically, there are three kinds of coaching wives: (1) those who know something about the game and become involved because they want to, (2) those who don't know much about the game and don't want any part of it, and (3) those who we can classify as ambitious wives. The ambitious wife becomes a problem only when she feels her husband is not being given enough credit for his contributions and begins to suggest that he really should be head coach. This is a potentially explosive situation, and the head coach's wife must work hard to make this wife feel that she and her husband are important to the program.

The happiest memories I have are of all the wonderful parents we got to know and became friends with, as we shared their sons through athletics. It is a nice feeling to be known by so many parents, and of course your paths cross while shopping, in church, or at other community functions. A coach's wife shares a lot with parents, especially during the athletic event itself. You both hope the team does well; if they do, you cheer with them, and if one or all the players don't do well, you share disappointment with them as well.

A coach's wife must also expect to receive telephone calls about her husband. Some can be very bad, but many can be quite complimentary. Why people call the coach's wife to complain instead of talking directly to him remains a mystery, but they do. One wife whose husband was a longtime famous coach at a major university used to completely disarm anonymous phone callers who would call to tell her that her husband was an incompetent coach. She'd say she quite agreed and thought the coach made some bad decisions during the game in question, too. This usually ended the conversation abruptly!

The fans who were the hardest to take were the ones who were critical of the players. When they criticized the coaches, the coaches' wives turned a deaf ear because we had come to expect this as part of the game, but it would make us angry to hear a grown person verbally attack a team member because he made a mistake in the game.

Getting to know the young athletes was a most rewarding part of being a coach's wife. I think athletes are extra special anyway, and to have them go out of their way to speak or call across the street to say hello gave me a real feeling of pride, because these fine young men were recognizing me as Coach's wife. If your husband establishes a close rapport with the team, they will find all kinds of excuses to drop in at your home, and frequently it will be around the dinner hour, as all young athletes are always hungry, it seems. So it isn't unusual to have company for dinner, even though you hadn't planned on it, and even though your visitor may have just gotten up from the dinner table at home before he decided to stop in to see the coach. I can't think of any kind of young people I'd rather have in my house around my own children than well-disciplined athletes.

Sometimes these visits would come late at night, when one of the team members had come up against some kind of problem and almost automatically came to the house to talk to the coach. The rest of the family learned how to make themselves scarce in a hurry.

We also felt it was a privilege to take these young men to college athletic events as they began to think about college, and when we did, our whole family went along. It was not uncommon to take a group to a Saturday afternoon football game and another group to a night game the same day. Often their mothers would send picnic lunches along, or a cake, and the trip became a big picnic.

It was a great pleasure to have some of the athletes who went away to college return to our home for a visit during their college days or after graduation. Often they would bring their new girlfriends along for us to meet. One of our proudest moments came when our family was invited to commencement at a prestigious university some years ago, when one of our former athletes, who had been elected president of the senior class, gave a commencement address.

As you might expect, the next step was receiving wedding invitations. This often put a dent in a coach's limited budget, but it was a very pleasant part of our lives, too. It was a good feeling to think that these young men thought enough of my husband to invite us to one of the most important events of their young lives. It never failed, though, that before the reception was over, a group of the athletes and the coach would be in the corner reliving past glories while the bride wandered about the room pretending not to notice.

One of the most important relationships the head coach's wife must cultivate is with the wives of the assistant coaches. The wives share many feelings and emotions during the course of a season, enough common ground upon which to develop the unique feeling of "in-ness" among coaching families. The larger the coaching staff, the more important this feeling becomes. Two problem areas may arise: the wife who doesn't join the group, and the overly ambitious wife.

The overly ambitious wife creates a problem that is much more serious. When a coach's wife is ambitious for her husband to the point where friction begins to develop within the group, this situation can destroy the unity among the coaching families, cause wives to draw up sides, and possibly spread to the point where the coaches themselves are affected.

At this point, if the head coach has established a good working rapport with his staff, he should sit down with the husband of this particular wife and calmly discuss the situation to see what the problem is. It may be that the assistant coach is not aware of the problem, or it may be that there are other reasons for his wife's behavior.

One of the most important contributions the head coach's wife can make is to serve as a committee of one to help the wives of new coaches get acquainted in the community as quickly as possible—in other words to be a one-woman Welcome Wagon hostess. It is easy for people who have been settled in a town for several years to forget the trauma that is often associated with moving into a brand-new community. If neither spouse is familiar with the community, their adjustment problems can be painful, and so the head coach's wife should take it upon herself to help ease the jolt of being "new" by helping these folks feel at home instantly.

There are so many ways she can help. One is to offer this young couple a place to stay while they look for a place of their own. She can also guide them around the community, showing them the various sections of town and possible living accommodations in relation to the location of the school and shopping areas. They need to arrange for a family doctor and dentist and should see where the various churches are located. It is a good idea, too, to take the new wife on a shopping trip, so she can learn something about the stores. This also provides a fine opportunity to introduce her as the wife of one of our new coaches to as many merchants as you happen to know. This is one of the first steps in making a new family feel welcome, and a good way to let them know that you are glad they are joining your coaching family.

Another method for creating the feeling of "in-ness" among wives is to arrange to go to all the games together. The wives can take turns driving to the games, but all meet at one house to save time. We always sat together at both home and away games, and after every game, we all met at someone's home for a postgame get-together. This I think was one of the best things we ever did, because it was one of the few opportunities the whole group had to be together and relax for a while during the season. If the team won, everyone wanted to be together to enjoy the win. If the team lost, we felt it was necessary to be together rather than brooding individually. I guess being together served as group therapy. Sometimes these sessions would last until three or four in the morning. Many cups of coffee were consumed as the husbands unwound and replayed the game over and over again. But these evenings were a wonderful part of coaching that helped create a real closeness within the whole group. The wives felt responsible for these get-togethers and looked forward to them. Sometimes the evenings were painful at the beginning because of a disappointing loss, but by the time the evening had ended, everyone felt better.

Then, too, there are the inevitable coaches' meetings. Rather than have each wife sit at home feeling neglected, we decided to meet, too. The wives with small babies would bring them along and put them to sleep in their car seats. We'd put on the coffee, talk, cross stitch or knit, and get to know each other better. Those who didn't know how to knit, learned, and sometimes when the coaches finished their meeting, they would come to the living room and have to wait for the wives because they were busy doing something of interest. They simply weren't ready to go home.

We soon discovered that after all these fun times together, we usually missed each other when the season ended, so we decided it was important to continue to do things together all year long. Coaches usually like to eat, so at least once a month we would all go out to dinner, have a picnic, or plan a progressive dinner, and we would take at least one camping weekend each summer. Another suggestion for "wives only" is a gourmet night. The wives got together, alternating houses, for a special dinner prepared by the hostess followed by cards or games. The only rule was the hostess had to prepare something she had never cooked before. Obviously, we didn't want anyone to feel that he or she wasn't an important part of a close-knit group, so we worked hard at it.

Another consideration is the wives of other coaches in the school— coaches of other sports. In order to prevent any misunderstanding about creating a feeling of "in-ness" within a coaching staff for one sport only, it is a good idea to invite coaches and their wives who are involved in other sports to some of the social functions your group has during the year. This helps create a good working relationship among all the coaches, and it can be an effective tool to help maintain harmony. The athletic director and his wife often joined us in these get-togethers. Occasionally, we would include the high school principal and his wife, or other faculty members who would enjoy the association with a group of coaches.

It is also important for a coach's wife to attend other functions in the school with her husband—school plays, concerts, PTA meetings, and so on—to show that those in athletics are not narrow and selfish in their interests but care about the total school program. Due to the nature of his position, your husband is highly visible in the community, and attendance at these functions does not go unnoticed.

Since we were primarily a football coaching family, the weeks during a season generally followed the same pattern. The first six days of every week our schedule revolved around Father's schedule, but we made certain that Sunday was a special day for the family. After church we always spent the day together, doing something totally unrelated to athletics. Everyone was fairly relaxed in the first part of the week, but as the days passed and game time approached, the tension in Father began to affect the whole family, so that by game night, dinner was a very sparse occasion, because everyone was too excited to think much about eating.

To make the children feel extra special, the coach always let them in on some special play that would take place during the game. Of course this made them feel quite knowledgeable when they went to the game and told their friends to watch for it, and then pointed it out when it happened. This was all well and good, but it backfired on us one night. Our daughter explained an unusual play in great detail to an inquisitive fan during a game, only to discover later that he was a scout for our next opponent.

One role a coach's wife rarely escapes is that of laundress. It isn't unusual for the coach to come home with one or two duffel bags full of dirty scrimmage vests or other paraphernalia to be washed in time to take back to school the next day.

She might also be called upon to chauffeur a group of athletes to a baseball game, tennis match, or other athletic contest when school buses aren't available. She may find herself hostess to thirty or more players for a team picnic, because her husband thought it would be a good thing. Or sometimes she will find herself going to the hospital with her husband late at night after a game to visit a player who has been injured. There is no question about it, a coach's wife is a lady for all seasons and a woman of many traits. It is truly an exciting way to live when you pitch in and join your husband.

Concerns and Advice

After this presentation a questionnaire was mailed to other wives of coaches. We asked them about the impact coaching had on their husbands and their families. The following are the most frequently reported concerns:

- The tremendous demands on a coach's time

- His time away from home, the children, and wife

- His health; for example, tension, anxiety, worry, exhaustion, and ulcers

- Irregular home schedule for meals, trips, and transportation

Their advice to a young woman considering marrying a coach was:

- Learn the sport that your husband coaches.

- Be prepared for long hours away from him.

- Support your husband in his coaching.

- Find some interest of your own.

- During the season be ready to be number two.

- Be patient, loving, cheerful, understanding, and a good listener.

- Learn to fix late, warmed-up meals.

- Understand that coaching is important to him.

- Be ready for losses by his team.

- Be prepared to be both mother and father during the season and to handle household problems, such as paying bills, plumbing/heating problems, etc.

If you are a man who intends to coach and get married, here is some advice for you:

- Include your wife in the sport; share with her your problems and concerns about the team. Take her to games and any social events surrounding the team.

- Let her know the amount of time you will be away from her and the family.

- Let her know it means a lot to you.

- Encourage her to find hobbies of her own.

- Don't let problems concerning the team cause problems at home.

- Marry the girl, not the sport.

- Find someone who likes sports.

- Be considerate of your time together.

Another factor that can develop unintentionally when men become coaches of girls' teams is some degree of jealousy on the part of wives. Everyone needs and likes attention, and when married male coaches seem to give their attention to the girls on the team, and little to their wives, it can become a problem. So be careful.

There is no doubt that a married man or woman's involvement in coaching does affect the spouse and family, for better or worse. This in itself is not necessarily a revelation to any married coach, but the important thing is to be able to put coaching, and particularly the time factor, into proper perspective. That is to say, more than one coach has devoted years of time and energy to "the team" and other people's sons or daughters, only to give up coaching one day and discover that his own family has grown up and moved on.

Coaching is certainly a demanding occupation. But it is also possible to be a considerate husband, wife, mother, or father and a coach at the same time. When a person quits coaching, and the scores of all those athletic events have long been forgotten by practically everyone, the family ties still remain. It may be that in the final analysis this is what really counts. At any rate, it would seem that a coach's family deserves at least the same kind of interest, concern, and dedication that he or she gives the team—if not more.

THE SINGLE COACH

This section of the chapter is obviously quite a bit shorter than that dealing with married coaches. By no means is this meant to diminish a single coach's concerns or personal/social considerations. The fact is that while all or most of the factors faced by married coaches can be shared by spouses, single coaches have no one else to rely on and, therefore, take on all these items themselves.

You need to be aware that although there are many similarities between you and your married counterparts (time constraints, taking care of a home or apartment), there are several important differences. The biggest difference between your private life (if you live alone) and that of married coaches is the lack of personal support. The need to go home after a game or practice and share what just occurred with someone who is willing to listen is not satisfied, thereby eliminating an important stress-reducing opportunity. Care of the house, cooking, and shopping are other important areas a single coach must deal with daily, without any support.

The demands of coaching can also affect your social life. If you are a full-time teacher, you will probably get to school at 7:30 A.M. and teach classes all day until 3:30. At that time your team will begin reporting for practice, and by the time you finish with the team and whatever else needs to be taken care of around the locker room, you probably won't get home until 7 P.M.

At that time, unless you pick up a hamburger on the way home, you will have to cook your own dinner and clean up the kitchen. It is now 8:00 or 8:30, and time to prepare for the next day's classes, practice, or game. If you are lucky, at about 10:30 you can fall into bed, exhausted at the end of another typical day for a coach.

Added to this are Saturday athletic events such as tournaments, district meets, and so on. If you are part of a coaching staff, you might also meet on Sundays, which makes your job a seven-days-a-week occupation.

If you become a college coach, life becomes even more hectic. When you add recruiting, long trips to away games, and longer seasons, you take on significantly more demanding responsibilities, all of which require more of your time—time that is already in short supply.

> I've never believed that any job is worth sacrificing one's personal life for. I have never believed that any success outside the home can compensate within it. It is important to hold on to your own values, or you will surely lose them.
>
> —David Gardner,
>   former president of the
>   University of California

The question is, when do you have time for a social life? The answer is, rarely—at least during your sport season.

Another consideration is that of establishing friendships, or the inability to do so outside the school environment. Because the demands on your time will be great and because many teachers in your school will probably be married, it can be difficult to develop much of a circle of friends. As a result, some single coaches tend to become friends with members of their team and do their socializing this way. However, this situation can cause problems: It is extremely difficult to be a pal and be in charge at the same time.

DISCUSSION QUESTIONS

1. Would you like to coach your son or daughter? Why?

2. What are some ways in which a coaching staff can involve their wives and husbands in their coaching?

3. How will you advise your spouse or children to handle critics in the stands?

4. Is it really necessary for coaches to spend so much time on the job? Explain your answer.

5. Should coaches involve their families in their jobs? Why?

6. How can having a husband or wife who is also in coaching create problems in a marriage?

7. What is your reaction to the advice from coaches' husbands? To the advice from coaches' wives? Is there anything in this advice that surprised you? Is there anything you take issue with? Are there other questions you would ask?

8. How do coaches' families become involved in the job through no effort on their part?

9. What mistaken assumption do coaches frequently make regarding those around them?

10. If a coach chooses to marry, when should he or she explain the nature of the profession to the intended spouse?

11. What are some of the differences between the life of a single coach and that of a married coach?

8

Of all the important issues surrounding high school athletics today, none has been with us as long as the recruiting of players by colleges. Recruiting actually began in the late 1890s, with the onset of student directed athletic club teams on college campuses throughout the country. During that period, team managers often recruited players from factories, mills, mines, railroads, or other workplaces. These players, referred to as ringers, were not students and were not affiliated with the colleges in any way. These first recruiting abuses led to faculty control of athletics. Nowadays, of course, high school athletes are the targets of college recruiters.

Even though recruiting is basically a college-initiated function, high school coaches need to take the initiative to exercise control over recruiting in their own schools. You should keep the following points in mind as we cover the recruiting process:

- Not every high school coach understands the recruiting rules as set forth by the NCAA.

- Not every high school coach is prepared to deal with the recruiting process.

- High school coaches should attempt to understand recruiting from college coaches' perspectives.

- High school athletes and their parents do not know the rules of recruiting, nor do they understand the process itself.

- High school athletes and their parents have significant misconceptions about recruiting and scholarship offers.

- Many parents have significant misconceptions about high school coaches' role in scholarship offers.

- Hard feelings can and do develop among athletes, parents, recruiters, and high school coaches because of misunderstandings and misperceptions of what is or is not supposed to occur before, during, or as a result of recruiting.

The recruiting process is an inescapable part of high school coaching and should be a positive experience for everyone concerned. This facet of coaching requires a lot of thought, planning, time, and understanding. Yet many coaches new to the profession are not aware of this until they are confronted with a recruiting situation.

Your first step is to order the pamphlet "NCAA Guide for the College-Bound Student Athlete" from the NCAA (P.O. Box 6222, Indianapolis, IN 46206-6222, Phone 317-917-6222, www.ncaa.org). This guide will enable you to effectively monitor the recruiting of your athletes by making certain that no rules are being violated. It is also important to stay abreast of rule changes, which occur from year to year.

The following excerpt is from a letter from a former student who was coaching basketball at a Division I university. It clearly illustrates the importance of the point I have been making:

> I feel bad for high school athletes today. Recruiting is too mind-boggling for adults—never mind 17- and 18-year olds. The NCAA recruiting rules are so complicated that it is taking me nights of studying to learn them. Many high school coaches barely know the rules—I was shocked when I would speak with coaches who knew nothing about the rules and didn't take part in advising their athletes. We will be having a workshop to help explain the rules to coaches and try to let them know what is helpful in recruiting (such as videotaping, keeping statistics, scheduling visits, etc.).

It should be a revelation to no one that the name of the game in college coaching is recruiting. If college X recruits better players than its opponents, it will probably win more than it loses. There is nothing mysterious about it—college coaches mainly survive in the profession on their ability to recruit. Because of the pressures associated with coaching high-visibility sports at the college level, including the demand to field winning teams, recruiting has a direct impact on high school coaches and athletes.

It has become standard recruiting procedure for outstanding high school freshmen and sophomores to be contacted by college coaches—not recruited, but contacted—because of some individual accomplishment in athletics, thereby planting a seed. Remember, these are 15- to 16-year-old youngsters. This is pretty heady stuff for a boy or girl of that age. The actual recruiting process normally begins in earnest at the conclusion of these athletes' junior year in high school, and this timing can create some problems for high school coaches. As a consequence, every high school coach should develop a set of guidelines or a strategy for dealing with the recruiting process *before* circumstances demand it.

THE RECRUITING PROCESS

You can deal with the recruiting of your athletes in three basic ways: (1) take a hands-off position if you feel this is not part of your responsibility, and allow the recruiters, athletes, and their parents to deal with the whole process; (2) participate in the process when requested to do so by athletes and their parents; or (3) take charge of determining precisely how recruiting will take place in your school, serve as a "bumper" between recruiters and athletes and their parents, and orchestrate the entire process. This third choice is the best if you have a bona fide blue-chip prospect who faces intense recruiting.

However you view your role, you have a responsibility to educate your athletes and parents about recruiting and all its ramifications. This education process should not be restricted to seniors but must include juniors, sophomores, and freshmen as well.

Many problems and misunderstandings occur between parents and high school coaches over recruiting, usually because parents lack understanding. They can become quite critical and angry when a son or daughter doesn't get a scholarship from a desired college, or when there is no scholarship offer at all. They typically place all the blame on the high school head coach. If a coach really cared and really worked at it, they believe, their youngster would have a scholarship. This potential problem can be alleviated somewhat by making sure you

have meetings to teach parents about the entire recruiting process and your role in it. These meetings should occur as soon as their youngsters begin participating in high school athletics. Some coaches will have college coaches from different levels come in and address their players and parents.

Among things parents need to understand is that a youngster can make a number of all-star teams, or even all-state, and still not be recruited. Parents often think recruiting should be automatic, and when it isn't they blame the coach. What they need to understand is that good high school athletes don't necessarily project as scholarship athletes.

Sometimes these misunderstandings begin when underclass athletes start getting mail from college coaches. The first thing parents and athletes must realize is that these initial contacts are not scholarship offers, nor are they necessarily a guarantee that an offer will follow. Parents should also know that Division I football programs, for example, have 500 to 2,000 players on a mailing list but only offer twenty or twenty-five scholarships out of that number. In short, getting that first letter from a college does not mean it is time for an athlete to start packing a suitcase.

What these initial letters really mean is that some coaching staff has become aware that the recipient of the letter has accomplished some special thing or has a special physical trait (size, speed, etc.) and that they will be watching the athlete's progress throughout the rest of the season or the rest of his or her high school career. Only later will the college coaches decide whether to actively recruit this youngster.

Another serious effect of these initial contacts is that they sometimes cause athletes to develop inflated opinions of themselves and their athletic ability because they think they are being actively recruited. In other words, they can get cocky and develop attitude problems.

Stages of Recruiting

The following stages in recruiting should help athletes be aware of how they stand with any college coaching staff:

- A form letter or multiple letters indicate that a college staff has somehow been made aware of the athlete.

- A handwritten note, a phone call, or a visit to the school by a college coach indicates moderate interest.

- A visit to an athlete's home by an assistant coach usually means there is a sincere interest in that athlete.

- A visit by the head coach indicates that the athlete is a top prospect for that college or university.

Athletes should understand that the recruiter is a coach who is also in the business of selling a particular university to athletes and their parents. The youngsters should keep this fact in mind as recruiters extol the virtues of their various institutions. The only way to really learn about a college or university is

to visit the campus and talk with athletes and nonathletes already enrolled there. As a rule, these people are not in the recruiting business and will be quite frank about the school.

Sometimes a college recruiter will make promises to a prospect that cannot possibly be honored. The usual approach is to promise a youngster a starting position at least by the sophomore year and to suggest that there is also a good chance of starting as a freshman. Far too often this ploy is merely a way to dangle the bait of instant success before an impressionable youngster. The only legitimate promises athletes should listen to are that the university can give them an education if they want one badly enough and that they will be given a fair chance to make the team.

To provide some assistance to senior members of your team, you might want to have everyone fill out a questionnaire similar to the one in Figure 8.1. The primary purposes of this questionnaire are to see whether any of the seniors want to go to college, to see whether any of them are interested in

Figure 8.1
*Recruiting
questionnaire.*

1. Name _____ Class Rank _____
   Height _____ Weight _____
   College Board Scores _____ Grade Point Average _____
2. Address _____ Phone _____
3. Do you plan on going to college? _____
4. Are you interested in playing college (sport)? _____
5. Preference of school (large, small, conference, state): _____
6. What course of study do you plan to follow? _____
7. Will your parents need financial aid to send you to college? _____
8. Are you willing to work while in college to help pay your expenses? _____
9. If you can, list your first three choices of colleges you would like to attend:
   1. _____
   2. _____
   3. _____
10. Do you want any assistance from this coaching staff in making arrangements to get into the college of your choice?
    Yes _____ No _____
11. List any individual honors you have received.
    _____
    _____
    _____
12. What is your best performance or season record?
    _____
13. What athletic performance records do you hold?
    _____

participating in athletics there, and to find out whether they want any help from you.

Suggestions for Athletes and Parents

Whether or not youngsters want direct assistance, you still have an obligation to offer some suggestions for the players and their parents to consider. For example, you should:

1. Encourage the better athletes to attend summer sports camps to gain visibility. Because many college coaches work at these camps, it is a good way for players to be noticed.

2. Explain the importance of choosing a college that offers a degree in the field of interest to an athlete. An athlete should not choose a college solely on its athletic reputation or simply because of an offer of financial aid. If aid is offered, it is sometimes helpful to ask the question, "Would I attend that college if no aid were offered?" It might also help if the youngsters faced the question of whether or not they would attend a specific college if they couldn't participate in sport anymore. A decision to attend any college solely on the basis of financial aid or athletic participation can be an unwise and, consequently, unhappy choice.

3. Discuss the size of the school and caliber of competition that might offer the greatest opportunity for success. Most players (and their

parents) tend to overestimate their ability in sport. This can create serious problems, especially with ambitious parents.

4. Suggest that students consider several levels of college if they are unsure of their own potential.

5. Encourage athletes to give serious thought to the colleges they are interested in and to narrow down the possibilities to just a few as soon as possible. In this manner, they are choosing the college rather than letting the college choose them. This approach also prevents them from being overwhelmed by recruiters from institutions that do not have what they want, academically or athletically. When a youngster is truly an outstanding athlete, this approach might eliminate some of the incredible pressure that great numbers of recruiters can exert on the athlete and the family.

6. Discuss the location of the college and its implications. Although colleges in another part of the country sound exciting, athletes should consider how many times they will be able to get home during a year (if this is important to them), and they should consider the fact that their family and friends might never see them play because of the expense of the trip. Athletes should understand, too, that if they attend college in a state a great distance from home, there is always the risk of competing for a position with an athlete native to that state. If they are equal in ability, politics will enter the picture—and the local athlete will probably play first. This can also happen when a player native to the state was sent to the school by an influential alumnus.

7. Make sure that parents know the total cost for a year's stay in the institution, in case only a partial scholarship is offered.

8. Help the youngster and parents try to determine the kind of stability a particular program has. For example: How long has the head coach been there? Has the head coach been making any noise about moving to another job? Has the head coach been under fire? Is the head coach one with a history of jumping from job to job every few years?

9. Encourage athletes to visit college campuses (or see to it that they do) and to attend practice sessions as well as a game or meet. It would be a good idea, also, to help them prepare a checklist of things to see, people to talk to, and questions to ask—for example, about the kind of academic support that is offered (study table and tutors). Incidentally, this is also a good way for high school coaches to learn about the various colleges.

10. Pay attention to what percentage of any particular college's athletes graduate.

11. Discourage athletes from waiting too long to make a decision—they could come up empty-handed.

12. Do not attempt to influence a player in any way in the final decision but, rather, give advice if it is solicited. The final decision should be the player's, not yours.

Unfortunately, some high school coaches do not hesitate to use an outstanding athlete to further their own ambitions. When this occurs, a coach will use every technique to influence an athlete's decision, because it might mean an opportunity to move with this prized recruit into a college coaching job, now or in the future. Some high school coaches attempt to establish a "pipeline" whereby they see to it that their best athletes each year always end up at the same college. Again, the motive is often selfish in that they hope this will provide them an opportunity to move to that same college some day as a coach.

There is nothing wrong with wanting to move into the college coaching ranks, but coaches must do so on their own merit rather than as a package deal involving blue-chip athletes. Coaches who operate this way are easily recognizable to recruiters, and in the long run their behavior might prove more harmful than helpful to their ambitions. The word does get around.

DEALING WITH RECRUITERS

High school coaches also have a responsibility to recruiters, since a recruiter relies a great deal on coaches' recommendations. Athletes have intangibles that don't always show up on videotapes, such as attitude, character, coachability, and competitiveness, and only the high school coach has this information. Therefore, you must be honest and frank not only for the recruiter's benefit but also for the athlete's sake. There is no advantage in putting youngsters into situations they can't cope with. This principle sounds simple enough, but it is violated repeatedly because some high school coaches tend to overestimate and oversell their athletes. They do so because they are often biased toward their athletes, but another reason might be ego involvement on the part of the coach.

College coaches on all levels can also become aware of prospective student athletes by sending a high school coach prospect cards on which to recommend potential recruits. Unfortunately, some high school coaches believe they can enhance an athlete's chance for a scholarship by inflating their statistics—listing an athlete on a prospect card as taller and heavier than he really is, for example. This information might attract the attention of college recruiters, and all of a sudden the athlete thinks he is a hot item, which gets his hopes up. The letdown comes when a recruiter visits the youngster described on the card and the real person walks in. Too many high school coaches do a real disservice to their athletes in this way. Therefore, you should avoid this temptation at all times.

Helping an athlete get into college, possibly with an athletic scholarship, will give you a certain degree of pride and satisfaction, which is normal. All teachers enjoy seeing students go on to bigger and better things, and if they feel that they played an important part in the process, so much the better. But seeing a student's success as a direct indication of your own ability as a coach, and as a personal accomplishment, could lead to some maneuvering not consistent with the basic obligations of a coach.

One impression you should avoid making on a college recruiter is that of trying to sell an athlete. This impression can be fostered by taking the initiative to contact a college to report the availability of a fine athlete, then immediately asking what the college can offer. A coach might also use this type of approach when the recruiter visits his or her school. When a high school coach operates this way, it can kill a scholarship possibility for a deserving athlete. This kind of coach can also earn an undesirable reputation as a "flesh peddler" among college recruiters. Some recruiters resent coaches who use this approach and, unless the athlete is an absolute superstar, they will probably thank the coach politely and say they are not interested. There are enough good athletes available, and recruiting is a difficult enough job without the recruiter having to put up with a high school coach who is selling athletes.

In addition, if athletes discover their coach is using this approach, they sometimes develop a warped idea of their own potential as college athletes. They can also get the wrong idea about the whole recruiting process. Then, instead of choosing colleges because of the education they can get, they allow themselves to be sold to the highest bidder. This is a sorry situation.

Although attempting to sell an athlete is to be discouraged, there is nothing wrong with taking the initiative in contacting college coaches to let them know that one or several athletes are interested in attending a particular institution. If videotapes are available of the youngsters in competition, the college coach should be made aware of them.

Many high school athletes are intelligent enough to gain admission to college and skillful enough to compete in intercollegiate athletics. Usually it is only the outstanding player—one who receives the most publicity or makes the all-star teams—whose name is noticed by coaches of large colleges or universities. But not every athlete has to compete in a big-time university athletic program. There are thousands of midsize and small colleges throughout the country where high school athletes can continue in athletics. Many of the smaller colleges have excellent athletic programs, but because of limited recruiting rules or budgets, they do not have the opportunity to scour the country for athletes.

Coaches at such colleges appreciate having high school coaches write to them about or send videotape of good athletes who might be prospective students. The normal procedure is for the college coach to follow up by getting in touch with the youngster, and possibly sending some literature on the college. The youngster might also be invited to visit the campus at a later date.

Another possibility to consider is arranging for seniors on the team to attend college games, particularly in the sport in which they are most interested. Although you might have to transport the youngsters in your own car, you will be giving them an opportunity to see college games and campuses and to meet some college coaches. Even if they choose not to go on to college, or if they do go to college but decide to give up participating in sport, the experience can be a good one for them. Keep in mind that high school athletes can receive three complementary admissions for as many college athletic events as desired. A high school coach can receive two.

Prior to a campus visit, you should take time to advise the athletes about their visit. They should be encouraged to present a neat, clean personal appearance and to wear suitable clothes. Torn blue jeans and T-shirts might be appropriate dress in a high school, but they do little to create a favorable impression on college officials.

If you have highly recruited athletes, remember that there is a limit to the number of official visits they can make to campuses. An official visit is defined as one in which the recruit's expenses are paid by the institution. The recruit is limited to a total of five official visits. Therefore, it would be a good idea to make sure that someone is actually offering them a scholarship before they make an official visit.

Athletes should also be cautioned about approaching college coaches with the attitude of "Here I am; what can you offer me?" However, there can be no argument as to the importance of finances in attending college today and the concern most families have regarding this matter. College coaches are well aware of this fact. Therefore, the conversation will eventually get around to college expenses as well as scholarship possibilities or the availability of other kinds of legitimate financial aid. If not, there is nothing wrong in asking for a clarification of the financial question, since it might have a bearing on a final decision about which college to attend.

Establishing Policies and Procedures

As a high school coach, one of your biggest priorities should be to establish policies with the school's athletic director, principal, guidance office, and the athletes as to how the recruiting process should take place for your sport in your particular school.

In other words, if I were a college recruiter, how would you want me to operate in your situation? The last thing recruiters want to do is upset you and make you angry, but that can happen if they don't know your policies or if you don't have any for them to follow. This is not to imply that you would be impeding the recruiter or getting in the way of an athlete's opportunities. But the fact remains that recruiting can become a real nuisance and a disruptive factor for any high school coach—particularly one with a highly prized recruit.

It doesn't take much to turn the head of a 17-year-old athlete, and publicity and recruiters are probably the most common causes. Consequently, some coaches will simply not allow any recruiter to talk with an athlete during the season. Of course, if a recruiter chooses to write or call an athlete at home, there is not much a coach can do except try to play the event down so the student doesn't get too excited too soon.

Most college recruiters have learned that the first stop when visiting a high school is the principal's office. You should have an understanding that office personnel are to direct the recruiter to you, not to the athlete the recruiter has come to see. This is one way to maintain some degree of control over the recruiting process. There may be several reasons you wouldn't want a recruiter talking to a member of your team at that moment. Maybe the sought-after youngster is developing an attitude problem; maybe the athlete has already made a decision and doesn't want to talk with any more recruiters; maybe the youngster doesn't want to talk with anyone from a certain college; or maybe the student is simply being pulled out of too many classes.

You should work out with the principal the question of pulling an athlete out of class to talk with a recruiter. Sometimes a recruiter will drop in on a school without any notification. The recruiter usually wants to meet a promising athlete and talk for a few minutes. At first glance, this situation doesn't appear to be a concern at all. But when a number of recruiters begin to show up to talk with the same person, it can present a serious problem. Teachers often object to having their classes interrupted, and the player can miss so much time that grades begin to suffer.

As a rule, a principal will not object to allowing an athlete to leave class once in a while for this purpose. But if the privilege is abused, the only alternatives are to have the athlete and recruiter meet at some other time—between classes, during the lunch hour, or after school. You should take the initiative and bring the question of recruiting to the principal's attention to avoid an embarrassing confrontation later on. Most school administrators will be agreeable to some reasonable solution to the problem, but if they find out by accident that recruiters are interfering with classes, they can become quite disagreeable. The tendency is for them to overreact and issue an edict that is unreasonable and possibly unfair.

Another solution to this potential problem is for you to let recruiters know the best time to visit the school. It is also a good idea for recruiters to have your telephone numbers both at home and at school. Recruiters are busy people, too, and they appreciate knowing the most effective time to visit.

Preparing for the Visit

You can do a number of things to prepare to assist recruiters. Recruiters are particularly interested in the items on the following list; if you have this material ready before a recruiter's visit, you will save everyone a lot of time.

1. Team roster

2. Each potential recruit's home address, telephone number, and email address

3. Parents' names

4. The level of competition on which each individual could be successful

5. Grade-point average for each athlete

6. Class rank of each athlete

7. Test scores (PSAT/SAT/ACT)

8. Each athlete's possible major in college

9. Videotapes

10. Copy of the student's transcript

11. Copy of student's current class schedule

Because of the timing of recruiting, many recruiters believe this information should be gathered midway through an athlete's junior year in high school.

It is helpful to both the recruiter and the athlete if you can arrange to videotape a game, meet, or other athletic event so that the college coaches can see the athlete perform. It is not necessary to do so in a competitive situation, and, in fact, the youngster might participate in a sport where no videos are ever used. There is no reason a coach cannot arrange to videotape an athlete in practice. The main purpose is for the college coaches to see the athlete in action.

ADVISING STUDENTS

You should be familiar with the types of scholarships and financial aid that are available. Not only will you be able to answer questions an athlete might have, but you will help parents understand the differences. Basically, there are NCAA scholarships, which can pay for some or all of an athlete's education based on athletic talent, and there are grants available based on financial need, as determined by a parent's confidential financial statement. Additional information on grants is usually available through high school guidance offices. Any other financial aid offer is illegal and should be reported to the NCAA at once.

You can also help in advising by learning as much as you can about various colleges. Information can be gathered by reading college bulletins or by visiting campuses to observe game and practice sessions when the opportunity arises. In addition, you can learn some things about colleges by talking with athletes who have visited campuses either on their own or as part of the recruiting process.

It can also be helpful to determine what kinds of athletes various colleges are looking for. This information can best be learned through experience and by talking to recruiters when they visit the school.

Another way to learn what colleges are looking for, and to get an idea of how your athletes compare with the competition, is to ask college coaches to comment on game tapes when they return them. This information might also prove valuable to you personally as far as coaching the team or individual is concerned.

College recruiters sometimes have trouble when they choose not to offer a scholarship to an athlete who comes highly recommended to them by the youngster's own coach. Some high school coaches take this rejection personally and become upset with the college. Some will be so upset that they vow that this particular college will never again get any athletes from their high school. This situation often arises because of the tremendous ego involvement of the high school coach. The coach might view this rejection as an attack on the quality of the athletes or as a negative reaction to the coachng. Instead of feeling this way, a coach should appreciate the frankness and honesty of the college staff in their evaluation of how a youngster would fit into their program. The college coaches might also be trying to keep a player from getting into a situation that is over his or her head.

The whole problem depends on the point of view. High school coaches naturally have tunnel vision. They see only the individual and know that he or she is a good athlete. They may also feel that they have an obligation to help youngsters get scholarships.

The college coaching staff, on the other hand, know what they want in an athlete, what kind of personnel they have returning, and what areas need to be strengthened, and, most important, they have the opportunity to compare a prospect with other outstanding players. Thus, an athlete who appears to a high school coach to be outstanding may be little better than average in comparison with many others. College athletic departments do not have unlimited financial aid, and they must pick and choose carefully.

It may be that an athlete turned down by one coaching staff will be accepted by another and will perform well. To say that the first staff made a mistake is not necessarily true. It might simply mean that their needs were different.

The point is that high school coaches need to understand the problems of college recruiters, and they should not become resentful when financial aid to an athlete is not forthcoming. If an athlete is determined to attend a specific college and participate in athletics there, the lack of a scholarship offer should not be looked on as the end of the world. The student can still enroll there and get permission to try out for the team. If the individual proves good enough to play, financial aid is still a possibility. If not, there are numerous opportunities for financial aid and loans in colleges today, over and above those given for athletics.

A high school coach not only serves an advisory role in recruiting but should also serve as a buffer between an athlete and recruiter. Rare indeed is the high school athlete who can cope with the persuasiveness of a veteran recruiter. When a youngster is approached by several super-salespeople, the problems are compounded.

Another area where you will need to be careful is in dealing with guidance counselors. In your haste and desire to help an athlete get into college, be careful not to infringe on the guidance counselor's role. If you have established a good working relationship with the guidance people, this will not be a problem. It is desirable to work in cooperation with the counselor to help the student. The guidance office can provide information about the size, curriculum, cost, location, and entrance requirements of any college in the country. Naturally, guidance counselors have a great deal of information on file about the student, and this is important to you also. Seeking assistance from the guidance office fosters mutual concern for a youngster's benefit.

One final important consideration for every high school coach is that NCAA regulations regarding athletes' eligibility for scholarships and participation in intercollegiate sport are based on their academic preparation in high school. Too many coaches rely totally on guidance counselors to monitor athletes' courses; this can be a serious mistake. Many counselors do not totally understand NCAA requirements. And so, once again, it becomes your responsibility to get to your athletes and their parents in ninth grade and to make certain they understand the kinds of courses required by the NCAA. You should also make sure that the guidance people in your school understand these requirements.

The requirements that need to be met by high school students wishing to compete in athletics on the college level change slightly every year. The consistent part is that a student must complete a set number of core classes along with achieving a minimum grade point in the core. A minimum test score is also required on either the ACT or SAT. Each year these standards come under review for possible changes. The best way to stay abreast of these rules is to write the NCAA to request updates. Most college recruiters will also have the current academic standards available to give to high school coaches. These rules apply not only to athletes who are potential scholarship players, but to "walk-on" athletes as well.

The NCAA also has a clearinghouse that determines the initial eligibility for college freshmen who wish to compete on an athletic team. High school coaches need to make certain the counselors are in contact with this clearinghouse so that all the proper materials are on file for each athlete who thinks he or she wants to participate in college athletics. Any student who intends on joining a college team as a freshman, regardless of being recruited, must apply to the clearinghouse. You can contact the clearinghouse by writing to NCAA Clearinghouse, P.O. Box 4043, Iowa City, Iowa 52243. The NCAA Clearinghouse also has an eligibility hotline (877-262-1492).

It would be criminal to allow youngsters to come to their senior year of high school only to discover that they do not qualify academically for an athletic scholarship simply because they failed to take the correct courses. Make sure that this never happens in your school.

ILLEGAL RECRUITING

Of all the problems in athletics, the pressures associated with recruiting rank at or near the top for college coaches. As a result, illegal recruiting will continue to occur. Far too often high school coaches see this as the colleges' problem. That is only partly true. You should do everything in your power to prevent your athletes from becoming involved in violations of recruiting rules, if for no other reason than to protect their eligibility.

High school coaches are in a perfect position to stop or at least curb illegal recruiting. You begin by learning the NCAA rules and teaching them to athletes and parents. You then instruct your players to report any questionable or clear

violations to you at once. If there is any doubt in your athletes' minds, they should still report the contact to you.

If a suspected violation occurs, you should then confront the recruiter to find out precisely what was said or offered. If you discover a clear violation, notify the recruiter that you are going to inform the college's head coach, the athletic director, and the NCAA. You should also let the recruiter's institution know that their representative is no longer welcome in your school.

When word gets around through the recruiting grapevine that you do not tolerate cheating (and it will), this will have an incredible impact on the recruiting process. It may be that college recruiters will welcome your stance, because they will know they are operating by the same standards as their competitors in your school.

Remember, college coaches need the goodwill and cooperation of high school coaches far more than high school coaches need them. College coaches' jobs often depend on how well they recruit—yours does not. You and others like you provide the lifeblood of intercollegiate athletics. I suggest that you and your colleagues simply say to recruiters, "Let's do this right."

The recruiting process is a hard reality for a high school coach, and one you should be prepared to handle. With some forethought, you can make the experience exciting for everyone concerned, because you are the one to determine the policies for recruiting in your high school.

One of the pleasant aspects of the process, other than seeing an athlete satisfied with a college choice, is getting acquainted with the college coaches who do the recruiting. In most instances they are fine people trying to do a job and to interfere as little as possible in high school athletic programs. When high school coaches treat these people with professional courtesy, permanent friendships often arise with the college coaches. Mutual respect is the spirit that should prevail between professionals interested in a student's welfare.

DISCUSSION QUESTIONS

1. Discuss the impact of recruiting on high school athletes and their families.

2. Discuss the important suggestions you will make to your prospective college athletes.

3. Why is it important for coaches not to influence or pressure athletes to choose a particular college or university?

4. What responsibilities do coaches have toward college recruiters?

5. Is it possible for high school coaches to oversell an athlete? What does this mean, and what are the ramifications?

6. Why is it important for high school coaches to involve other members of the high school staff in the recruiting process? Who are these people, and what are their roles?

7. How can the availability of scholarships serve as a tool for motivation?

8. How can the egos of high school coaches enter into recruiting?

9. Why should high school coaches establish recruiting policies?

10. What are the differences between athletic scholarships and financial aid?

11. What responsibilities do recruiters have toward high school coaches?

12. What are some ways you could deal with an underclass athlete who has developed an attitude problem because of attention from a college coach?

13. List other questions high school athletes should ask or things they should look for when they visit college campuses.

14. Why is it important to involve parents in prerecruiting orientation meetings? When should this involvement occur?

15. How would you deal with a situation in which one of your athletes was being recruited in clear violation of NCAA rules?

OFF-SEASON PLANNING

The time to begin making plans for the next season is the day after your current one ends. With the past season fresh in everyone's mind, it is an excellent time to sit down and evaluate all that happened in the preceding weeks and months. This is an ideal opportunity to think about the good things that occurred as well as those that were not so good. Did you accomplish all your personal goals and team goals? Could you have done a better job of coaching? Were mistakes made that are correctable for the next season? Now is the time for a thorough evaluation by you and your staff, not for going on a nine-month vacation from coaching.

The purpose of this end-of-season evaluation is to lay the plans for the next year. Coaches who decide to wait until the next season approaches to begin planning will have lost a great deal of valuable time and will probably not do as good a job of organizing and coaching. This chapter discusses a variety of areas for you to consider as you look at the season just passed and the one coming up.

EVALUATING THE PAST SEASON

Your first priority in the off-season should be a reevaluation of everything you believe in regarding athletics and coaching. It is important that you know exactly what you believe in and why. Coaches can take less for granted now than they could a few years ago, so your beliefs about all aspects of the sport you are coaching should be clear, in your own mind at least.

> A journey of a thousand miles
> Begins with a single step.
> —Lao Tzu

It is your personal vision that will provide the direction and guidelines for the conduct of the entire program the following season and that will help pinpoint the area in which you can have the greatest impact on the overall program. It once again bears mentioning that your attitudes and beliefs will be reflected by the team you coach. If you are aggressive, well disciplined, and well organized, and if you believe in playing by the rules, the team will probably reflect this attitude. If you are lackadaisical and disorganized and believe in winning at any cost, this attitude will be apparent in the team's performance. It is therefore

171

imperative that you clarify your beliefs if you are to provide any degree of leadership to your staff and the team.

It is critical for coaches not only to evaluate the past season but to involve the players in this process. It makes little difference how coaches view a season just concluded, including all the facets of the coaching that took place, if the players' perceptions are different. Too often we organize and conduct programs the way we, the coaches, believe is best, on the assumption that we know better and that the athletes will accept our methods without question.

This is poor leadership technique; failing to include the opinions of athletes can lead to serious problems. After all, the athletes are the ones who play the game, not the coaches. If you have an idea that you happen to believe is great but turns the athletes off, you need to know they don't like it and be willing to rethink your position.

To be fairly certain that any evaluation of you and the season is frank and honest, it is best to involve the seniors only. And even their responses should be anonymous.

The best time to have the players complete an evaluation is immediately after the season, to assist you as you begin the long period of off-season planning. Their responses might also cause you to adjust something in your personal philosophy of coaching. The sample in Figure 9.1 contains some questions that could be included in a senior evaluation. The key here is to include questions directed to whatever specific information you would like to have from the members of the team.

CONDUCTING AN EQUIPMENT INVENTORY

Taking inventory at the end of a season is a must so that you can intelligently purchase new equipment for the following year. Unless you are lucky enough to have a full-time equipment manager, this task will fall to you.

For some coaches this process is fairly simple, because some teams are small or require little special equipment. For other coaches equipment inventory can be a formidable task. It should be accomplished as quickly as possible, not only to get it out of the way, but to help you in devising your budget and purchasing for next year.

PREPARING A BUDGET

As a general rule, preparing a budget is the responsibility of the head coach and should be done as soon after a season ends as possible. Your first step in a new coaching situation is to ask the athletic director what the procedure is at your school. It is highly unlikely that you will ever have to create a budget from scratch. For example, budgets from previous seasons should be on file to at least give you a starting point, and if prior budgets are not available, the

Figure 9.1
Questionnaire to give to seniors.

SENIORS' EVALUATION

In order to improve our program, it is important to take stock of our accomplishments, shortcomings, and objectives. We, as a coaching staff, will do this, but another valuable source of information is the seniors on the squad, whom we are now asking to help us. Will you please take the time to give us your frank and honest views and ideas? We'd really appreciate it. You need not sign this form.

Thank you,

Coach

1. Did anything happen during the season to make you upset with your coaches, teammates, opponents, teachers, administration, or student body?

2. Did you feel that you were ever called upon to do something for which you were not properly prepared?

3. List any personal criticisms that you think will be helpful to our team for the future.

4. Did you really enjoy the season? Why?

5. Did you hear any comments by parents, fans, or others about the games or players that you feel would be helpful to the team or coaches?

6. How can we, as coaches, help our players perform better?

7. What was your opinion about our scouting reports? [If appropriate to your sport]

8. How did you feel about squad morale?

9. How can we improve our total program?

10. What do you think of our notebooks (quantity, form, quality, clarity, etc.)?

11. How did you feel about our equipment and uniforms?

12. What do you think of our video sessions?

13. Are there any ways you feel we could better use our facilities?

14. Do you have any ideas regarding our total organization?

15. What do you think of our promotional ideas and activities? Do you have any other ideas along these lines?

16. What are your feelings about our warm-up activities and organization?

17. Do you feel you were well drilled in fundamentals?

18. What are your comments about our training room procedures?

19. What do you think about the way we planned and organized practices?

20. Regarding our younger team members: Who do you feel will be our best players next year?

21. Were there any players on the squad who you feel were playing out of position, or who should have played more? Was there any player who you feel should have played ahead of someone else?

22. What is your opinion for or against special awards?

23. Do you feel you were given a fair chance to show your ability?

24. What do you think about the scout team?

25. Do you think you were well prepared to compete?

26. What are your views on electing captains for the season?

27. List any other points or ideas you feel would be helpful.

Thanks a lot for taking the time to help us evaluate our program. It has been a pleasure having you on the team.

athletic director or other head coaches should certainly be able to give you concrete suggestions on how to proceed. The budget process is not all that complicated.

Your second concern is to find out exactly what is to be included in your budget. You might have to include transportation, training room supplies, ticket takers, police, officials, and custodial work for example; or, your budget might simply reflect equipment purchases or a combination of these items.

The next step is to find out whether it is up to you to determine where to purchase the equipment or whether that is done by an administrator in the front

office. You also need to know whether the final decision is based on bids or your recommendation. Once you have the answers to these points, you can begin putting a budget together.

When you order/purchase new equipment, your decision should be based on the equipment inventory, replacement equipment needs, and the number of youngsters involved. And, finally, shop around before you buy.

With any luck, your equipment has been purchased wisely in the past, so that you only need to add small quantities to replace discarded gear. A major purchase, such as all new game uniforms, should be avoided if possible because of the great expense. Using standardized styles, colors, and designs will also help your budget.

Figure 9.2 presents sample budget information requests from the athletic director to head coaches.

PURCHASING EQUIPMENT

There are two basic ways athletic equipment is purchased in high schools. You may be permitted to purchase needed equipment directly, or you might be required to submit a list of equipment needs and specifications through the athletic director to a central purchasing agency in the school system. The purchasing agent, in all probability, will then ask sporting goods companies to submit bids.

Regardless of a school's purchasing policy, equipment should be ordered many months before it is needed, since delivery on athletic supplies is notoriously slow. If the equipment company makes mistakes in delivering the order, you will also have plenty of time to have them corrected. There is no excuse for starting a season without all your new equipment and supplies on hand. The time

ATHLETIC DEPARTMENT MEMO
TO: All Interscholastic Athletic Head Coaches (_____) Sport Level (_____)
FROM: Athletic Director
DATE: 00/00/00
SUBJECT: Interscholastic Athletic Budget Preparation

Step 1 - Understanding Our Athletic Department Budget Procedures
The following principles about the budget process are important for all of us in the Athletic Department to understand so that we may work together effectively:

1. The overall interscholastic athletic budget allocation and individual sport allocation for next year will be the same as last year. There will be no increase.

2. Budget allocations for each sport level will be strictly adhered to. Each head coach should be knowledgeable about his/her current account balances and therefore responsible for planning so that funds are spent wisely and accounts are not overspent.

3. The total dollar amount allocated for each sport level is the amount of money that you have to operate your sport in the categories of:

   • Cleaning and repair

   • Rental

   • Travel expenses

   • Supplies

   • Equipment

   • Dues/fees

   You do *not* budget for salaries, transportation, officials, security, or post-season tournament expenses.

4. Transfers of money from one category to another within a sport level budget can be made by the head coach through the Athletic Office.

5. Special requests for any operational expenses that cannot be covered from the sport level's allocation may be submitted by a head coach to the Athletic Director at budget preparation time. A written rationale should accompany the blue request form. All special requests will be considered and prioritized on a rotating basis by the Athletic Director in May/June of the fiscal year. The funding of special requests will depend upon the availability of money in the total athletic fund at that time.

Step 2 - Planning for the Operational Needs of Your Sport Level
The total budget allocation for your sport level (_____) is $_____

Based on your sport level for last year, I suggest that you allocate the following amounts in certain budget categories:

Cleaning and repair of equipment and uniforms $_____
Rental of practice facilities $_____
Travel expenses for scouting and clinics (include mileage, meals, lodging, and registration) $_____
General supplies $_____
New equipment $_____
Replacement equipment $_____
Dues and Fees (league dues and entry fees to regular season invitationals) $_____

Additional considerations in planning your budget include:

• The current travel mileage reimbursement is 32.5 cents per mile.

• Catalogs for ordering supplies, equipment, awards, and information relating to league dues and invitational fees are available in the Athletic Office.

• Be sure to add shipping and handling expenses when planning supply and equipment costs (10% above the cost of the item is the usual amount that we must pay).

PLEASE COMPLETE THE DETAILED BUDGET SHEET ATTACHED TO THIS MEMO AND SUBMIT IT TO THE ATHLETIC OFFICE BY JANUARY _____

Figure 9.2
Sample budget information request forms.

Figure 9.2
(continued)

AREA HIGH SCHOOL

ATHLETICS OFFICE MEMO

Date: January

To: All Head Coaches

From: Athletics Director
             Secretary

Subject: Budgets

Our office is currently preparing budget projections for the next school year. You will find the following information listed in the table below:

Column 1 – Description of your budget accounts

Column 2 – Original amount deposited in your accounts for the year

Column 3 – Adjusted amount (reflects transfer of money to/from account to cover your expenses during the year)

Column 4 – Projected budget amounts to be deposited in your accounts for the year

Column 5 – Adjustments that YOU would like to have made to the *distribution* of your total budget amounts for next year based on last year's expenditures

In acknowledgment of projected budget allotments and distribution, please sign, date, and if necessary, amend Column 5 of this form, and return it to our office by Monday, January 00. As always, if you have any questions, please contact our office.

_____   _____
Signature   Date

Sport:	Swimming/Diving	Head Coach:	
Supplies (610):	2600.00	2575.00	2600.00
Travel (582):	200.00	200.00	200.00
Dues & Fees (810):	100.00	125.00	100.00
( ):			
Total:	2900.00	2900.00	2900.00

to prepare an equipment order for next season is as soon as possible after the current one ends.

Generally, it is best to purchase name-brand equipment from long-established companies, since such companies will stand behind their products when others might not. This is not to say that you should never consider purchasing lesser-known brands from smaller companies, but remember that the least expensive product might turn out to be the most costly in the long run if it doesn't hold up. And with the cost of athletic equipment rising all the time, you need to learn how to get the most for the least amount of school money.

The three guiding principles for purchasing athletic equipment, in order of importance, are (1) quality, (2) cost, and (3) service (will the person who sold you the equipment provide prompt service in delivering, repairing, or replacing defective equipment?).

If timing is not a problem, it is best to order athletic equipment in early January, when many suppliers reduce prices in an attempt to clear out their stock before inventory and tax time. The January bargains can really stretch your equipment allowance.

Many coaches pass old, worn-out equipment down to the junior varsity or freshman teams. You should avoid this practice. If equipment is not good enough for a varsity player to wear or use, and if it cannot be reconditioned, it should be discarded. Also, protective equipment originally purchased for varsity teams is generally ill fitting for younger athletes and therefore unsafe.

Worn-out, poorly fitting equipment can lead to injury. Sometimes coaches forget, for example, that when two 90-pound people collide in a contact game, it hurts just as much as when two 200-pound people collide. In addition, athletes on reserve and freshman teams are not as highly skilled as varsity players, so their need for protective equipment is just as great as, if not greater than, it is for varsity athletes. Providing adequate protective equipment is really a moral and legal obligation of a coaching staff, and you must see to it that this obligation is fulfilled for every member of all the teams in your program.

Providing proper equipment for every athlete in a program should be one of your primary goals. Finances are always a problem, but they should not be an excuse to outfit youngsters in old, cast-off equipment.

PROVIDING STRENGTH TRAINING

The next decision to be made is whether to organize an off-season strength-training program for players not participating in another sport. Coaches who choose not to organize a weight training might find their athletes at a disadvantage when competing against others who have worked hard to increase their strength over a long period of time. As a result, weight training has become a must in athletics.

Intelligent, well-planned, and carefully supervised strength-training programs can and do have many advantages for athletes. However, misconceptions and just plain lack of knowledge continue to surround this kind of training. One of the most widespread myths is that training with weights will cause girls to develop muscular definition similar to that of men. However, this is absolutely untrue; women's physiological makeup prevents this. Strength training can be as beneficial for women as it is for men and is therefore a legitimate part of their training as well.

If you are interested in initiating or improving your strength training program and do not have information at hand to guide you, contact strength coaches at any college or university in the country. These people are generally willing to help in any way possible. There are also a number of books on the market dealing with this topic. If you choose to incorporate strength training into your program, make certain that you know what you are doing.

CHOOSING STUDENT HELPERS

There is a huge difference between working hard and working smart. Working hard usually means trying to do everything yourself; working smart means being willing to delegate, delegate, delegate. Know what kind of work to let others do, and then surround yourself with good people who are competent and dependable.

One of the great, often untapped sources of people who can take some of the pressure off you is the student body of your school. Any number of bright, eager students could assist you and would be more than willing to volunteer if you only took the time to approach them. And making an announcement over the school PA system is not the way to go.

You have to seek out good people and talk to them personally, one on one. You need to offer them the opportunity to be an important part of the team by working for you in a special capacity. Make sure they understand that what they do will be of great value to you and to the team. When you carefully select student helpers and give them proper guidance, they can move mountains for you.

Secretary

One of the earliest lessons you will learn in coaching is that a lot of paperwork is involved, such as typing and reproducing forms, notices, and correspondence. Doing this paperwork is time-consuming, and unless you are very lucky you will have no secretarial help.

A good way to lighten some of this load is to find a student secretary. First, you will need permission from the principal; then check with the word-processing teacher to get the names of some of the best students, and interview them to see whether any can be recruited.

Your student secretary can do work for you during study hall or during some other free time. If you handle this situation right, the principal might even provide a small space and some office equipment for the student.

You might consider starting out with a sophomore or a junior who will, when a senior, be able to train a replacement for the following year. This approach will also save you time. This arrangement can be highly advantageous to you and your program, and it can be a worthwhile experience for the students.

Managers

Good student managers are worth their weight in gold; bad managers can and do create unnecessary problems. Therefore, you should select these individuals just as carefully as you do any other student helpers.

The ideal arrangement is to have a junior or senior and at least one freshman or sophomore as managers. This way, the younger students can learn about the job; then, when the number one manager graduates, an experienced manager will be available to take over. If the team has a lot of athletes organized into varsity, JV, and freshman teams, it is a good idea to have four managers: a freshman, a sophomore, a junior, and a senior, with the senior in charge.

You can use either of two methods for picking managers. The primary source is the team itself. There may be someone who cannot continue as a player because of injury, someone who simply does not have the ability to play, or someone who is so small as to be in danger of serious injury and who should possibly be cut from the team. In such situations, you can tactfully suggest that the student consider becoming a manager, not as a demotion but as a way to perform an important function for the team in a capacity other than as a player. Surprisingly, youngsters often take this option willingly because they enjoy still being a part of the program.

Another source of managers is physical education classes; you can get to know students well there if you are a physical education teacher. When you find someone who displays the qualities necessary for a manager, you can try to recruit this boy or girl for the position. Such students often have a great deal of interest in sport but are not participating as players for one reason or another. Being a manager gives them an opportunity to be an integral part of the team.

One of the coaches on the staff should be assigned the responsibility for supervising the managers. To make sure the managers know their duties and what is expected of them, this coach should develop a checklist of things to do throughout the season and post it in the managers' area. This list also serves as insurance; in the excitement of game day, managers are less apt to forget something if they have a checklist to refer to.

It is important to impress on the team that the managers are not servants or personal valets. Rather, team members should look at managers as people who work for you, the coach; who are there to help in any way they can; and who are to be treated with the same courtesy extended to anyone doing someone else a favor.

One way to make managers feel they are an important part of the team is to recognize them at the banquet at the end of the season. In one of my schools, the head manager always gave a short speech at the banquet. One year the manager had found an old leather football helmet and mounted it on a piece of fine wood. He autographed it and made a ceremony of passing it along to the next year's head manager, as a symbol of the authority of the position. This ceremony was a big hit at the banquet. Recognition is important to young people and adds another dimension to the experience and fun of being a special part of a special group. Adults tend to forget how important small gestures like this are to teenage students, but it is on these little things that tradition, esprit de corps, and high morale are built.

Good managers are invaluable, and after growing up through the system they begin to anticipate what you want done and how you will react in certain situations. As a result, they can be a step ahead of you most of the time, helping make your job easier.

Trainer

Choosing a student trainer requires careful thought. This person should be bright, dependable, and cautious. Among the trainer's responsibilities are keeping the training room or training area neat and clean, caring for minor hurts such as blisters, keeping an inventory of supplies throughout the season, and, eventually, taping ankles and applying first aid to minor injuries, of course being careful when dealing with an injury where blood is present. These guidelines need to be clear (see Chapter 11). All of these tasks must be performed under a coach's direct supervision, because of the legal ramifications associated with the treatment of athletic injuries.

Many training room supply companies provide correspondence courses or workshops for high school student trainers. Such courses offer a fine opportunity for a youngster interested in athletic training. You might also find similar opportunities at a college campus near you.

Incidentally, if you haven't had a course in treating athletic injuries, you should enroll yourself in one of these workshops at once.

Statistician

If keeping statistics of any kind is important to your program, this is another area for which student help should be considered. The process of selecting a statistician is the same as for all the other student areas.

Media Liaison

In many locations the number of coaches and athletic teams is far greater than the number of sports writers. Reporters simply cannot cover every athletic event, and as a result many coaches become upset over the lack of publicity for their teams.

All colleges have someone working in sports information. Your high school can and should. Having a media liaison is an excellent way to help sports reporters help you. They will appreciate your efforts, and you will make some good friends in the media as a result.

In selecting a student liaison, you might want to begin by asking an English teacher or the school newspaper adviser for some recommendations. The basic requirement, of course, is the ability to write a simple sentence.

The student liaison has two primary responsibilities. The first is to call every radio and TV station in the city immediately after a game, meet, or contest to notify the sportscasters of the score and to answer any questions they might ask about who scored, who pitched, whether any records were broken, or whether there were any gems of an unusual nature that sportscasters like to mention. As long as the information given out is fact, and not opinion, you will have little cause for concern.

The second responsibility of the media liaison is to meet with you the morning after an athletic event to write down any comments you want printed concerning the game or, most important, the people who participated in it. The student then submits these comments to the newspapers. This is an excellent way to publicly recognize deserving youngsters, and you should try hard to get as many athletes' names in the paper as possible during a season. Doing so does wonders for morale, and it might be the only time in some athletes' lives that they will have a chance to see their name in the sports section of a newspaper.

This exercise is also a great way to publicize the contribution of an assistant coach, not only on the varsity level but on the JV and freshman levels as well. When an assistant deserves credit, it never hurts to give it publicly.

A mandatory rule for the student liaison is that the only information written or telephoned to any sports writer comes from you and not from the student. Having this rule is vital. Often, newspapers and radio or TV stations offer the added incentive of pay for students who call in scores and other bits of material. The student you enlist should not freelance and become a source of information but rather should remain a liaison.

You should clear your media procedures through the athletic director and the sports writers involved. If the student is conscientious and responsible, the newspaper people will be appreciative and will rarely refuse to print any news item submitted to them. Incidentally, this method is a sure way for teams sometimes unfortunately labeled as minor to receive their fair share of publicity.

By using this kind of initiative, you are dictating what is being written about your team, and all of it will be positive. Once again, this takes valuable time, but the benefits make it all worthwhile.

PREPARING A CHECKLIST FOR REQUIRED PAPERWORK

Because the first few days of preseason practice involve collecting a lot of paperwork from the athletes, recordkeeping can become a problem and a nuisance. This is particularly the case when many athletes are involved. For example, if 100 youngsters come out for a team and each one has to turn in just four pieces of paper, you will be handling 400 papers, plus trying to remember who did or did not bring in all the required forms. A simple checklist, such as the one in Figure 9.3 for which a manager or assistant coach can be responsible, will reduce confusion and remove another chore from the head coach.

Figure 9.3
Checklist for required paperwork.

Name	Physical Card	Insurance	Self-Addressed Envelopes	Eligibility Form
H. Bee	✓			✓
J. Burkham	✓	✓	✓	✓
C. Bodie		✓		
M. Christine	✓			✓
B. Francis		✓		✓
J. Krikorian	✓		✓	✓

It helps if junior varsity and freshman teams have their own checklists. It then becomes the responsibility of the coaches of those teams to make sure that each athlete has handed in the required materials.

To prevent collecting forms from becoming a problem throughout the season, it is a good idea to set deadlines for handing in each item, including some kind of penalty for being late. If you don't, some of the athletes will never turn in what they are supposed to, and you will have to nag them all season long. There really is no reason why most forms can't be completed within two or three days after the start of preseason practice.

There is one exception to this schedule, and that is the physical examination card. Under no circumstances should any athlete be permitted to begin practice without handing in a completed physical examination card. Without this policy, you are taking a tremendous risk of legal action. The simplest way to enforce this deadline is to refuse to issue equipment to any youngster who doesn't hand in a completed card. Such students should be prohibited from beginning practice, and perhaps some kind of penalty should be imposed for each practice session they miss. Enforcing such a policy can save you a lot of aggravation, as well as protect a youngster against possible serious physical problems.

ESTABLISHING PRACTICE TIMES

Unless you are sharing a facility with other teams and an overall schedule is set by the athletic director or principal, there is no reason you can't determine practice times long before the season begins.

This planning becomes more important when your season is interrupted by a holiday. You owe it to your athletes and their families to let them know by the beginning of the season what the practice times will be. Surprising the families of your athletes with a last-minute change of practice plans, especially over a holiday, can create serious public relations problems. The last people you want to alienate are the parents of your athletes, and planning ahead is one way to avoid this.

DEALING WITH FAMILY VACATIONS

Family summer vacations always create problems for pre-season practice that begins in August; Thanksgiving and religious holidays do the same thing for winter and spring sports. Long before a season begins, the coaching staff should settle on a policy covering this potential problem. When writing letters to athletes and parents before the season begins, spell out your policy to avoid misunderstanding later on. The sad thing about this problem is that it is the players who get caught in the middle. A coach says there will be practice, while the parents insist that the youngster go with them on vacation.

Family vacations in August present additional problems. Players who are gone in August will miss getting their equipment issued; will miss all the initial meetings, in which a great deal of information is disseminated; and, most important, will miss a number of preseason practice sessions and the physical conditioning that accompanies them. The only way to deal with this situation is to let parents know early how much of a disadvantage it will be for their son or daughter. If they choose to go on vacation anyway, you have two choices: refuse to allow latecomers to try out for the team, or allow them to report late and take their chances.

MEETING WITH PROSPECTIVE PLAYERS

Off-season meetings can fulfill many purposes, one of which is to get a good idea of who plans to try out for the team the following season. Knowing this information is useful in your final preseason planning, particularly as you look at depth charts by position, plan for equipment issue, and set up a preliminary roster, by class. Information can be gathered through the use of a simple form prepared by your student secretary. Obviously, the items on the sample in Figure 9.4 can be adjusted for specific sports.

The player information form provides a handy mailing directory and can easily be sorted by class or position. The answers to item 7 should be used only

Figure 9.4
*Player information
form.*

PLAYER INFORMATION

1. Name_____ Class next year _____
   ht. _____ wt. _____
2. Home address _____ Phone _____
3. Summer address _____ Phone _____
4. Name of parent or guardian _____
5. Position last year: Offense _____ Defense _____
6. What position would you like to play next fall? _____
7. List the name of one person in our school who is not out for the team, but who you think could
   become a good player _____
8. List the five people you think will be our outstanding players next season:
   1. _____
   2. _____
   3. _____
   4. _____
   5. _____
9. Do you need a new mouthpiece? _____
   Do you have the plaster impression of your teeth? _____
10. What are your goals for next season? _____
    _____
    _____
    _____

when one or two students' names reappear on several forms. It may be that a potentially fine athlete has not attended the initial meeting, and you might want to find out why. You should never become so independent or callous that it is beneath your dignity to ask people why they missed the meeting and to inquire as to whether they have any interest in trying out for the team. A small gesture like this can do a lot for a youngster's self-confidence, and it might help him or her become a fine athlete. If so, you will have done a great service to some boy or girl. Don't confuse this inquiry with coaxing a student to come out for your team; coaxing should be avoided at all times.

Item 10 might be the most important part of this brief questionnaire. It forces youngsters to give some thought to what they hope to accomplish for themselves and the team, and it will give you a great deal of insight into the individuals on the team. However, knowing players' goals will be of little value unless you follow up and use them in individual conferences with the players before the season begins. Young people might not understand what it takes to realize their goals. Some athletes' expectations may be unreasonably high or low, or in conflict with team goals. During the individual conferences you can help bring all these things into proper perspective, clarify a youngster's perceptions of the goals, and spell out precisely what he or she will have to do to accomplish them.

Goals stated by the athletes can be used during the season. If athletes are failing to live up to, or to try to reach, their goals, you can use the goals to remind and motivate the players to get back into the proper frame of mind. Having youngsters state goals also serves to enhance performance, foster better communication between coach and athletes, improve self-confidence, and create a more positive commitment on the part of the players.

As an aid to the players, you might list a number of goals for them to consider, simply because they may not realize all the possibilities for themselves and the team. The athletes can then pick the ones that apply to them, and of course they can add their own if they choose to do so. The important thing is the individual conferences after these forms have been collected. Many coaches have found this exercise to be of great value.

All this information can be obtained at meetings in the high school and junior high schools—after first getting permission from the principal—at a time when youngsters won't have to be pulled out of class. This should be done far enough in advance so you can use the information in planning for the start of preseason practice. You don't need any big surprises on the first day of practice.

CORRESPONDING WITH PLAYERS AND PARENTS

If you are involved in a sport that begins in the fall or late summer, it is necessary to correspond with all the members of the team over the summer months. Summer mailings are the only certain way to give players pertinent information and materials, such as physical examination cards, and also to start them thinking about the sport before the first practice. The mailing also serves as a method of keeping in touch with the players over the vacation period, and it lets them know you are thinking about them and the coming season regardless of the time of year your season begins. Letter writing is also the best way for getting information directly to the parents. Do not expect your athletes to hand carry information to their folks—it will never get there in most cases.

The following is a sample of a letter sent to parents of female basketball players prior to the beginning of the season.

> Dear Parents,
>
> I would like to take this time to explain my philosophy of coaching and describe how your daughter will be involved with our Basketball Program.
>
> I strongly believe that the foundation of a successful program is discipline. The discipline that I am referring to is explained in our guide booklet under our team commitments. I expect our basketball players to abide by all school rules and regulations as well as our own team commitments.
>
> Since your daughter has elected to try out for our team, I want to address the questions of participation. Basketball is an extra-curricular activity. It is completely voluntary, but once she makes the decision to try it, I hope you will encourage your daughter to be committed and participate fully until the end of the season. If a player makes the decision to leave the team, I would want to discuss that decision with the player and her parents to make sure all sides involved have the opportunity to express their ideas and concerns. Once the decision is made, we need to stand by the decision.

I also believe it needs to be stated that no player is guaranteed any playing time whatsoever. Playing time is earned with quality practice time. It is the responsibility of the coaching staff to make that determination.

A common question that arises is, who will play JV basketball? JV basketball is reserved for all sophomores and juniors. Any freshman choosing to not play freshman basketball for reasons other than participating in a different fall sport must get permission of the coaching staff, administration, and parents, before the freshman season, to try out for JV or varsity basketball. Those players choosing to participate in a different fall sport will be given the opportunity to try out for JV or varsity basketball.

A major part of our program centers on academics. We are governed by the P.I.A.A. which requires a student-athlete to be successfully passing a minimum of four credits. This is monitored through bi-weekly and tri-weekly grade checks.

To improve our chances of accomplishing our goals for this program, we need several things to happen. First we need to avoid injuries. Second, we need to show our athletes that the value of education is first and athletics are second. If an athlete is not eligible, she cannot participate. Finally, we need to accept our roles in the game. The coaching staff realizes that we can't please everyone all of the time. My job is to operate a program that will provide for a sound educational experience for our players. Remember your role is to provide encouragement and support for your daughter. I'm sure she will experience both success and disappointment at some time in life. It is my hope she will learn how to deal with both and discuss both situations with you and me alike. It will be very helpful when discussing basketball to do it in a very positive, encouraging manner for the betterment of our team.

Looking forward to seeing you in the stands.

Varsity Head Basketball Coach

The following letter is a sample of one that could be mailed to soccer players:

Dear Player,

I certainly hope your summer is going well. I also want you to begin physically preparing yourself for the upcoming soccer season that is only 5 weeks away. Defending the Division IV Championship will not be an easy task as no team has ever repeated in our division. If everyone comes to preseason fit, perhaps we can put ourselves in position to repeat. However, if you decide to rest on your laurels, the opportunity will be lost. The choice is yours.

As for this summer, I'm attempting to play a few "friendly's" with other towns. I'll give you a call about when and where we will be playing. You really need to make an effort to be there.

Training for all students entering grades 9-12 who want try out for the varsity team should meet on the field Monday, August 22, at 5:30 p.m. If you prefer a less rigorous pace and wish to play JV, please show up on Thursday,

August 15, at 5:30 p.m. We encourage you to come out for either team. Any player who does not make varsity will automatically play JV—we will cut no players from the program.

Preseason prep:

1. Buy your "boots" soon and get them broken in. One pair of molded and one pair of studs is the ideal combo for all conditions. If you decide to get one pair, I suggest the molded.

2. Wear two pairs of socks when playing, to prevent blisters.

3. Shin guards are mandatory!

4. Set up your physical appointment ASAP. Every athlete must have one every two years.

5. Bring $3.00 to rent a lock/locker.

6. Bring a completed physical/permission/insurance/medical form to the first practice. These forms are included in this mailing.

Minimum physical requirements for the fall (varsity):

1. Boras—Sprint goalline to goalline in 18 sec.; jog back in 30 sec.; 30 sec. rest; repeat 10 times.

2. 75 crunches without rest.

3. Doggies—Sprint from goalline to 6 and back; goalline to PK mark and back; goalline to 18 and back; goalline to top of D and back; 35 sec. rest; repeat 10 times.

Our tentative preseason schedule is on the back of this letter. Also included are both the JV and varsity schedules. Remember, you must make 10 preseason practices before you can play! This is a State Principals' Association rule.

We look forward to your participation in the Fall. Come and join us for some soccer fun in August.

Sincerely,

Coach

The following are samples of two letters sent to girls' hockey team members by their coaches.

Dear Hockey Player:

I hope you are having a good summer. I am having an "exciting" summer going to school. Actually, I am enjoying going to school instead of teaching for a while. Going to the hills for a little camping has helped maintain my sanity.

Just a few reminders before we take off for hockey camp:

Arrive at camp: Tuesday, August 27, by 12 noon; lunch at 1 p.m., play at 3 p.m.

Reminder of fee due: $50.00

Address: The Hockey Camp, [address]

Bring: Bedding or sleeping bag, towels, rain gear, hockey shoes, lots of wool socks, at least three or four white tops to wear with kilts, Ben-Gay, cards, Monopoly.

NOW (TODAY!!!) is the time to start conditioning! Wear your hockey shoes. Jog lightly 1/2 mile for warm-up, sprint 25 yards, jog 100-200 yards, sprint 25 yards, and continue this routine until you get tired. You might put in a few yards of walking if you want. Then build up the amount of time and distance you jog-sprint so that you are jog-sprinting at least 30 minutes. In addition, running up steps and hills is great! Goalie conditioning: Along with some of the above, running in your goalie pads, you need to sharpen your reaction and movement times by kicking (very quickly) a ball (hockey or tennis) into a backboard or wall. Also, sprint sideways, front, and back in a 12' x 12' area.

Good luck! Get going on that conditioning! See you at camp.

Sincerely,

Coach

Dear Hockey Team,

Believe it or not, the time has come to get ready for hockey camp. So here are a few reminders:

Camp: [address]

Dates: Leave from parking lot of the high school (by the gym) at 1:00 p.m., Sunday, August 17. Camp: Monday through Friday, August 18-22, 8:30 a.m. to 12:30 p.m. Return to town Friday, August 22, immediately after camp, arriving, hopefully, by dinnertime. (If we plan properly, we should be able to return campers directly to their homes.)

Lodging: [address]

REMINDER: $40.00 fee due for week's room and board.

Equipment:
Sleeping bag, towel, washcloth, soap, shampoo, etc.
Neat clothes to practice in—no rags, please!
Socks (preferably wool) and hockey shoes (or sneakers)
Hockey stick
Shin guards (you may buy your own, or borrow some from school on Sunday)

Sweater (one) or sweatshirt for cool weather

Some neat jeans or something to relax in—remember, we're staying on a farm

Bathing suit

Some spending money for snacks, lunch, and $10 each to pay for gas (that will cover the round trip)

One roll of adhesive tape

(All equipment except the sleeping bag and hockey stick must fit into one small duffel bag or laundry bag. We will not take any suitcases.)

You may want to pack a deck of cards or a paperback book for evenings. AND START RUNNING NOW! Put on your socks and shoes, and for the first two days do the following: jog 1/2 mile, then sprint 20 steps, jog 20 steps for the remaining half mile. For the next two days jog 1/2 mile; sprint 50 steps, jog 50 steps for the remaining half mile. For the rest of the days, jog 1/4 mile; sprint 50 steps, jog 50 steps for the rest of the mile.

REMEMBER: When we meet Sunday at 1:00, you will have four things with you: one hockey stick, one sleeping bag, one laundry bag full of what you need, and your money.

DON'T FORGET TO SHOW THIS TO YOUR PARENTS! Let me know if there are any problems—see you Sunday.

Sincerely,

Coach

Not only do youngsters have questions in their minds about the upcoming season, but so do parents—especially if this is their first daughter or son to go out for a team. Consequently, it is worth writing to all the parents to answer some of their questions, too—especially about the matter of a vacation falling during the season. They will appreciate your thoughtfulness. The following is an example of a letter to parents. It should go in the mail several months prior to the beginning of the season—whatever the sport.

Dear Folks:

Last week we had a meeting of the eighth-grade boys to sign up for high school football for next fall. We had 57 boys indicate that they intended to play football in ninth grade, which is the largest turnout we've ever had. Your son was at this meeting and expressed interest in ninth-grade football. I hope that he does come out for the team, but before he does, I believe you should have an understanding with him that once he decides to come out, he cannot quit and must finish the season. I think this is very important to the boy, and you will be doing him a real favor if you make him stick to this arrangement.

Practice begins on Friday, August 20, at 7:00 a.m. Every year problems arise because this conflicts with family vacations; therefore, I will try to explain our policy to you. If your boy is on vacation with you and reports late for practice, he can still come out for football, provided we have any equipment left. We do not save equipment for anyone, nor can we give it out early. In other words, it is first come, first served for the ninth graders; and while we think we will have enough for everyone, we are never sure how many boys will report the first day. One other factor to consider is that we practice twice a day, and each day a boy misses puts him that much further behind his teammates, which makes it tough on him physically as he tries to catch up.

On Wednesday, May 19, at 7:00 p.m., local dentists will be at the school to fit each football player with a latex mouth guard. This is a mandatory piece of equipment, and we are fortunate to have dentists in our community who are willing to do this for us free. Make sure your boy is present. If he misses this opportunity, he will have to have a mouthpiece made on his own, and that will be very expensive. Incidentally, he will need a metal nail file to spread the latex on the mouthpiece later. If you have any questions, please do not hesitate to call me.

Sincerely,

Coach

Later on, a second letter, like one of the following, should be sent to the parents of every student planning on coming out for the team to bring them up-to-date on the latest plans for the coming season:

Dear Parents,

It won't be long until another football season gets under way. This is the time of year I look forward to, but I suppose some of you have mixed emotions about football. Some of you look upon it with anticipation, others with skepticism, and this is natural when you are concerned about your son's welfare.

I can tell you this—"football fever" seems to be running high among the boys this year, and to me this is a good sign. The interest is high, the competition will be keen, and this is what brings out the best in the boys. Football, to many of our boys, is one of the most important phases of their high school career. Being on the team fills a great need for them—to be a member of a group, to be accepted by their friends, to have the respect and admiration of their classmates, and to have an opportunity to pit their courage against an opponent in a contact game.

Football is a game that demands great physical courage on the part of a participant, and this is why I have so much respect for the boys who play this game.

Our practice schedule this year will be as follows:

7:30 - 9:30 A.M.　　—Practice

9:30 - 10:00 A.M.　　—Shower

10:00 - 10:30 A.M.　—Light Lunch

10:30 - 10:45 A.M.　—Meetings

11:45 - Noon   —Dress

Noon- 1:30 P.M.   —Practice

This will get us done before the hottest part of the day.

You are all welcome to attend any or all of our sessions, but please—no coaching from the sidelines. You might show up the coach.

We are having our first annual "Parents' Football Clinic" on Tuesday, August 31, at 7:00 p.m. in the high school gymnasium. We'd like very much for all of you to attend, if possible, so we can show you how and what we are teaching your son, in order to help you enjoy our games more. You are welcome to bring along your whole family, if you like.

By the way, season tickets will be on sale at the high school office from August 19 to 25 for you parents only, so if you are interested, you can have first choice of the best seats in the stadium.

Sincerely,

Coach

Dear Basketball Parents,

Here we go again! Another basketball season is upon us. I know how hectic things can get; early morning practices, late practices, several meals to prepare, out-of-town trips, and many other things. We really appreciate your hard work and support.

We are having a "Tip-Off and Picture Night" Wednesday, December 1, at the North Building gym beginning at 6:45 p.m. All players and coaches in our 7th and 8th grade, 9th grade, Junior Varsity, and Varsity programs will be introduced. We will then have individual and team pictures taken for the program. We invite you to bring your camera and take some shots of your favorite players. Members of the media will also be on hand at this time to interview coaches and players and take pictures as well.

Following brief intersquad scrimmages for each team will be a booster club meeting in the cafeteria. Feel free to bring any family members, friends, or fans to this event. Hope to see you there!

Sincerely,

Coach

CONDUCTING A PARENT CLINIC

An area that many coaches often neglect is parent involvement, which is a big mistake because the people most concerned about the program, aside from the coaches, are the parents of the athletes. Because they will be involved one way or another, why not take the initiative and involve them in a positive way? In general, parents are extremely eager to understand the program. They want to know what their sons or daughters will be going through, what is expected of them, and what the coaches are trying to accomplish, and they want to feel more a part of their youngster's experience. This is especially the case for parents whose sons or daughters are going out for a sport for the first time or for parents who have just moved into a new community and do not know anything about you and the program.

One good way to involve parents is to organize a clinic at the school some time early in the season or, preferably, during preseason practice. You should schedule the date and location of the meeting through the high school office, plan the agenda, and have your student secretary prepare announcements resembling the sample shown in Figure 9.5. It is possible to send these notices home with the athletes, but as every teacher soon learns, things sent home with students do not always get there. So rather than take a chance, you should require all athletes to bring in a stamped envelope addressed to their parents. It takes a manager very little time to put the notices into these envelopes and into the mail.

A meeting like this also serves a valuable purpose in giving the coaches an opportunity to meet the parents. The entire coaching staff should be at the door or gate, so that each player can introduce his or her parents to each coach as they come into the meeting. The coaches might decide to include their wives or husbands in this receiving line so that parents can meet them as well. All this takes time, but it is time well spent, and it teaches some social graces to the athletes. These introductions might seem like a simple matter, but some youngsters will get so nervous that they sometimes forget the coaches' names as they introduce their parents.

During this meeting you can bring the team to the front of the room and have all players introduce themselves and their parents. As the players speak, their parents should stand up so that other parents can see who they are. This can help eliminate unfortunate incidents during a contest, such as when a parent criticizes

Figure 9.5
Sample parents' clinic announcement.

PARENTS' CLINIC

Where: High School Cafeteria
When: Wednesday, August 31
Time: 7:00 p.m.
Why: A. Meet the Coaches
        B. Meet the Team
        C. Display of Equipment—Past and Present
        D. Explanation of our Program
        E. The Philosophy Behind Our Plans for this Season

This is for parents of freshmen, sophomores, juniors, and seniors. Here is your chance to learn, firsthand, exactly what your youngster will be doing this season. It will be a fine opportunity to have your questions answered.

Hope to see you there,

Coach

a player whose parents are sitting nearby. If the parents at least recognize each other, they will be a little more careful in the stands.

There are other possibilities for bringing the parents together. For example, a swimming coach could invite the parents into the pool for some fun races, or a basketball coach could invite the parents down on the floor and have the players attempt to teach their folks some of the skills of the game through drills, followed by some short competition. This activity might help parents appreciate what their children are required to do in a sport. Such sessions can be a lot of fun, and they certainly won't hurt the program.

The parent clinic is particularly important to a new family in town. A gathering like this can help them get acquainted quickly with a lot of people who have something in common—a son or daughter participating in athletics. People who have lived in the community for a long time, including the coach, often take it for granted that everyone knows everyone else.

An exercise of this sort also helps parents feel more a part of the program, and this should be one of your goals. When people feel a part of something, such as an athletic team, and understand what the coaches are trying to do, they are less apt to become critical as the season progresses. Generally speaking, parents appreciate a coaching staff that takes the time to talk to them about the upcoming season. It is a great public relations gesture. (This is a good way to make points with the superintendent also!) The coaches are telling the parents that they are a special group and that they merit some inside information about the team.

The basic purpose of this kind of meeting is to give you a great opportunity to make very clear what you are attempting to do, why, and the ways you intend to do it. This is the perfect time to discuss the most sensitive topics before they become problems, including playing time, cutting, quitting, and picking the team (see the sample agenda in Figure 9.6). And since the parents hear all of this firsthand, misunderstandings and problems will be less likely to occur later in the season. Obviously, conducting such a clinic will take a lot of your time, but it is well worth it in the long run. If you do it right, it should reduce the number of phone calls and questions from moms and dads later on in the season. This is the ideal time and place to become a "fire preventer" instead of having to be a "fire fighter" throughout the season. Do not be bashful! It would be a good idea to include the athletic director, principal, superintendent, and president of the school board as well. That way, everyone concerned is hearing the same message.

AGENDA

1. Introduce coaches
2. Introduce coaches' wives or husbands
3. Introduce school officials
4. Introduce players; players introduce parents
5. Organization of whole program
6. What we expect of players
   A. Promptness
   B. Hard work
   C. Respect
   D. Loyalty
7. What parents can do to help
   A. Training rules - Yes or no - Why
   B. Support the coaches
   C. Not allowing youngsters to quit the team
   D. Do not criticize the coaches in front of youngsters

E. Morale - Give a boost when needed
F. Do not support complaining
G. No coaching on the part of a parent
H. Problem? Make sure to get both sides
I. Attendance at practice
8. What we coaches stand for
9. Practice organization: times, dates, etc.
10. Parent concerns
    A. Playing time
    B. Strength training
    C. Weight control
    D. Recruiting and scholarships
    E. Drug abuse
    F. Cutting the team
11. Demonstrations

It is easy to tell parents what you expect to do with their sons or daughters and why, but it is also important to know what the parents expect of you, and what their primary concerns are. For you to assume that you know what these expectations and concerns are could be a serious mistake. The only way to know for sure is to ask. Appendix D contains a questionnaire designed to elicit this information. If you expect to win the support of the parents, you better know what they expect of you. If their view is different from yours, you can address it at the parent clinic.

ARRANGING FOR MEDICAL CARE AT ATHLETIC EVENTS

Off-season is also the time to arrange for physicians to be present at home games, meets, or contests. In some sports, the rules require a doctor's presence. Even when a doctor is not required, you should try to arrange for one. Sometimes there will be doctors for the varsity teams but not for the junior varsity or freshmen. The absence of medical personnel or a qualified trainer at athletic contests poses a real danger both physically—for the well-being of the players—and legally for the coach. Actually, arrangements for medical care are the responsibility of the athletic director, but you should double-check to make sure they are being taken care of.

According to the medical profession, the following factors should be considered:

- Every athlete participating in an outdoor sport where there is danger of a
  spike wound or similar injury should have up-to-date tetanus immunization.

- An emergency vehicle should always be present at every football game to save valuable time in an emergency. This vehicle should be parked as inconspicuously as possible.

- Each athlete should fill out an accident card listing the family doctor, home telephone, and phone number of someone else to call in case the parents are not home. These cards should be kept on file near a telephone that is convenient to the practice area.

- The telephone number of the local emergency service (normally the fire department) should be posted by this same telephone.

- A reserved parking space should be set aside for the doctor at the game site. Sometimes a doctor cannot get to the game early and arrives when there are no parking spaces left. A reserved space is also convenient in case the doctor has to leave for an emergency.

- An athlete's physical examination should be given by the family doctor, because the family doctor knows the youngster's medical history. Such knowledge is critical in determining whether the student should be allowed to compete in athletics. Using one doctor to examine an entire team at one time is generally not recommended. However, school policy might dictate otherwise. Make certain you check with your athletic director in this matter.

The easiest way to implement the last item is to have the student secretary or manager mail athletes a physical examination card before the season begins, have them arrange their own physicals, and have them bring the completed cards to hand in when equipment is issued. Other possibilities would be to have students pick up the cards at the school office or at various places in the community, such as the swimming pool, or have the coaches carry a supply with them for the asking.

STAFF CLINIC

The next step in off-season planning is to plan a clinic for the coaching staff, whether you have one other coach or several. During the course of a school year, various coaches attend clinics conducted by other coaches from all over the country. During the off-season they might also have read articles or books about coaching or about a particular sport; as a result, they might have picked up ideas good enough to adopt in your immediate situation. The quickest way to share these ideas with the entire staff is to write them all down and then meet to discuss them. This is also an excellent way to indoctrinate coaches new to the staff.

Staff clinics are particularly useful when only the head coach is given the opportunity to attend clinics during a school year. A coach who shares the ideas heard at these clinics helps the staff grow in their knowledge of the sport, and it eventually benefits the athletes they teach.

If noncertified part-time coaches are on the staff, attendance at coaching clinics becomes absolutely essential. It can serve as training for people who have had little or no professional preparation for coaching.

ORGANIZING YOUR STAFF

Organization is no problem if the staff consists of one or two people, but in a large school system with a junior high program and possibly some involvement of the upper elementary grades, anywhere from three to fifteen or more coaches

might be involved in a single sport. In this situation it is imperative that everyone know precisely what his or her role is in order to conduct the program efficiently.

The decision as to who will coach a freshman team or a reserve team or serve as a varsity assistant must be made by the head coach. Perhaps the best method of arranging the system (to prevent morale problems and still maintain a fine coaching staff) is to attempt to convince the superintendent of schools of the importance of hiring qualified, high-level assistant coaches who have or will develop the qualities and knowledge expected of varsity assistants. Then when a varsity opening occurs, everyone who wants to has an opportunity to move up, and the new person moves in at a lower level on the staff. Unfortunately, the hard reality of high school coaching shows very clearly that not all superintendents employ coaches in this way. In far too many instances superintendents do not involve head coaches in the hiring process. As a result, assistant coaches are sometimes hired to fill specific coaching vacancies without the head coach's knowledge. Such procedures can create serious problems for the head coach.

It is also true that not every assistant wants to be a varsity coach. Some prefer to coach at the freshman level, for example, and do a good job there. In such situations, a varsity opening can sometimes be filled with a new coach. There are two main disadvantages to this practice. One is that an assistant coach with no desire to move up can become too comfortable in one position and not put forth the effort the head coach would like to see. The other drawback is that assistants hired right out of college, regardless of their capabilities, may be limited by a lack of experience. Some recent graduates, however, begin making a significant contribution right away.

Because a teaching vacancy must exist before a new coach is hired (in some states), it may be that the only person who can fill it is not qualified to coach at the required level. In this situation the head coach will have to reevaluate everyone's responsibilities, do some realigning, and then personally coach the area that is left. If the staff is a good one, filled with people who are knowledgeable, this situation is not too difficult to manage.

ISSUING EQUIPMENT

Although not too complicated for a cross-country, swim, or golf team, equipment issue can become a gigantic problem for other types of teams. If plans haven't been well thought out in advance, chaos can occur. The four things that complicate equipment issue are (1) the time it takes for one person to draw a complete uniform, (2) the importance of everything fitting properly, (3) the fact that some youngsters do not know the proper way to put on the various pieces of equipment, and (4) the necessity of recording the number on each piece of equipment issued to each athlete for the purpose of equipment control.

To solve all these problems and outfit a large number of athletes in an hour or less, the following method can be used. Lay out all pieces of equipment in two lines down the gymnasium floor. The various items should be laid out separately, rather than in piles, and in the order in which an athlete would put each thing on while dressing. As the youngsters walk down the line—varsity on one side, everyone else on the other side—they choose and put on each piece of equipment. By the time they reach the end of the line, they will be completely dressed in full gear. In the meantime the coaches can wander up and down the line to give whatever assistance is needed—such as checking proper fit.

When the athletes get to the end of the line, a manager hands each one an equipment record card; as the players undress in the locker room, they record the number painted on each piece of equipment and then turn the card back to another manager. This method is efficient, is easy to control, and creates an atmosphere of careful organization and attention to detail that serves as an example to the team.

ORDERING MOUTH GUARDS

Athletes involved in contact sports must have mouth guards. Each student can purchase an assembly-line model at a sporting goods store for a nominal fee, or each individual can have one made to fit by a dentist. The latter method is expensive, unless dentists in the community are willing to donate a few hours one night to make them for every member of the squad. Getting mouthpieces donated is not impossible if a coach goes to work soon enough to try to arrange it. A good approach is to enlist the aid of a local dentist who can then get some colleagues to participate.

ARRANGING FOR CLASSROOMS

If you need to hold team meetings in a school classroom at any time, you will need to make arrangements through the principal's office ahead of time. This planning ensures that there will be no conflict in the use of the room (especially a room used for videos) or with the custodians.

BRIEFING THE ATHLETIC DIRECTOR

Before the opening practice, make a point of meeting with the athletic director or faculty manager for a briefing on your plans for the season, especially dates for preseason scrimmages or practice contests if the athletic director has to arrange transportation. The director should also be made aware of any special events, such as a parent clinic, meet-the-team night, banquet, holiday practice, and so on. The athletic director will have plenty of time to take care of your plans if you notify him or her far enough in advance.

CREATING PLAYER NOTEBOOKS

Another decision you will have to make is whether to create a notebook for every member of the team. Writing a notebook, having it produced, duplicated, assembled, issued, collected, and revised every season is a big undertaking and can be extremely time-consuming. But with a little planning you can arrange for members of the team to do most of the work. The production and duplicating can be done by a student secretary. A potential problem is that an athlete might lose a notebook, which could end up in the hands of an opponent.

On the positive side, however, is the fact that a tremendous amount of information can be put into a notebook and disseminated to a great many people (including parents) without taking away a minute of valuable practice or meeting time. No one can ever say, "I didn't know the rules," "I didn't know this or that," or "You never told me," because it is in writing and every team member has a copy. Also, alerting parents at the parent clinic and encouraging them to read the notebook will save you a lot of phone calls during the season.

The National Interscholastic Athletic Administration Association (P.O. Box 20626, Kansas City, MO 64195) has published a lengthy set of guidelines for athletic handbooks called *Game Plan for Athletics*. You might want to look for a copy in your school to assist you in putting together a notebook. In the meantime, here is a list of the kinds of information you could include in the players' notebook:

1. A brief summary of past accomplishments and traditions of this particular sport

2. A brief summary of the outstanding accomplishments of individuals in the program

3. A brief recap of the preceding season

4. Season schedule

5. Coaches' phone numbers

6. Practice procedures and schedule

7. Training rules

8. Use of training room

9. Conduct in the locker room

10. Conduct in school

11. Conduct on the sidelines

12. Conduct for traveling

13. Care of equipment

14. Injury prevention and care

15. Diet and nutrition

16. Controllable factors (factors we need to focus on because we can control them):

   • Our own physical condition

   • Our own mental attitude

   • Our own desire to win

   • Our own effort

   • Our own skill

17. Uncontrollable factors (factors we have no control over and therefore should not worry about):

   • The weather

   • The officials

   • The other team's preparation

   • Injuries

   • The opponent's skill level

   • The spectators (at away contests)

18. Inevitables (if we play long enough, sooner or later some or all of these things will happen, so don't get upset and lose your poise when they do happen):

    - Injuries

    - Bad calls against us

    - Losing

    - Playing in bad weather

    - Turning the ball over

    - Penalties

    - Making mistakes

    - A poor playing facility

    [Obviously a more specific list would have to be made for a specific sport.]

19. A list of don'ts [again, specific to a sport; many of the items are fundamental for a smart team—but some are "little" details that can and do get lost in preparing for a game or meet]:

    - Don't foul a player going in for a shot with two seconds on the clock when we're ahead by three points (basketball).

    - Don't ever get called out on strikes with the bases loaded and two outs.

    - Don't ever look back over your shoulder when leading in the hurdles.

    - Don't ever false-start (track).

    - Don't ever retaliate.

    - Don't argue with officials.

    - Don't criticize a teammate.

    - Don't incur a penalty inside your opponent's 20-yard line (football).

    - Don't rough the punter (football).

20. We must:

    - Be prepared physically and mentally to play our best.

    - Be aggressive.

- Ignore adversity.

- Control our own performance.

- Exhibit good sportsmanship at all times.

- Take advantage of sudden changes in the contest (when a situation swings the momentum in our favor).

21. Technique and safety sheets. (This section should contain detailed safety precautions before, during, and after practice sessions or games. It should also contain detailed instructions on the correct way to perform certain fundamentals of a sport—e.g., tackling in football. The purpose is to help prevent injuries, to alert youngsters to risks involved in the sport, and to protect the coaches against lawsuits. It would be a good idea to require athletes to sign these pages as an indication that they have read the material.)

You might also want to include drills, offensive plays, and defensive schemes. Many coaches who choose to include plays do not draw them up. Instead they have the athletes draw the plays as they are explained. This method might improve comprehension, and the plays will be added to the book only as they are needed.

Putting information on paper is one thing—getting athletes to read it is another. If the players do not read the material in the notebook, the coaches will have wasted a tremendous amount of time and effort. There is only one quick way to find out if the players have read the material, and that, as every teacher knows, is to give them a test. The test doesn't have to be long or complicated, but it should contain enough questions to indicate whether the members of the team have read the material. The head manager can grade the papers. An athlete who fails to score whatever grade you think is satisfactory will have to pay some penalty. Unless you follow up like this, the whole project will have been a waste of time.

Obviously, the decision to create notebooks for an athletic team is a big one. The task is enormous, but the books are an excellent way to disseminate a lot of necessary information. The benefits far outweigh the time spent.

A COACH'S CHECKLIST

Another tool you will find helpful in the off-season is a checklist of things that have to be done before the beginning of preseason practice. As a program grows and you have more things to remember, a checklist becomes more important as a way to make sure that nothing is left undone before the first practice begins. The following is an example of such a checklist. Obviously, not every item will apply to every sport.

1. Check on condition of practice area

2. Arrange for plastic cover for dummies

3. Arrange for planks for board drills

4. Pick up tires at local service station for agility drills

5. Arrange for classrooms

6. Ready accident cards in case of injury

7. Make sure phone is in operation

8. Arrange with cafeteria for a refrigerator for training room

9. Arrange for socks to sell to team

10. Arrange for team pictures—date, time, place, rain date

11. Prepare notebooks

12. Number equipment

13. Clean training room

14. Set up scouting schedule for assistant coaches

15. Set up parents' club

16. Arrange for play cards for scout team

17. Send letter about parent clinic

18. Arrange for Labor Day practice at night

19. Arrange to display pictures of individual players in town

20. Plan for holiday practice

21. Send letters to athletes

22. Set agenda for preseason meeting

23. Notify athletic director about preseason practice games, meets, scrimmages

24. Arrange for travel

25. Arrange for officials

26. Check in new equipment as soon as it arrives to make certain no errors were made in the order

The next section of the checklist should include every phase of the game or meet that absolutely must be covered before the opening of the season. The items in this checklist should be incorporated into the master plan for the preseason practices. As a result, no phase of the game will be overlooked. For example, a football coach would include items similar to these:

1. Kickoff—field goal—extra point

2. Return—punt and kickoff

3. Punt

4. Offense

5. Pass cuts

6. Quick kick

7. Defense

8. Huddle-cadence

9. Objectives of defense and offense

10. Pass-defense highlight video

11. Offensive highlight video

12. Defensive highlight video

13. Two-minute drill

14. Defensing weird formations

SELECTING TEAM CAPTAINS

Whether or not to have team captains is another consideration. There are advantages and disadvantages to both choices. The greatest advantage, which might outweigh everything else, is the leadership that team captains can provide, not only during an athletic event but in every other aspect of a particular sport, in season and out. Unless you are firmly opposed to the idea of captains or are convinced that captains are a good thing, you should leave the decision up to the players. They can choose whether they want a captain or co-captains, whether seniors only should be chosen, and whether they want to vote or have you appoint someone.

Coaches who support this idea frequently have the team select the captain or captains immediately after the season ends. This gives the captain a good opportunity to grow into the role before the next season begins. More important, it gives you an excellent link to the team throughout the entire off-season. Such a link can be positive for everyone concerned.

The biggest danger is that the captaincy can become strictly a popularity contest and lead to cliques on the team. This situation must be prevented at all cost. Popularity and leadership ability do not necessarily go hand in hand, and having captains who are not leaders can create problems that defeat the basic purpose of the whole concept. Therefore, before captains are elected you should describe the qualities needed for the role so the team can make an intelligent choice.

The only other criteria I ever gave a team was to tell them to look at their teammates and figure out who they would look at as the "go to" player if we got in trouble in a game; that is the person they should vote for.

PLANNING A MEDIA DAY

One thing that irritates a coach is to have a newspaper photographer walk in and ask to take some publicity pictures when the team is in the middle of a practice session. Not only does the photography disrupt practice, but the team usually has on practice gear, which doesn't look very good in a picture. By giving this matter some thought in preseason planning, you can avoid such interruptions.

As you look at the preseason schedule, simply pick a date when the team could use a break from the daily routine and monotony of practice, and set that day for pictures. It is not necessary to cancel a practice session to do this; just shorten the practice, make sure the athletes wear their game uniforms, and turn everything over to the media.

After setting the date, time, and place (including a rain date for outdoor sports), you can have your student media liaison phone or write every area newspaper, the yearbook photographer, local television sportscasters, and the photographer for the game programs, inviting them to come to the school to take all the pictures they want. This planning can be accomplished two or three months in advance to give all the media folks plenty of notice. You will find that they really appreciate your effort, and you will be finished with this task for the rest of the season. This event creates a big-time atmosphere and is a great morale booster during preseason practice. Colleges do this all the time—why not high schools?

WORKING WITH CUSTODIANS

During the off-season, you need to consider the role of the school custodians and how the beginning of a new season will affect them and their work at school. Like so many other factors, this is of more concern to coaches whose season begins at the end of summer vacation or straddles a school vacation period.

The sports that begin before school opens in the fall may run into problems with the facilities if the custodians aren't alerted in advance, because the school building and locker-room areas are usually in great disarray as the custodians clean and prepare the building for another school year. Unless they are notified that field hockey practice, cross country, or football practice will begin in mid-August, the custodians probably won't be ready. The result can be real confusion when athletes move into locker rooms that aren't ready for them.

Unusual practice hours during winter holidays, when heat in certain parts of the building might be a problem, are another reason for keeping custodians informed of practice plans. The athletic director should take care of these details, but you should at least check to make sure everything is arranged ahead of time.

Custodians appreciate this notification and are usually more than willing to cooperate and help in any way possible. You should cultivate the friendship of the custodial staff to receive the kind of assistance necessary for the good of the program. If you treat these people as servants rather than as friends and co-workers in a school, you will eventually run into some problems that otherwise would never occur.

PLANNING PRESEASON PRACTICE GAMES/MEETS/EVENTS

In any off-season planning, you might have to decide on opponents, locations, and times for preseason scrimmages or practice meets, and arrange for officials if an event will be at home. In many states, the exact number of preseason scrimmages is fixed for some sports, in which case you have little choice. After your decisions have been made, the athletic director should be notified and then you can carry on with the details.

In arranging practice contests, take care not to always schedule a weak opponent. The advantages to be gained from playing a weak opponent are negligible, and your team or individual players might get a false impression of how good they are. At the same time, you should not deliberately schedule a team that is too strong. In contact sports, an uneven contest increases the chances of injury, and if the team gets handled rather easily, morale could be affected to the point where the athletes lose confidence in themselves, their teammates, or their coaches. The idea that strong competition will make a team better is true, within limits. The only time scheduling a weaker team for a scrimmage is justified is when you are a new coach fielding your first team and trying hard to sell yourself and a particular system to the team. If the athletes do well, even if it is against a poorer team, they will gain a lot of confidence in you. This is an important consideration for a new coach in any sport.

SCHEDULING ATHLETIC BANQUETS

Banquets are traditional in athletics, but the expense involved can be significant. As a result, many schools no longer sponsor them. Whatever the case, decisions involving these affairs should be made before a season begins. If the season is highly successful, everyone will want a banquet. If it is unsuccessful, you should want one to create good feelings that will carry over into the off-season and into the next year.

Kinds of Banquets

There are three basic kinds of banquets: (1) one all-sports banquet at the end of a school year; (2) seasonal banquets involving all teams for a specific season; (3) individual banquets for each sport.

The advantage of the all-sports banquet is that it is a one-time event that theoretically creates unity among all the teams, both boys' and girls'. The main disadvantage is that if youngsters participate in a fall sport only, a banquet six months later means very little to them. A banquet seems to be most effective when it takes place the week after a season ends. An all-sports banquet also presents the problem of accommodating a large number of people.

The seasonal banquet is good because there is no danger of a major team having a better banquet than one of the so-called minor teams. The disadvantage is having to work out the logistics for handling large numbers of people, plus the fact that if a main speaker is featured, that speaker usually ends up talking about one sport (the one he or she coaches), and the athletes on other teams have little interest in what is being said.

Specific-sport banquets allow far more flexibility but can be the most costly if the school is financing them. Of course, one way that all these banquets can be financed is by selling tickets to parents or to the community at large. One of the concerns in doing so is that some athletes' families may not be able to afford to buy tickets, which puts them in an uncomfortable situation.

The easiest type of banquet is one sponsored by a civic organization. The primary drawback is that normally only a few select teams in the school are so honored, and the rest are ignored. This selectivity sometimes causes hard feelings, so a coach should not actively encourage it. But if such a banquet is offered, you cannot afford to say no unless the school has a policy against banquets of this type.

The least expensive type of banquet, and a kind that every coach can organize with little expense for anyone, is a potluck at the school—or at the coach's own home if the team is small enough. To arrange the potluck, figure out how many team members, managers, coaches, coaches' spouses, school officials, and parents will attend. Then plan a menu that is fairly simple to prepare, decide how big each portion should be, and then determine how many players will have to bring each item. For example, if there will be 60 people, and if a single cake is big enough for ten servings, six athletes will have to bring cakes of this size. Such arrangements can be made in just a few minutes of a team meeting. There will normally be more food than needed, because the athletes usually bring a surplus of their contribution. I have never seen anyone go away hungry from this kind of banquet.

To keep the coaches and their families from carrying the whole burden of planning and working on the banquet, the team captains' parents can be recruited to help, and—to create continuity for the next year—you can give them the names of some juniors' parents also. Try to include the parents of the athletes most likely to be next year's captains. If there are no captains, just choose a few parents and ask them to help. These parents can then take care of getting the food set out. To keep anyone from being overwhelmed, another group of parents can be asked to decorate the tables, with a different set of parents being responsible for decorating each table. This process provides a lot of variety, imagination, and involvement without undue imposition on anyone.

Programs and Speakers

One activity that can easily become a tradition and the highlight of a banquet is the tapping of the next year's captains. The final event of the banquet can be a brief talk by the outgoing captains about the season and what being captain has meant to them. As they finish their comments, they begin walking among their seated teammates and, on a prearranged signal, slap the new captain or co-captains (who up until that point have been unknown to everyone but the outgoing captains and the coach) on the back and bring them up in front of the group, where their first official function is to make a short speech. When handled properly this ceremony is very effective and exciting.

The next decision to consider in conjunction with a banquet is whether to have a speaker. College coaches are often sought for this purpose because doing so has become traditional and because it adds prestige to the affair. Usually these people have a canned speech that they change slightly to fit a particular situation, and many times they spend a great deal of time talking about the sport at their particular university. Sometimes these presentations are very good; sometimes they are not. And sometimes they cost a lot of money.

If finances are a problem, an outside speaker is not necessary. Instead, a number of school officials and coaches, limited to about five minutes each, can talk about the team; some of the athletes can speak for a few minutes; the outgoing manager can pass on the symbol of authority to next year's manager; awards can be passed out; and parents can speak, too. For example, a mother of a player and father of another player, one whose youngster played regularly and one whose youngster did not, can be asked to say a few words.

One of the finest speeches I ever heard at a banquet was given by the mother of a substitute who got into only one game all season, and then only briefly. She was superb.

The point is that a lot of people are intimately involved in an athletic program, and they have a lot of talent and tremendous interest in the youngsters who participate. It sometimes seems like a waste not to take advantage of this situation and instead bring in an expensive college coach who really couldn't care less about the situation unless there happens to be a prospective athlete to recruit. And being a college coach does not necessarily guarantee a lot of skill in public speaking.

THE FIRST TEAM MEETING

Plans for the initial team meeting should also be formulated well in advance. Since such a meeting generally occurs before the opening practice, the length of the meeting is not critical. It is therefore an excellent opportunity to talk about all the details the youngsters need to know as they go into a new season. Communication is essential, and the better understanding the athletes have of every facet of the program and precisely what you expect of them, the better the entire organization will become. This is the time to give direction to the program and to let the members of the team know what they can expect of the coaches. The following agenda illustrates the kinds of topics that might be covered before the first practice:

1. Introduce coaches

2. Explain the role of captain(s)

3. Introduce manager-trainers and explain roles

4. Explain insurance

5. Make sure all players have had physicals

6. Collect registration cards for emergency in case of injury

7. Double-check eligibility with athletic director

8. Explain how to get season tickets for parents

9. Mention socks, T-shirts, and so on are for sale through athletic department

10. Make sure players have mouthpieces for contact sports

11. Ask students to provide stamped envelopes—addressed to parents or guardians

12. Announce team pictures—date, place, time

13. Announce schedule for scrimmages/practices against outside opponents

14. Give information about meeting rooms for whole team or by position

15. Discuss care of blisters

16. Discuss prevention and care of injuries

17. Discuss drug abuse

18. Discuss locker-room conduct

19. Discuss recruiting/scholarships (NCAA rules)

20. Discuss care of equipment

21. Discuss training rules—Nutrition

22. Give out notebooks

23. Discuss practice procedure

24. Announce the team clinic

25. Discuss cutting the team—criteria

26. Announce parent clinic—date, time, place

27. Discuss team goals for the season

28. Discuss players' expectations of coaches

29. Break—then meet with seniors separately

Item 29 is an important part of a pre-season meeting. When the general meeting is over, the seniors should be asked to stay for a short while. After everyone else has gone, explain very clearly the role seniors have to play on the team regarding leadership and attitude. If you do a good job at this point, problems associated with "senioritis" will be lessened or eliminated. The main point is that this is the last season these people will ever participate in this sport at this high school, and for some it is the last athletic participation ever. As a result, it is important for seniors to try to provide the younger students with the kind of leadership necessary to ensure a successful season. The seniors also need

The Face in the Glass

When you reach your goal in the world of sports
And you have worked the big game that day
Just go to the mirror and look at yourself
And see what the face has to say,
For it isn't your family or friends or the coaches
Whose judgment upon you must pass,
The person whose verdict counts in your life
Is the one staring at you from the glass.
You may fool the world down the avenue of years
And get pats on the back as you pass,
But your only reward will be remorse and regret
If you have cheated the face in the glass.
　　—Author Unknown

to be aware that the performance of the team as a whole might have some bearing on scholarship possibilities. When senior athletes look at a season this way, they tend to approach it from a new point of view.

In conjunction with the seniors on the team, one of your concerns has to be *senioritis*—an undesirable frame of mind seniors sometimes develop in which they think they have it made and don't have to hustle like the underclass students who are trying to make the team. With boys, this attitude is normally an individual matter, but the problems it creates can negatively affect the whole team. With girls senioritis often becomes a group problem. On girls' teams it sometimes manifests itself in the form of cliques. The seniors think the team belongs to them, and they can become highly resentful if one of their group is benched in favor of an underclass athlete. When this occurs, senior leadership has a negative effect on the other people, morale suffers, and the team will not reach its greatest potential.

Consequently, in the off-season you should spend time planning ways to create a positive attitude in the minds of the upcoming seniors. Another

reason senioritis develops is the fact that many seniors consider themselves at the end of their playing careers, which seems to dampen motivation in some of them.

In an effort to combat this particular attitude, you should encourage athletes who intend to go on to college to consider participating in athletics there. Too many high school players assume that they have to be super-athletes in order to participate in college athletics, and this just isn't so, except in large universities. There are many smaller schools with fine academic standards and fine athletic programs where good high school athletes can compete.

There are several ways to encourage youngsters to set higher goals for participation in athletics beyond high school. One possibility is to publicize the athletes from your school who have gone on to compete in college. You can do so by taking seniors to college games to see some of their former teammates perform or by hanging framed photographs of former athletes who competed in college athletics in the locker room. These photos should be labeled by name and college; they are generally available through college athletic publicity offices. Another possibility is to hang college banners or pennants in the gymnasium area, and list the student athletes under the appropriate banner.

Such motivational tools can help prevent senioritis. Another benefit is that if young people can be encouraged to participate in college athletics, their college experience can be more meaningful, more complete, and more enjoyable, in spite of what critics say about the evils of college athletics.

TEAM CLINIC

As a part of the initial team meetings, you might consider a team clinic as well. This approach would enable you to deviate from the mechanics of getting a season under way and to plant the seed for the kind of mindset you want to permeate the entire squad. This agenda also gives you the opportunity to go into detail concerning goals for the season and the steps necessary to realize these goals. At this point in the initial team meeting you can let the team know the decisions that have been made by the staff regarding the style of play to be used during the season and the reasoning behind these decisions. This is the time to set direction for everything that is to follow. A likely agenda might be:

1. This will be a championship year, therefore we must:

   - Think championship

   - Talk championship

   - Practice like champions

   - Play like champions

2. How do we do all these?

   - Work harder than our opponents

   - 110% effort all the time

   - Fewer mistakes than our opponents

   - Superior physical conditioning

   - Superior mental discipline

   - Superior mental attitude

   - Superior technique

   - Superior desire

   - Superior defense

   - Superior offense

- Superior organization

- Pride in our team, teammates, school, and coaches

- Loyalty to our team—make each other look good, associate with each other

3. Team goals

4. Whether you make the team depends on how well you measure up to these criteria, on your ability, and on whether you show the coaches that you are a winner.

5. Mutual respect between coaches and athletes

6. Personal conduct in and out of school

7. The person listed as number two at a position is not necessarily the number one substitute at that position.

8. Cuts (if cutting is part of the program) to be based on:

- Individual cases

- Attitude

- Effort

- Hustle

- Overall effect on the team

9. Offense: objectives—priorities (general picture) (when appropriate)

10. Defense: types of defenses and why (when appropriate)

Item 6 on this agenda deserves careful attention. Too often coaches get so wrapped up in the details of a coming season that they forget to discuss the ways in which athletes are expected to conduct themselves, not only at an athletic event but in and out of school as well. Assuming that players know how to behave in an acceptable way is asking for trouble. You owe it to everyone to clarify appropriate behavior at the outset of every season. This is a great time to begin teaching youngsters how to behave like decent human beings.

In this regard you should remind students what it is like to be a role model. Many young athletes fail to realize that they themselves could be looked up to by some youngster in the community at this point in their athletic lives. They thus have certain responsibilities and obligations. Whether they like the idea or not does not matter; it is true. The following poem can help drive this point home and serve as a constant reminder to members of your team when they are tempted to do something foolish.

Like You

There are little eyes upon you, and they're watching night and day;
There are little ears that quickly take in every word you say;
There are little hands all eager to do everything you do,
And little children dreaming of the day they'll be like you.
You're the children's idol, you're the wisest of the wise;
In their little minds about you no suspicions ever rise.
They believe you devoutly, hold that all you say and do
They will say and do in your way when they are grown up just like you.
Oh, it sometimes makes me shudder when I hear a youngster repeat
Some careless phrase I've uttered in the language of the street;
And it sets my heart to grieving when some little fault I see,
And I know beyond all doubting that they picked it up from me.
There are wide-eyed little children who believe you're always right,
And their ears are always open and they watch day and night;
You are setting an example every day in all you do
For the little girl and boy who's waiting to grow up to be just like you. [See pg. 214.]
          —*Author Unknown*

When people understand why they are being asked or told to do certain things in certain ways, they are more likely to get the job done— or at least to pursue it with a more positive attitude. This is one of the primary reasons for a team clinic. You are trying to create an attitude or frame of mind in the athletes that will make them want to give their best in whatever they are told to do during the season. Because this session is usually a beginning coach's first official team meeting, its importance cannot be overemphasized.

Off-season planning takes a tremendous amount of time, thought, and energy, but it is crucial as a first step in successful coaching and should not be minimized. Off-season planning on your part serves as the initial step in preparing for the long season ahead.

DISCUSSION QUESTIONS

1. What are some important points for a head coach to consider in organizing a staff, a team, or a program?

2. How does a team reflect the personality of the coach?

3. Should parents be permitted to attend practices? Why?

4. How can you use videotape in coaching your sport?

5. What do you view as your role in an athletic booster club?

6. Should every athletic team have a captain or co-captains? What are the advantages and disadvantages?

7. Should coaches encourage parent involvement in a sport? Are there limits? If so, what are they?

8. Define "senioritis." How can it affect an athletic team?

9. Are cliques more of a problem in girls' athletics than in boys'? How should you deal with them?

10. In what capacities can other students in the school become involved in the athletic program? How can they be chosen?

11. Do you believe notebooks would be of any value in your sport? Why?

12. How would you deal with a situation in which a supercritical parent is affecting a player's performance?

13. How can coaches use a player's individual goals as a positive factor in coaching?

14. What kinds of information would you include in a notebook, in addition to what is listed in this chapter?

15. What would you include on an agenda for a team clinic?

16. What are the three basic considerations to follow when purchasing equipment?

17. Interpret this statement: "The harder I work the luckier I get."

18. Ideally, physicals should be given by an athlete's family doctor. Why?

19. On what should a particular sport's budget be based?

20. What is the best way to prevent problems from arising over family vacation time and practice for a team?

21. Interpret the saying "Chance favors the prepared man."

22. When should coaches begin making plans for the next season? Explain.

10

Chapter 9 presented a number of ideas for long-range planning during the off-season, which covers a period of many months. This chapter deals with the short period right before practice begins.

During this time you need to finalize as many of your preseason plans and deliberations as possible so you can be well organized for the beginning of practice. It is to your advantage to make as many decisions as you can before you meet the team for the opening of preseason practice.

Although most coaches are hard workers, there is a big difference between working hard and working smart. Avoid making work for yourself and staff merely to be busy or seemingly organized, but do whatever is necessary to make your program successful.

Consider this anecdote:

> A factory worker injured at work was sent to the clinic next door for medical attention.
>
> He walked into a beautiful, antiseptically clean white room. No one was there, but there were two doors. One had a sign on it that said Cash; the other had a sign that said Insurance.
>
> He went through the Insurance door and found himself in another beautiful, antiseptically clean white room. No one was there, but there were two doors with signs on them. One said Internal Injuries; the other said External Injuries.
>
> He went through the door marked External Injuries and found himself in a room just like the first two. The signs on the doors said Life Threatening and Non-Life Threatening.
>
> He went through the Non-Life Threatening door and found himself out in an alley near the factory entrance.
>
> He walked in, and the boss said, "Glad you are back. What happened?" The worker said, "Nothing, but they sure are organized."

Be careful to avoid falling into a similar trap of a lot of organization with little or no results.

STAFF MEETINGS

If you are a head coach with no assistants, every decision regarding the team is yours to make. If more than one coach is involved, schedule a staff meeting before the beginning of practice. Depending on the sport, the number of coaches, and how well you are organized, staff meetings can require just a part of one day, several days, or the better part of several weeks.

At these preseason meetings you present ideas and plans and encourage the assistant coaches to question, challenge, offer other ideas, and, finally, reach some agreements. Rarely, if ever, will everyone on a staff agree on every point; consequently, final decisions reflect a series of compromises made by the staff. After everyone has had an opportunity to speak, you, as the head coach, must cast the deciding vote, and the staff has to understand this fact.

President Harry Truman was fond of telling the story of how, during the Civil War, Abraham Lincoln's entire cabinet voted "no" on a crucial agenda item. When they finished, Lincoln said, "I vote yes, therefore the motion passes."

The first purpose of a staff meeting is for you to reaffirm your views of coaching. Doing so serves as a review and reminder for the assistant coaches who have been on the staff and as guidelines for the new ones. It also gives everyone a sense of direction in carrying out coaching duties during a season. The head coach's beliefs are also important because they set boundaries within which each coach must work (specifically in regard to the athletes), the attitude toward winning and losing, the way the program will be run, and the way coaches should conduct themselves at practice, among other things.

Once this is clear, the entire staff will feel more comfortable, simply because they understand what you believe in and the way the program is to be conducted. Each coach can then determine the best way to carry out individual responsibilities within this framework.

A Short Course in Human Relations
The 6 most important words are:
   "I admit I made a mistake."
The 5 most important words are:
   "I am proud of you."
The 4 most important words are:
   "What is your opinion?"
The 3 most important words are:
   "If you please."
The 2 most important words are:
   "Thank You."
The 1 most important word is:
   "We."
   —Author Unknown

GOALS

The next order of business is to establish and clarify goals for the season. In the business world this is called *management by objectives*. In athletics we can refer to it as *coaching by objectives*. These goals or objectives can be directed to the overall program, the athletes themselves, the season, and the coaches. The important thing is that the staff agrees with and supports this exercise.

Figures 10.1 and 10.2 illustrate just two of any number of techniques that can be used as teaching aids before, during, and after a season.

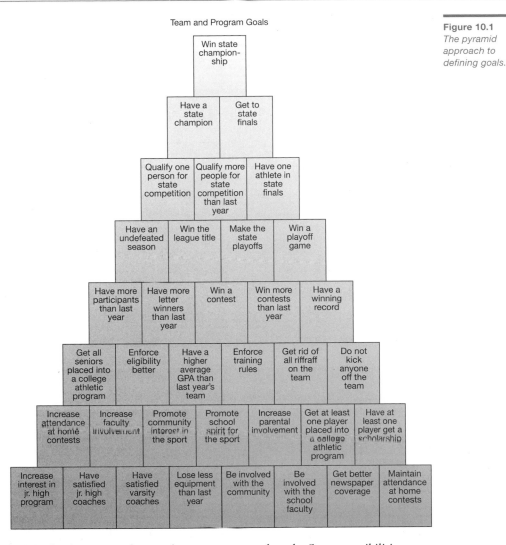

Team and Program Goals

Figure 10.1
*The pyramid
approach to
defining goals.*

It is also important for coaches to set personal goals. Some possibilities are:

- Be more positive.

- Be more patient.

- Do a better job of teaching.

- Give more youngsters a chance to play.

- Do a better job of preparing the players for each contest.

- Have a plan for everything.

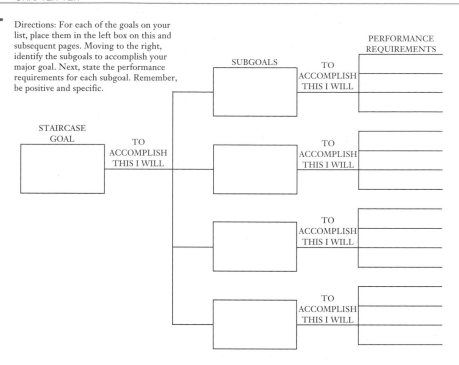

Figure 10.2
Staircase for goal-setting.

Directions: For each of the goals on your list, place them in the left box on this and subsequent pages. Moving to the right, identify the subgoals to accomplish your major goal. Next, state the performance requirements for each subgoal. Remember, be positive and specific.

- Pay more attention to the benchwarmers.

- Get the athletes in top physical condition, and maintain that level all season long.

- Learn to recognize individual differences and ways to deal with them.

- Set a positive example for the athletes.

- Do everything possible to help all youngsters achieve their maximum potential.

- Be a better coach than I was the year before.

As mentioned in Chapter 9, all athletes should also have identified goals for themselves and the team before the beginning of the season. With any luck, their goals, at least for the team, and those of the coaching staff will be similar.

Unfortunately some coaches overlook this aspect of planning by simply assuming that they and the athletes expect the same thing out of the season. The coaches therefore decide on team goals themselves. This can be a big mistake. What matters most is what the athletes want to accomplish or expect to accomplish. They are going to play the game, not you. If there are significant differences, you will therefore need to plan some meeting time with the players in an attempt to resolve whatever the differences are. Failing to do so could mean that the coaches and players will operate at cross-purposes, which will likely lead to disaster.

It is highly unlikely that a list of objectives for one coach or player will be exactly like the list of another. The point is that every coach or coaching staff should develop a list of objectives. Coaching by objectives will help everyone know exactly where the team is going and why. Setting goals does take time and thought, but it certainly should make a season run more smoothly and make coaches more confident in formulating plans.

Goals can also serve as an evaluation tool. At the end of the season you can see whether the goals that were established at the beginning of the season were accomplished. If they were not, it is important to try to figure out why. This should help in planning for the next year.

STAFF CLINIC

During the off-season you will have an opportunity to attend one or more coaching clinics, to do some reading about coaching, to meet with other coaches, or possibly to visit a college campus to observe practice and talk to the coaches. Not everyone on a staff will be able to do all of these things, but a program will certainly benefit from any new ideas shared with the entire staff. If there are new coaches in the group, they also need to learn more about the existing program (terminology, practice procedures, and other important matters). The easiest way to arrange for this information exchange is to conduct a coaching clinic for the staff.

For efficiency, all this information should be gathered from the entire staff, put on paper, duplicated, and passed out before the meeting. No item or idea is too insignificant to be included, regardless of its origin or of the sport involved. Some pertinent idea from a baseball clinic (related to motivation or discipline, for example) could be of value to a volleyball coach.

You and your coaches do not need to agree with every point covered at this clinic. What is important is to know what others believe and why, which provides a means for you to reevaluate what you and your staff believe. Of course, if some of this information comes from a coach whose team you will be competing against, you had better pay attention. Your agenda may also trigger ideas in your staff that will benefit your program.

COACHING ASSIGNMENTS

Before the staff clinic, you should have determined each coach's specific assignment for the season. As the size of a staff increases, so does the importance of clarifying additional duties and responsibilities for each coach. The first step is to make a master list of every item that must be covered.

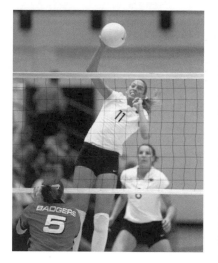

Coaches can then volunteer for these responsibilities or be assigned to them. The list should be put in writing and posted on the office bulletin board. This reduces the chance that something important will be left undone because everyone thought someone else was going to take care of it. Figure 10.3 lists the responsibilities for a staff of eight people. Coach A is the head coach; coaches G and H are the newest on the staff.

The staff scribe is responsible for taking notes at every staff meeting and seeing to it that everyone on the staff receives a copy. These notes serve as a permanent record of what is discussed and decided. This record is important for a high school staff whose members are teaching a full schedule every day or working elsewhere and who have a lot of other things on their minds. And since high school coaches do not have time to meet during the day, or may not see other members of the staff until practice, the minutes serve as a reference and help prevent misunderstandings regarding what was said or what decisions were made.

Figure 10.3 lists public relations and several other items for every coach, because these items cannot be delegated and are responsibilities of every coach. One coach should always be designated to represent the staff at faculty meetings

during the season. This practice keeps the principal happy and will be noticed by the faculty. A staff that takes the initiative on this matter can avoid the possibility that other teachers will grumble about coaches not attending faculty meetings. It might also keep the principal from insisting that every coach be present at these meetings, forcing you to cancel practices. Generally, as long as the principal is satisfied that the information is getting back to the coaches, this arrangement should be satisfactory.

In addition to overall assignments for the season, daily assignments and game-time assignments should be clarified and put in writing. Once again, this type of organization helps eliminate confusion and keeps important details from falling through the cracks.

At some point during the days preceding the opening game or meet of the season, the coaches, their husbands and wives, boyfriends or girlfriends, should set aside time for a picnic, progressive dinner, or other social gathering. This is an opportunity for everyone to get acquainted with the new

COACHES' ASSIGNMENTS

Coach A

Morale and discipline	Film grading	Team pictures
Offensive game play	Scouts and scouting	Banquet
Defensive game play	reports	Parent night procedure
Clinic notes	Managers	Practice plans
Checklist	Review periodicals	Film study room
Public relations	Notebooks	Orientation

Coach B

Defensive game play	Press box	Practice plans
Offensive game play	Staff scribe	Orientation
Clinic notes	Review periodicals	Coaching clinics
Public relations	Coaches' preseason	Summer jobs
Promotional gimmicks	picnic	Summer conditioning
Weight training	Office decoration	Projector
Film grading	Personnel board	

Coach C

Offensive game play	Film grading	Practice plans
Defensive game play	Equipment issue	Orientation
Clinic notes	Managers	Coaching clinics
Checklist	Checklist for managers	Summer jobs
Accident and illness cards	Weight training	Summer conditioning
Public relations	Review periodicals	Grade card check

Coach D

Clinic notes	Tires	Cafeteria duty
Checklist	Practice plans	Classroom assignments
Public relations	Orientation	Meetings
Review periodicals	Coaching clinics	Grade card check
Physical cards	Summer jobs	Scout
Eligibility	Summer conditioning	Weight training

Coach E

Checklist	Weight training	Coaching clinics
Clinic notes	Office decoration	Summer jobs
Public relations	Personnel board	Summer conditioning
Promotional gimmicks	Music	Grade card check
Review periodicals	Practice plans	Film exchange
Training room	Orientation	Eligibility

Coach F

Clinic notes	Review periodicals	Summer jobs
Checklist	Notebooks	Summer conditioning
Public relations	Practice plans	Grade card check
Drill file	Orientation	Scout
Library	Coaching clinics	

Coach G

Scout	Roster	Representative to
Physical cards	Accident illness cards	teacher's meetings
Eligibility		

Coach H

Emergency file	Scout	Duplicator
Socks		

Figure 10.3
Sample coaching assignments.

staff members and to involve the spouses or special friends in the coaching family. If staff meetings take several days or evenings, a social event with the whole group offers a good break in the routine just before practice begins. It is at this time that after-game parties or other get-togethers can be planned if you think having them is important.

PRACTICE PROCEDURES AND POLICIES

In the interest of order, discipline, and efficiency, it is essential that all policies dealing with practice be carefully thought out and explained thoroughly to the athletes. It doesn't make any difference how many years some of your athletes have been on the team; every year is a new year, and you cannot afford to skip over any detail. Explaining policies will eliminate the problem of athletes violating them because nothing was explicitly spelled out for them. We said it before: Do not assume anything where youngsters are concerned.

Here are a few items that athletes must know about before the first practice begins. Certainly there are others specific to a particular sport:

1. Practice times

2. Practice uniforms or dress

3. Length of warm-up

4. Type of warm-up

5. Equipment problems

6. Types of drills

7. Holiday practices

8. Excuses from practice because of injury or illness

9. Reporting late to practice

10. Foul weather practice procedures for outdoor sports

11. Use of bulletin boards for announcements

12. Conduct during practice

13. Visitors at practice

14. Injury care during practice—especially with only one coach

15. Transportation to and from practice

16. Taping time

17. Protection of valuables in locker room

18. Excuses from practice for other commitments

19. Where to report for practice after getting dressed

20. Squad meetings—time and place

21. How soon to clear the locker room after the day's practice ends

22. Use of training room

23. Language (swearing)

24. Locker-room discipline

25. Skipping practice

Setting Practice Times

Agreeing on practice times and procedures is complicated only when the number of coaches and athletes involved is such that facilities and space become a problem. That fact that practice for sports like football, soccer, field hockey, and cross-country begins before the school year creates additional concerns for the coaching staff. Some of the problems that must be recognized as affecting two-a-day practice sessions in August are heat and humidity, family vacations, members of the staff attending graduate school, transportation for athletes in rural areas, and the work responsibilities of athletes who live on farms.

During the school year, practice times are not as great a consideration (except for holidays) because practices are usually held immediately after school or in the evening. If a particular facility is overcrowded, you could find yourself holding some practice sessions in the morning before school begins.

Creating a Depth Chart

A depth chart is a useful organizational tool, particularly when large numbers of players are involved. One of its biggest advantages is its efficiency: You won't waste time in practice by picking out a team or players one by one to do something. Having a depth chart is also a good way to make sure the number of people per position is fairly balanced. If you know your players and know what you want done, creating a depth chart is not too difficult.

The first step is to write all players' names down beside the position they played in the preceding season or the position they indicated they want to play when they filled out the questionnaire described in Chapter 9.

The staff's next job is to create a depth chart, making sure that every letter winner is listed somewhere on the first team, if at all possible. Doing so some-times means changing positions for someone, and that is where evaluation comes into play. But it must be done; otherwise some letter winners will be listed behind other letter winners while other positions on the first team will be assigned to inexperienced players. Unless you are blessed with an incredible number of talented athletes, keeping players at a specific position is a waste of talent and playing experience. Since the staff has determined what the team will be designed to do, changing players' positions to fit the overall scheme should not be difficult. When such changes are made, however, it is important to talk to each player involved to explain why the change was made, to prevent morale problems.

As the depth chart is being completed, deciding who the best five, nine, or eleven players are becomes the primary challenge confronting the staff. When this list is completed, these players should be assigned a position on the first team. It makes no difference how many people sign up for a team—there will always be five best, eleven best, and so on. It is your job to try to anticipate who these people are before practice begins. After these people and the letter winners have been assigned positions, the other positions should normally be filled by seniors who have game experience, then juniors, then sophomores.

Many coaches believe that after letter winners have filled certain positions, the seniors who have not lettered should get first chance at the open positions in the lineup. The reasoning is that normally the seniors bring some playing experience to the team, and generally a senior team stands a better chance of winning than one made up of younger players. Another reason for using seniors is to give them a fair chance to show whether they can do the job. In many cases they have been working hard for the team for several years, and now they deserve this chance. Whether they make it or not depends on them and the persons listed behind them on the depth chart. If a senior is a competitor, he or she will rise to this challenge and make a real contribution during the season.

Keep in mind, the primary purpose of a depth chart is for organization. The players need to understand this at the outset. They must also understand that their initial position or place on the team as listed on the depth chart is no guarantee that they will remain there and that responsibility for creating changes in the lineup rests with those listed on the second or third teams. If they prove to the coaches that they are better than the players listed ahead of them, they will move up on the depth chart.

To ensure that no one is overlooked or is in the wrong position, every youngster on the depth chart should be evaluated by you or the coaching staff after each preseason practice session. Changes in the lineup, if they are warranted, should occur at that time. This evaluation provides continuous motivation for everyone on the squad, including those listed on the first team. The players should be aware that this evaluation is ongoing. The "down-the-liners" need to know they aren't being overlooked, ignored, or—worse yet—forgotten.

Depending on the type of team, the number of positions to be filled, and the number of youngsters trying out, a depth chart can be made of:

- A manila folder

- A large sheet of poster board

- A plain piece of plywood or similar material

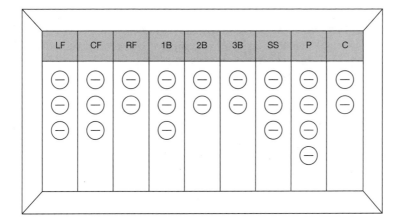

Figure 10.4
Sample depth chart.

- A permanent "board" painted in the school colors and mounted on the wall of the coaches' office

- Any other piece of material on which names can be attached with tape or tags so that they can be moved easily without damaging the chart

Figure 10.4 shows a depth chart for a baseball or softball team. If the chart is made of wood, screw hooks or nails can be put into the board under each position. A round key tag, available in any stationery store, can be used for each player. Such tags are easily hung on the hooks and easily moved. A shop teacher might be willing to make one of these boards for you, or allow a student to make one, thereby saving you valuable time. Someone on the team, a manager or a parent, might also be able and willing to make one.

Without organization of this type, initial practice sessions can be chaos and can remain so until the team shakes down and positions are assigned. By creating a depth chart ahead of time, you save valuable time and prevent a great deal of confusion.

Preparing the Preseason Master Schedule

Another important tool is the master schedule for every day from the first practice to the first game, meet, or event. The first step in drawing up a master schedule is to list every aspect of the sport that must be covered in order to get the players ready for the first competition. Each item should then be put on a calendar that includes every practice session up to the opening of the season. It is absolutely essential that this schedule be adhered to each day, regardless of the players' progress, if they are to be ready for the opening of the season.

When you develop each practice plan based on the master schedule, the athletes will have been exposed to every phase of the sport necessary for the opening of the season. Naturally, they won't master everything immediately, but by reviewing each day, and by continuing to practice on all their shortcomings for the rest of the season, you will eventually resolve most problems. Most coaches find that trying to continue to teach many new things once a season has begun is not as satisfactory as doing the bulk of the teaching in preseason. The rest of the season can be devoted to polishing the rough spots.

Preparing this schedule is really nothing more than budgeting the limited preseason time to make certain all facets of the sport are covered. Sometimes coaches become concerned because the players aren't executing a skill properly, so they continue to teach that particular skill at the expense of some other phase of the sport. As a result, they begin to run out of time and at the last minute have to concentrate a lot of teaching into a short period. This is poor planning, a poor teaching method, and rarely satisfactory.

Avoiding Electrical Storms

Be wary of storms if your team practices or competes outdoors in the spring or summer. Thunderstorms can and do crop up very suddenly. When they do, get your athletes indoors at once. Do not wait for that first bolt of lightning. There are far too many recorded instances of lightning striking athletes or coaches because someone failed to exercise good judgment. No practice or event can be that important.

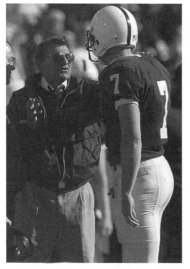

Preventing Heat Exhaustion and Heatstroke

Heat exhaustion and heatstroke are the only preventable catastrophes in athletics. The ultimate tragedy in athletics, death from heatstroke, is not an accident. Because it is preventable and totally predictable, its occurrence is inexcusable.

Heatstroke is a major health hazard among athletes who begin preseason practice in hot weather. It can occur at night as well as during daylight, and it can happen to distance runners, soccer players, and wrestlers as well football players. However, its incidence is far greater in football players primarily because the uniform is a very effective heat trap.

Coaches should begin to pay attention to heatstroke prevention in early summer. You must impress on athletes the importance of getting their bodies used to performing in hot weather. It is foolhardy to expect youngsters, some of whom spend most of a summer lounging around swimming pools or living in air-conditioned homes, to begin full-scale practices in August, ready to cope with abruptly increased demands on their bodies.

Youngsters can normally become acclimated to practice conditions in 10 to 14 days. Acclimatization can be brought about by gradually increasing the intensity of practices throughout this period. An athlete becomes acclimated through running, agility drills, conditioning drills, the physical demands of practice sessions themselves, and increased liquid intake. A number of liquids are suitable for use during this process, including water. While water is still satisfactory and less expensive than commercially prepared drinks, the prepared liquids have some benefits not found in plain water.

In preventing heat illness, you need to consider the practice uniform, especially for football. Because one of the ways a body dissipates heat is through the skin, it is important that as much bare skin as possible be exposed. Knee-length stockings should not be allowed. The jersey should be short-sleeved and of mesh material. Football helmets should be removed at every opportunity. Since a great deal of body heat escapes through the head, wearing a helmet is similar to putting a lid on a chimney. A football player should never be encouraged or permitted to wear any kind of "sweatsuit" under his pads as a means of speeding up weight loss. Doing so is extremely dangerous. The player would lose only body fluid, not fat, increasing the chances of dehydration and heat illness.

To predict heat exhaustion and heatstroke, pay close attention to temperature and humidity. Weather information can easily be obtained from local weather reports. Figure 10.5 outlines practice guidelines for certain combinations of humidity and temperature.

During practice, athletes should take rest and water breaks at least every half hour, with no limit on fluid or ice intake. Remember, it is impossible to harm an athlete—externally or internally—with water. Coaches should also drink fluids during these breaks, since they too are susceptible to heat illness, and they should set a good example for their players.

PRACTICE GUIDELINES		
Humidity	**Temperature**	**Guidelines**
Under 70%	Under 80°	No limitation
Under 70%	80–90°	Full practice; water players; watch weight loss
Over 70%	80–90°	Shorts with minimum pads; frequent rest
Under 70%	90–100°	Change wet shirts
Over 70%	90–100°	Exercise caution
Over 95%	Over 100°	NO PRACTICE

Figure 10.5
Practice guidelines for preventing heat illness.

AILMENT	SIGNS AND SYMPTOMS	TREATMENT

Heat Cramps	Muscle twitching and cramps
	Muscle spasms occur in some cases
	Muscles most commonly affected:
	   those of arms, legs, and
	   abdomen
		1. Apply firm pressure with hands, or gently massage the cramped muscle.
		2. Give the victim sips of salt water (1 teaspoon of salt per glass): half a glass every 15 minutes for one hour.
		3. If symptoms persist or worsen, medical referral is indicated.

Heat Exhaustion	Pale or gray skin that is clammy
	Profuse sweating
	Fatigue and weakness (possibly
	   faintness)
	Loss of coordination
	Mental dullness or
	   light-headedness
	Elevation of body temperature up
	   to 103°F
	Slow pulse
		1. Give the victim sips of salt water (1 teaspoon of salt per glass): half a glass every 15 minutes for one hour.
		2. Have the victim lie down and elevate feet 8 to 12 inches.
		3. Loosen victim's clothing.
		4. Apply cool, wet cloths and fan victim or remove to a cool environment.
		5. If victim vomits, cease giving fluids and transport to hospital where an intravenous salt solution can be provided.
		6. Advise victim to avoid exercise and heat stress for several days.

Heat Stroke	Hot, reddish skin Little or no sweating Headache Loss of consciousness Rapid pulse Elevation of body temperature to 105°–106°F	1. Take immediate action to cool the victim, but take care to prevent chilling once temperature drops below 102°F. 2. Remove clothing and repeatedly sponge victim's skin with cool water or rubbing alcohol, apply cold packs, or place victim in a tub of cold water. 3. Use fans or air conditioners to promote cooling. 4. Do not give stimulants. 5. Seek medical assistance immediately.

Salt tablets are *not* a prevention or a remedy for heat illness. Coated or uncoated, they are of no value and can in fact be harmful. When taken without water, they can produce intense gastric and intestinal irritation and enhance the toxic level of an incipient heatstroke victim.

There are three degrees of heat illness: heat cramps, heat exhaustion, and heatstroke. When symptoms appear, immediate first aid must be given to prevent heatstroke. Warning signs of the onset of a heat–related problem can be observed by coaches. Some of them, along with American Red Cross–recommended first-aid treatments, are described in Figure 10.6.

Heat-related problems can be a matter of life or death. One of your goals must be the elimination of heat illness as even a possibility in your athletic program.

TRAINING RULES

At one time, training rules were as much a part of sport as the equipment a team used. However, the trend in many locations of the country today is to water down rules or eliminate them altogether. Many coaches do not establish training rules because they say they are difficult to enforce. Furthermore, these coaches say that high school boys and girls are old enough to decide for themselves whether they should drink and smoke, among other things. In lieu of official training rules, some coaches will discuss the subject with their team and hope youngsters will refrain from using alcohol, tobacco, and other drugs.

Some people believe that coaches, regardless of their college major, are also health educators and have an inescapable obligation to teach youngsters the importance of maintaining a strong, healthy body. To ignore educating youngsters about the harmful effects of alcohol, tobacco, and other drugs and about the good effects of proper nutrition is to ignore an important obligation of coaching. The ease with which youngsters can obtain cigarettes, liquor, and other drugs compounds the problem. Training rules that are established and enforced can do a lot toward preventing youngsters from developing bad habits in their formative teenage years.

If you or the team decides to establish training rules, it is equally important to determine possible penalties for violating the rules. Any offender, regardless of position, ability, or any other factor, must pay some price for breaking a training rule. Otherwise training rules will be totally unenforceable. It might be a good idea to keep penalties purposely vague at this point. Doing so allows you a lot of leeway in dealing with a rules violation rather than finding yourself boxed in a corner. Contrary to what some believe, observing reasonable training rules is not a sacrifice for an athlete. When boys or girls learn to avoid habits that can harm their health, that can hardly be termed a sacrifice.

More often than not, parents appreciate athletic training rules, because such rules give them another tool in their own efforts to prevent a son or daughter from drinking, smoking, or pursuing other bad habits. Concerned parents usually see to it, as best they can, that the rules are followed.

The argument as to whether or not smoking, drinking, or using other drugs hinders a high school student's athletic accomplishments is relatively immaterial. Prohibiting these behaviors is a matter of mental discipline and concern for a healthy body, both of which are important ingredients in sport and in life. What better reason could there be to help youngsters avoid these habits?

One final point—put the rules in writing and have each athlete sign them, and possibly parents as well. Doing so can prevent some serious problems later on.

DISCIPLINE

The purpose of discipline is not to punish but to correct. You, your staff, and the players all need to understand this fact.

There are two other reasons for discussing this topic at staff meetings. First is the need to maintain discipline in every phase of the program where youngsters are concerned. Second, every effort must be made to ensure consistency among coaches. This consistency applies not only to discipline among the athletes, but also to coaches' self-discipline, practice discipline, and game-time discipline. When there is strong discipline, each member of the team knows what to expect from the coaching staff. Overzealous disciplinarians and weak disciplinarians on a staff must compromise and agree on the kinds of discipline necessary. Such agreement gives the staff solidarity and consistency in this important area and lessens the chances of any coach being labeled an iron hand or a soft touch.

CONDUCT OF PLAYERS AND COACHES

The way coaches and players conduct themselves during practice sessions, in the locker room, before and during an athletic contest, and while traveling to and from an athletic contest is very important. The behavior you expect is a direct reflection of your beliefs. You should make sure that all your coaches and players know what is expected of them and how they can do their best to make the season successful and to keep from embarrassing themselves, the team, the school, or you. Putting your expectations in writing is recommended in order to make sure there are no misunderstandings between parents, athletes, and you in this matter.

Figure 10.7 is an example of one way (a "contract") to deal with the expectations for athletes.

Most head coaches tell athletes what is expected of them, but they often neglect to do the same thing with their staff. As a head coach, you owe it to your coaches to let them know what you expect of them, not only in coaching, but also in their behavior around the players. Your expectations need to be clear before any problems occur—not after.

COACHES' PERSONAL APPEARANCE

A great deal of research has been done over the years regarding personal appearance and the impression it has on others. The clear message that has emerged is that your personal appearance does affect those around you, for better or for worse.

Figure 10.7
*Athlete's team
membership
contract.*

CONTRACT
APPLICATION FOR ATHLETIC TEAM MEMBERSHIP

I. Pledge and Declaration

A. I, _____, promise to abide by all the rules and regulations set up by the school district, the school, and the coaches. I will attend practice faithfully and work as hard as I possibly can to learn the fundamentals and to develop the skills necessary for becoming a championship player. I will always conduct myself in a manner that will be a credit to my family, my school, my community, and myself. I will try to maximize the interest of others in sports, to help players younger than myself, to encourage fair play at all times, and to respect the judgment and advice of all personnel associated with the school and the team.

B. I am proud to be an American and a participant in the school's athletic program. In appreciation of these privileges I will strive to prove myself as a worthy citizen and athlete. My goal will be to assist the team in being one of which everyone can be proud—a team of *Champions* and a *Championship Team.*

II. Standards and Understandings

A. I hereby agree to:
1. Be neat and clean and have my hair above my ears and collar.
2. Not have evening dates prior to practice or game days.
3. Be home by 10:00 PM and in bed early before school days.
4. Never miss a practice, unless sick. If sick I will notify one of the coaches.
5. Not be tardy for practice.
6. Be modest in attire. (Good appearance is important since athletes are always on parade.)
7. Not curse.
8. Display good sportsmanship at all times.
9. Be courteous to officials.
10. Never fake an injury.
11. Not smoke or use tobacco products.
12. Not drink alcoholic beverages or use any type of illegal drug.
13. Keep in top physical condition (eating properly, working out in the weight room, etc.).

B. I understand that:
1. If I fail to keep my pledge, if I exhibit behavior inconsistent with my above declaration, or if I do not observe all of the foregoing standards, I will be disciplined or dropped from the team (at the discretion of the coach and the athletic director).
2. Neither the school district (including the school) nor any of its employees (including coaches) can be held liable for any injury I may sustain or be held responsible for the payment of any medical costs I may incur (including hospital, doctor, or pharmacy charges).

_____   _____
Date   Candidate's Signature

III. Parental Request, Acknowledgment, and Certification

A. I, the undersigned, hereby request that my son/daughter, _____, be permitted to participate in the sport of _____.

B. I acknowledge my recognition and acceptance of the condition of team membership that neither the school district nor any of its employees can be held liable for any injury my son/daughter may sustain or be responsible for any medical costs that my be incurred by them.

C. I certify that I hold insurance that will pay any medical costs that may be associated with _____'s participation in the sport of _____.

_____   _____
Date   Parent's Signature

Courtesy of Coach John McKissick, Summerville High School, S.C.

> . . . Garments that will lend dignity
> to his work.
> —Exodus:28, *The Living Bible*

Because coaches, especially, teach many lessons through personal example, how you look is important. Appearance applies not only to how you dress for school, practice, or athletic events but also your physical condition. For example, it would be difficult to teach athletes proper nutrition and appreciation for fitness if you were dramatically overweight or delivered your lectures while smoking a cigarette.

If you insist on certain standards of dress for practice, for travel, and for competition, you should follow the same policy. There is little question that dress also affects the way a person behaves. If your school designates one day a year as "dress down" day, take a careful look at the behavior on that day; you will probably find the school in an uproar. Likewise, if you permit your athletes to come to practice sloppily dressed or dressed like clowns, they will probably act that way.

On the other hand, dressing appropriately creates an entirely different atmosphere—one that is positive and businesslike and therefore tends to be more productive. Here are some additional reasons for attention to personal appearance:

- Unity in dress gives the appearance that there is also unity in thought and purpose within the staff.

- Attention to your own personal appearance makes it easier to impress the same thing on a team.

- A neat, clean coaching uniform is an example of attention to detail, which is a lesson members of a team need to learn to be successful.

- A professional appearance adds "class" to the coaching staff.

- A staff that dresses like professionals tends to act more professionally in dealing with the members of a team.

- A professional appearance enhances the image of the coaches.

SCOUTING ASSIGNMENTS

The preseason coaches' meeting is also a good time to make scouting assignments (if doing so is appropriate to your sport). If the decision has been made to scout, the number of times each team will be scouted and which coach will scout which team should be listed on a master schedule posted in the coaches' office for the duration of the season.

Each coach is responsible for finding out the location of the games to be scouted and for double-checking the dates and starting times. Scouting passes are normally handled by the athletic director or faculty manager. If the sport is one for which games are filmed, and a film exchange has been worked out with the next opponent, the scout should also be sure to make arrangements for the exchange.

Scouting forms should be revised and reviewed before the season begins. It is a good idea to keep the forms in a central file for easy access.

CUTTING PLAYERS

One of the most difficult decisions facing a coaching staff is whether or not players should be cut from a team. The question is not so difficult if coaches feel little empathy for the young people. But if you look at the situation assuming that it is your daughter or son who is being cut, you discover an entirely new point of view.

To boys and girls who have grown up dreaming of the day when they can participate on the high school team, being cut from the squad can be extremely traumatic. The disappointment and sense of failure can be so severe that it sometimes affects their personalities, behavior, and work in school. The phenomenon of athletic exclusion can have far-reaching effects that we do not totally comprehend.

Ideally, no one should be cut from a team unless it is for disciplinary reasons or for safety. The ultimate in absurdity is a policy of cutting youngsters who try out for junior high school teams. This is a stage for teaching skills and creating interest. It is not an occasion for junior high coaches to pick the high school varsity, which is basically what is happening when they cut youngsters. Cuts at this level are usually for the convenience of the coach and for no other legitimate reason. Having too many people and not enough equipment or space is not a reason for cutting at the junior high level—they are excuses.

There is no proof that daily practice sessions for junior high school athletes will make them better performers as seniors in high school. Likewise, there is no proof that a two-hour practice in junior high school is better for youngsters than a one-hour session. Therefore, if space or equipment seems to be a problem, there is no reason a squad cannot be broken down into small, workable groups for practice purposes. In this way, several groups can practice for short periods each day after school or on alternating days.

The purpose of junior high school athletics should be to give every youngster a chance to participate and to develop a love of sport. Only under special circumstances should junior high school coaches be permitted or directed to cut their squads. Winning is fun, but it should never become the number one priority in junior high school athletics.

Young, ambitious coaches tend to be quick about picking out the best junior high athletes and cutting all the rest. They are eager to win in order to demonstrate their superior ability as coaches. Therefore the head varsity coach must make sure the junior high coaches know the priorities of the program. Every experienced coach knows that the smallest, meekest, and most awkward 12-year-old youngster could easily grow up to be the finest varsity athlete of the senior class—that is, if the youngster is allowed to participate and mature without the threat of being cut during junior high school. The junior high coach who can look at a group of youngsters and predict with 100 percent accuracy which ones will become varsity athletes has not yet been born. And when junior high school coaches make cuts, that is effectively what they are doing.

On the high school level it would seem that the only justifiable reasons for cutting youngsters are (a) serious disciplinary problems, (b) attitude problems that are having or could have adverse effects on the team, and (c) the possibility of serious injury because of a gross lack of size or motor skills.

There is one other possibility to consider in cutting a team. When space, facilities, and number of coaches are limited, having unskilled upperclassmen on the roster can be detrimental to the team. A junior who has never played tennis and decides to try out for the team might fit this category. When such people take turns in practice, they are using up valuable practice time for the highly skilled performers, thereby hampering their development. Seniors who sit on the sidelines can become unhappy, which can cause problems too.

There does not appear to be a simple, clear-cut solution to the issue of cutting players. As a general rule, if circumstances dictate a policy of cutting, it should not occur in junior high school or on the freshman and sophomore levels. By the time the players become juniors, they should have had several years to demonstrate some characteristics necessary for being athletes. If they have not done so, and if in the opinion of the staff cuts must be made, this might be the time.

You will also discover that, as time goes on, some youngsters will elect not to try out for the team another year for a variety of reasons. Doing so is fine as long as they don't quit once a season begins. In effect they have cut themselves.

If you decide to make cuts, announce this to the squad at the first meeting you have with them. They should also know when the cuts will be made, how many will be made, and the criteria involved. This message should also be made clear to the parents and can easily be included in a preseason parent clinic.

In fairness, you should have the decency to meet with each individual being cut and carefully explain why the action is being taken. This task is never easy, nor is it pleasant. But the practice of putting a list on the locker-room bulletin board and then retreating to the safety of your office is cowardly, and it is not consistent with the image coaches should try to project.

Many coaches adopt the attitude that if practices are hard enough work, people will quit the team on their own, thereby eliminating the need for cutting anyone. There might be some truth to this belief. The biggest error lies in the fact that an entire squad could pay the price of too much work over a long season because you cannot or will not make a decision about cuts. The whole question deserves careful thought and discussion on the part of the entire staff. The final decision should be based on a thorough consideration of all the ramifications and alternatives. Once again, the time to do so is before the season begins, so your athletes will be aware of your policy and the reasons behind it.

TRAVEL CONDUCT

Every interscholastic athletic team travels to away events. If the trip is short, teams sometimes dress at school and travel to the game in uniform. For some teams this is impractical, regardless of the distance, so a decision must be made as to how the team will dress for the trip. Some teams are provided with blazers, some are told to wear dress clothes, and still others wear bluejeans and sweatshirts. Again, this attire reflects the personal desire of the head coach, but keep in mind that a team does represent a school and community, and their personal appearance will make a positive or negative impression on people from another community.

Another thing you need to clarify is the way the players are to conduct themselves on the trip. Nothing can be more embarrassing to a school than to have members of a team hanging out of the windows of a schoolbus shouting wisecracks and obscenities or just being obnoxious. Some coaches of girls' teams, especially male coaches, often think such behavior will not be a problem with the girls because they will be "ladylike." But girls can be just as obnoxious and foul-mouthed as boys.

Criticism regarding such behavior will always fall on the coach, and rightfully so. Consequently, you must establish rules of conduct for away games beforehand to prevent embarrassment for everyone concerned.

STUDENT HELPERS

In order to help student aides (managers, trainers, etc.) help you and the team, you should write out their duties and responsibilities and post them in the appropriate areas. If you do so, the youngsters will not have to run to you all the time to ask a lot of questions; they can simply refer to the list posted where it is convenient and readily accessible to them.

PREGAME AND POSTGAME PROCEDURES

Preseason is also the time to decide on the procedures to be followed for pregame warm-up at home and away, at halftime (if this is appropriate), and after the event.

The value of pregame warm-up is questionable, but it is traditional and probably has a settling effect on a team. Whatever a staff decides to do before the beginning of a contest, it must be planned to prevent last-minute confusion.

Halftime plans usually consist of getting to the locker room or sidelines quickly and budgeting the time so that all needs can be taken care of. The actual conduct of a coach at halftime depends on the situation and must be given a great deal of thought. You should have a general idea of what to say when the team is behind, ahead, tied, playing well, or playing poorly. Experience is the best teacher in this situation.

Postgame planning must include what to do when a team loses and what to do when it wins. Most coaches know what to do when the team is victorious but give little thought to how to conduct themselves in a locker-room atmosphere gloomy with defeat. You and your coaches should discuss and consider various possibilities because situations in a locker room or on a bus on the way home after a loss vary, and you must be prepared to deal with them. Remember— have a plan for everything.

The staff should also discuss plans for the day after a game. If the game is played on a day preceding a school day, postgame discussion is no problem. But it is a different matter entirely when a game is played on a Friday or Saturday.

Unless plans are made to get the team together, you probably won't see the players until after school on Monday, two or three days after the event.

If the contest was lost, some of the athletes will waste a great deal of time brooding over the loss. And if a player discovers an injury the morning after a game, you might not find out about it for several days. The time lost in treatment could delay the healing process and might prevent a youngster from competing in the next contest.

Bringing a team together the morning after a game has several advantages. Bumps, bruises, and other injuries can be cared for immediately, thereby saving valuable time in the healing process. If the team won, they will have a chance to enjoy the win a little longer with their teammates. A relaxed, informal workout can be good for morale, and if the game was taped or filmed and the development service is good, you can all take a quick look at the game films.

Most important, you can tell the squad some things about the next opponent to start them thinking ahead instead of celebrating too long or feeling bad too long—whatever the case may be. These workouts seem to make Monday practices a little easier too, because they cut down on the layoff between the game and Monday's session.

PEP RALLIES

One of the questions that should be decided early is whether to have pep rallies. For some high-visibility sports, weekly pep rallies were once as much a part of a season as the game itself and were used to give the student body an opportunity to participate, to create an atmosphere of excitement, and to develop school spirit. The effect of a pep rally on a team has always been questionable, because such rallies are usually held several hours before a game (or on the day before if the contest is on a Saturday), and any positive emotional effects on a team have usually worn off by game time.

In some schools pep rallies are no longer as integral a part of a season as they once were. Some coaches prefer not to have pep rallies at all because the emotional pitch can become so high that the players are drained by game time. It is generally felt that if a team is not being mentally prepared all week, a short pep rally on game day will not help them anyway.

However, you and the team will have to decide not only whether you want pep rallies but also, if so, how many. This information is important to the principal for scheduling purposes. The faculty also appreciate having predetermined and publicized dates so that they can plan accordingly.

Some members of the faculty resent time being taken from their classes for pep rallies. There is no way these absences can be completely avoided. If the faculty can be shown that well-planned pep rallies are a way to create unity in a school and to give the student body an opportunity to feel a part of an exciting school function, they might be more understanding and patient.

Establishing good rapport with the cheerleaders and their adviser can be of great help as well. They can hang signs and posters throughout the school, tape various materials on the players' lockers, and possibly decorate the locker room for a special game. They are usually willing to help in any way possible and are very receptive to suggestions.

AWARDS/TROPHIES

Another item on the agenda for the preseason staff meetings is awards/trophies to be given out during and after the season. Some schools have adopted policies stating that the only awards granted to athletes are letters given by the school, based on playing time in the games or points scored in meets. In other schools, awards are issued weekly as an incentive, and in some schools various awards are given to individuals at the end of the season (e.g., most valuable player or most improved player). These awards may be given by the school to players the coaches choose, or they may be given by businesses or individuals in the community.

The head coach should decide what kinds of awards are given. It is important that you not go overboard in the number of awards. Otherwise, they become gimmicks, their value is lessened, and their purpose becomes meaningless. For example, giving trophies or other awards to the most friendly athlete on the team, the athlete with the neatest uniform, or the athlete with the best form while swinging a bat, or giving ten special awards to an eleven-person team seems absurd and probably has little or no effect on points put up on the scoreboard.

It is possible that some of the value placed on awards/trophies by the athletes themselves has lessened over the years because of participation in youth sports programs. That's because in many of these activities every girl and boy is given a trophy at the conclusion of the season, just for being on the team. By the time these youngsters get to high school they might have a dozen trophies lying around gathering dust, so how important is another trophy in the whole scheme of things?

Allowing community members not directly connected with the school to pick certain players for awards has no place in high school athletics either. Often these awards are excuses for free advertising for a business, and the objectivity of the selections is always questionable. Instead of having a positive effect on a team, these awards (and also the ones given by the coaching staff) can cause bad feelings within a team and sometimes with parents. There are enough problems in coaching without adding to them by getting involved in promotional gimmicks.

Recognizing an outstanding player or two every week on the basis of game films or judgment of the staff might be the extent of in-season awards. Awards should not necessarily be anything concrete or material, but rather a form of recognition for a job well done. If athletes are properly motivated, their rewards will come from competing and playing well. Presenting a number of trophies and other awards simply leads youngsters to expect awards. Getting awards should not be an objective in athletics, nor should this idea be perpetuated.

In this same light, you might be confronted with a request to establish or accept an award or scholarship in memory of an athlete or coach. The thought behind such awards is certainly understandable, particularly when the current coaches knew the person to be honored. But there are drawbacks to such memorial awards. Generally it becomes your responsibility to select an athlete to receive this award, and doing so always presents problems. Singling out one athlete to be honored can be difficult, because there are usually several outstanding and deserving people. When new coaches join the staff, the name on the memorial award is unknown to them, so the whole exercise has little meaning. Eventually, the coaches who permitted the establishment of this award will be gone, and so will all the students who knew the individual. Then it becomes just another award that long ago lost its special significance.

Instead of an award, a permanent gift to the school in the honoree's name or a self-perpetuating scholarship could be considered. It is easy to accept the idea of special awards. But you must remember that once they are established, the athletic department will have to live with them for a long time.

DRILLS

Drills are an excellent way to teach parts of a game, so a great deal of preseason thought should be devoted to them. For many coaches, drills are the basis of most practice sessions. Setting up every practice session as a full-team scrimmage or practice game is not generally the best way to teach youngsters the fundamentals of any sport. As a matter of fact, "game play" can be a poor way to teach the fundamentals of a sport because the athletes normally concentrate on things other than executing fundamentals properly—like the score or the stopwatch.

Some coaches record drills on 5 x 7 cards and file them by category for the use of all the coaches on the staff. When several coaches are contributing to a file, it can become very worthwhile, particularly to new coaches. There are six main sources of drills: your own playing experience, books or magazine articles, clinics, visits with college coaches, your own imagination, and working at summer camps.

Drills themselves have four broad uses: for developing agility, for developing reaction, for conditioning, and for teaching. Here are fourteen guidelines for evaluating the suitability of a drill:

1. Every drill should simulate a "game" condition.

2. When possible, every drill should accomplish multiple results.

3. Every drill should have a definite purpose. The athletes should know the purpose and the correct way to perform the drill.

4. Group drills should be kept short. This could mean anywhere from one minute to a maximum of fifteen minutes (see #5).

5. Drills should have enough variety in content and time to prevent monotony and boredom.

6. Do not break the continuity of a drill to take time to correct one person. This is a tremendous waste of time.

7. Do not use your best athletes for "dummies."

8. Stack the deck: When teaching something new, arrange the drill so that the people who are to learn have a sure chance to succeed. Success breeds confidence and, ultimately, success.

9. Arrange for maximum participation. Use drills that keep everyone moving, not standing around too long waiting a turn.

10. Keep drills simple. (KISS: Keep It Simple, Stupid)

11. Use drills to focus on particular problems.

12. Use a checklist to make sure drills cover all possibilities athletes could confront in the contest.

13. Be quick, but don't be in a hurry.

14. Don't mistake activity for achievement.

One final thought regarding the use of drills is, *Repetitio est mater studiorem* (repetition is the mother of learning).

PRACTICE PLANS

Every good teacher relies on carefully prepared lesson plans. For teachers of athletics, these are practice plans, and they are a must for organization and efficiency. Practice plans should be kept on file after they have been used, not only for reference but for legal reasons. In case of a lawsuit dealing with injuries incurred during practice, coaches are usually asked for their practice plans by the court to see if the practice session itself was a contributing factor in the injury. Without any written plans, you could be in some difficulty in a court of law.

The best-prepared practice plans are relatively worthless if the time schedule is ignored. To ensure that everything in the plan is covered, each coach has to follow the plan to the minute. Ignoring the time schedule when a particular part of practice is not going well can cause some real problems, especially if several coaches are involved. Generally, if something doesn't go well, move on when the schedule dictates, and include the problem area in the next practice plan.

Practice plans should be prepared at least a day ahead of time so that each coach can plan accordingly. A good time for making plans is after practice, before the coaches leave for the day. The plans should then be posted so the athletes also know what is in store for them. Last-minute planning should be avoided if at all possible, because the pressure of time prevents careful thought. The following guidelines should be helpful when writing practice plans:

1. The first team should never lose in practice, ideally.

2. Practice plans should have a lot of variation.

3. Practice plans must be well organized.

4. Practice plans should provide for maximum participation.

5. Practice plans should allow for efficient use of time.

6. Practice plans should make maximum use of space and facilities.

7. Practice plans should show progression in teaching skills.

8. Practice plans should serve to teach new things, to review, to correct, and to prepare for the next contest.

9. When teaching something new, use the whole-part-whole method.

10. Practice plans should be adjusted for time and intensity as the season progresses.

The practice plans in Figure 10.8 illustrate close attention to time, length of time periods, use of drills, and progression. The exact terminology used here is not important as long as what you use is understood by the coaches and players.

After practice plans have been developed and it is time to begin teaching, it would be helpful for you and your assistant coaches to remember Thorndike's laws of learning: the law of readiness, the law of exercise, and the law of effect.

The Law of Readiness

Youngsters learn best when they are ready to learn—when they have reached the proper growth level (maturation) and have a great desire to learn. Coaches can recognize readiness when a youngster can learn a skill with ease, is self-motivated to master the skill, and succeeds. All three elements must be in evidence. More simply stated: Unless a youngster is ready, it won't make any difference how skillful a teacher you are, because little or no learning will occur.

Tell me, and I will forget
Show me, and I might remember
Involve me, and I will understand

SAMPLE TENNIS PRACTICE PLAN (BEGINNING OF THE SEASON)

A. Objectives
   1. Develop endurance, strength, speed, and agility.
   2. Develop stroke competency.
   3. Improve game strategy, singles and doubles.
B. Situation
   1. Coach
   2. 2-hour practice
   3. Adequate courts and equipment
C. Practice
   1. 2:00-2:15—two per court rally—forehand crosscourt shot. Emphasis: ball control for good placement and recovery to middle of court after every stroke.
   2. 2:15-2:30—repeat "1" above with backhand crosscourt.
   3. 2:30-2:45—forehand and backhand crosscourt and down-the-line shots.
      Player A sends ball crosscourt and recovers to middle (ball kept in play continuously.) Alternate positions.
   4. 2:45-3:00—player A practices serves to right and left courts working on placement in outside and inside corners. Player B practices returning ball deep crosscourt and down-the-line.
   5. 3:00-3:15—player B serves, player A returns as above.
   6. 3:15-4:00—play pro set (round robin) to determine ladder positions. (This takes about a week.)

MIDSEASON

Work with individuals on particular problems of each. May be done for 2 hours—or if near a match date, for one-half of the practice period. Second half should be devoted to challenge matches.

SAMPLE WRESTLING PRACTICE PLAN

3:30-3:40 Calisthenics—announcements
3:40-3:50 Warm-up drills (reaction-spike drill)
3:50-4:00 Demonstrates new takedown and counter
4:00-4:15 Work on takedown and counter by the numbers
4:15-4:20 30-second escapes
4:20-4:35 Takedown tournament
4:35-5:00 Pinning combinations
5:00-5:10 Chain wrestling
5:10-5:30 One-minute matches—live

SAMPLE BASEBALL/SOFTBALL PRACTICE PLAN

3:30-3:40 Loosen up—throw
3:40-3:50 Pepper
3:50-4:00 Base running
4:00-4:10 Sliding—demonstration and practice
4:25-4:40 Shag flies sideline to sideline on the run
4:40-5:00 Outfield shag—infield practice
5:00-5:30 Hit (infield and outfield continue)

Figure 10.8
Sample practice plans for tennis, wrestling, baseball/softball, basketball, football, and soccer. Please see Appendix F for more sample practice plans.

Figure 10.8
(continued)

SAMPLE BASKETBALL PRACTICE PLAN—SATURDAY

9:30 a.m. Prepractice	Passing—Coach C
Rebounder—Coach A	Agility—Coach D
Defense—Coach B	
9:45 a.m. Clean 2 and T	
9:50 a.m. Talk	
9:52 a.m. Lap and warm-ups	2 to break
2 Ball with moves	Gut
4 Man	T to break
10:00 a.m. Gazini	
10:05 a.m. Over the top	
Drake	
Cal	
Block out	
10:15 a.m. Defensive disposition	
10:20 a.m. Scrimmage	
10:25 a.m. Defensive split	
No touch and checks—Coach A	
Defensive principles—Coach B	
10:35 a.m. White split	
10:45 a.m. White	
10:50 a.m. White game	
11:00 a.m. ½ Set	
11:10 a.m. ½ Motion	
11:20 a.m. M.F.	
11:25 a.m. 10 possessions	
11:40 a.m. Scrimmage	
11:55 a.m. Out of bounds	
12:05 a.m. Red 50 and spread	
12:15 p.m. Circle to hold	
12:25 p.m. Run 2	
Cal	
Fouls	
Bounces	

SAMPLE FOOTBALL PRACTICE PLAN—OFFENSE

3:30-3:40 Calisthenics—loosen and stretch—reaction
3:40-3:50 Run tires, antifumble (backs and ends); seven-man sled (tackles, centers and guards)
3:50-4:00 Run sidelines (backs and ends); two-man sled (tackles, centers, and guards)
4:00-4:10 Demonstrate new play to full team
4:10-4:25 Run plays—pass cut—line scrimmage
4:25-4:55 Full team dummy scrimmage—Red and White versus Blue Shirts
4:55-5:00 Live punt
5:00-5:15 Full team live pass offense
5:15-5:25 Full team live scrimmage—goal line offense
5:25-5:30 Fun time (sprints)

Figure 10.8
(continued)

SOCCER PRACTICE PLAN #6
4:30–6:30 Baker Field 18 players

1. 4:30–4:35 Miscellaneous
   a. Review weekly schedule
   b. Collection of medical forms
   c. Review weekly duties
   d. GK's work with GK coach
2. 4:35–4:50 Warm-up & Stretch
   a. Individual moves in center circle—pull backs; step overs; scissors
   b. "Knock Out" game—all players in center circle
   c. Combination play in pairs—overlapping runs; 1–2's; takeovers; double pass
   d. "Double Trouble"—play in groups of 8 in half field area
3. 4:50–5:00 Short-Short-Long
   a. emphasize 3rd man attack (disruption)
4. 5:00–5:15 Playing Away From Pressure
   a. 3 v 1/3 v 0–5 passes and switch the point of attack
   b. 4 goal game
5. 5:15–5:30 Restarts with GK's
   a. Defensive & attacking corners
   b. Free kicks in the "D"   "Twin State" & "Butch"
   c. Defending & attacking long throws
6. 5:30–5:50 Conditioning Game
   a. "Team knockout"—2 teams of eight, play in half field
7. 5:50–6:10 8 v 8 Scrimmage with GK's
   a. Play 2 touch
   b. Can only score after executing a combination
   c. No restrictions—last 10 minutes
8. 6:10–6:20 Shooting & Finishing
   a. 1 v 1 in penalty box
   b. 1 v 2 in penalty box
   c. Pass & Pound from 18 yd line
9. 6:20–6:25 Conditioning
   a. 5 "Boras"—18 seconds to goal line; back in 30 seconds; rest 30 seconds; repeat
10. 6:25–6:30 Cooldown
   a. Team stretch led by captains

The Law of Exercise

People learn by doing, but only if they practice the right way. Therefore coaches should say little and have the athletes practice frequently, correctly, and successfully. The key is not to talk too much. Talking is not necessarily teaching.

You must also resist the temptation to overcoach, the results of which could be similar to the following:

> The centipede was quite happy until the frog, in fun, said, "Pray which leg comes after which?" This wrought her up to such a pitch, she lay distracted in a ditch considering which leg came after which.

This is a prime example of "Paralysis by analysis."

The Law of Effect

How athletes feel about what they are doing is as important as what they are doing. They will react positively only if what they are doing is fun, difficult enough to be a challenge, and meaningful enough to be considered important. A clever coach will find it relatively easy to create a situation in which all of these factors are present. If not, problems will occur, and learning will be hampered.

In his book *The Paul Brown Story*, the highly successful Coach Brown said, "In every training camp I applied the basic laws of learning—seeing, hearing, writing, then doing again and again. We constantly emphasized doing everything one proper and precise way."

It has been said that practice makes perfect. This is not true. Practice makes permanent. It is perfect practice that makes perfect. Therefore, the fundamental purpose behind every practice plan and practice session is to "habitize" the athletes and to insist that whatever is done is done as nearly perfectly as possible.

> Habit is a cable; we weave a thread of it every day, and at last we cannot break it.
> —Horace Mann

Because perfection for all athletes is an impossibility, it becomes necessary for you to define a "range of correctness" in your own mind when teaching skills. This means that although you expect athletes to become as nearly perfect as possible, there are degrees of properly executing any skill that you will find acceptable.

PICKING THE TEAM

Of all the items on the agenda for preseason staff meetings, none is more crucial than a thorough evaluation of the athletes involved. When going through this process, everyone on the staff must understand and adhere to four basic principles for consistency:

> Of all sad words of tongue or pen The saddest are these: It might have been.
> —John Greenleaf Whittier

1. *Potential.* Under no circumstances should players be played on potential alone. Violating this principle will prove costly to you and to the team. A lot of coaches have a tendency to stay too long with people of potential; we call these players coach killers.

There are basically three kinds of players: those who can do, those who cannot do, and the question marks. The real test is to reach the question marks, the players who have the skill but aren't getting the job done— for whatever reason. The point is that at some time in preseason or during the season an athlete will do the job or not. If not, this person should be benched at once in favor of one who does get the job done, regardless of potential. Athletic events are won by people who do what is expected, not by athletes who might do it—someday.

This particular problem can be one of incredible frustration to coaches. To see talent going to waste is something a dedicated teacher simply cannot comprehend or fully accept. Working with such youngsters will challenge every bit of imagination you can muster in an attempt to get them to perform to the best of their ability—and sometimes you will fail.

The three saddest words in the coaching profession in this regard are *if, would,* and *could.* When the season is over, you should never have to look back and say, "*If* player "X" *would* ever have played up to her potential we *could* have had a good year." This is inexcusable on your part, and also futile.

2. *Desire and ability.* Players should be selected on both ability and desire. As Sam Snead, of golfing fame, said, "To win, an athlete has to have talent and desire—but desire is first." It is easy for you to pick an athlete with both talent and desire out of the crowd. This boy or girl is commonly referred to as a blue-chip prospect or, better yet, a golden nugget. Such kids are not just good athletes, they are great, and like real golden nuggets, they are rare in the normal high school situation. Obviously these athletes are your number one choice.

However, the typical athletes that come to high school coaches are high in talent but low in desire, low in talent but high in desire, or somewhere in between. Desire becomes all important simply because it can cover up some deficiencies in skill. The great players are going to play, but the ones who will win for you are the ones who aren't great but don't know it. You have to have "winners" and you have to be able to recognize them.

Desire in this context is defined as

- The desire to play

- The desire to win

- The desire to work hard

- The desire to learn

- The desire to get better

- The desire to compete

In short, youngsters with these qualities just love to play the game. They may not always be winners on the scoreboard, but they are "gamers" because they only know one way to compete and that is to put out maximum effort all the time, regardless of the score or any other circumstances. This trait is also referred to as *constant competitiveness.* Gamers have thunder in their hearts.

Figure 10.9
The relationship between ability and desire.

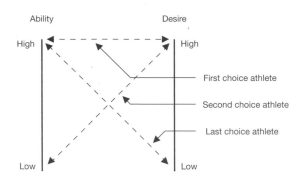

The last choice in picking personnel is individuals with ability but little or no desire. These people will be losers in athletics—not a pretty word, but true. They will look bad, and chances are great that you and the team will look bad also. A real loser can always give you reasons why he/she lost. A winner only gets beat on a scoreboard—never in the heart. The relationship between ability and desire is diagrammed in Figure 10.9.

3. *Your priorities.* As you look at the team, you need to decide what qualities or skills are most important in your athletes. For example, basketball coaches might decide that their number one priority is shooters; a softball coach might decide on hitters; a football coaching staff might look first for people who like to hit other people. Other top priorities could be speed, intelligence, strength, size, attitude, or general athletic ability. The only thing that matters, really, is that the staff knows what the priorities are so that all the coaches are looking for the same thing as they determine who will make the team.

4. *Game play.* In the final analysis, players have to be chosen on the basis of their performance in the "game." This is the bottom line. If doing so is not possible, then you must look at their performance in gamelike situations such as scrimmages, practice meets, or matches, ideally with other schools.

Generally speaking, there are three kinds of athletes in regard to game-time performance: those who look great in practice and who also perform well in competition; those who do not practice particularly well but who are great game-time athletes; and those who look great in practice but rarely, if ever, do well in competition. There is no way to predict with absolute certainty how athletes will react in competition. Therefore, the ultimate test in evaluating personnel has to be "the game."

Evaluating players should be one of the primary purposes of interschool preseason scrimmages, events, or meets. This is the time to find out who the players are rather than worry about which team is scoring points in an informal scrimmage. Coaches who go through lengthy scrimmages without videotaping the entire session and without giving every member of the team an opportunity to compete are misusing one of the finest evaluative tools in athletics.

Grading Forms

Other possible methods of evaluating personnel should be discussed and agreed on during initial staff meetings, because player evaluation should be a continuous process throughout the season. Grading forms for use in conjunction with game videos should also be considered. The three basic kinds of forms are those that are used for a percentage grade, those that use written comments only, and a combination of these two.

Sociograms

Sociograms can be another help in deciding on a starting lineup. Players sometimes see each other quite differently than the coaches do, and the use of sociograms can point out discrepancies in this regard. The method is particularly useful if you believe team unity is important. If the majority of a squad rejects a teammate for some reason, a sociogram will quickly point this out, whereas the coaching staff might not detect this situation until later in the season. By then some damage probably will have already occurred. A coaching staff can use sociograms as a guide in making whatever changes they think necessary, and they may also find these diagrams useful in counseling youngsters and in identifying specific problems.

The sample sociogram in Figure 10.10 deals with rejection. Ten players' names have been put on the form in a random order. Any question that will force the group to make decisions about their teammates can be posed. Each athlete then completes the form and gives it back to you unsigned. It is up to you to interpret the results. The question posed for this example was, "Which players would you least like to sit beside on the bus for an away game? Name three, in order; the one you list first will be considered the person you would most dislike having sit next to you."

The results from the sample (mapped here as a sociogram) make it obvious that Harry has a problem. Now you need to do some investigating to see why this youngster's teammates reject him. It might be a relatively simple matter that can

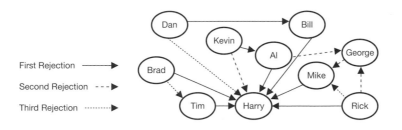

Figure 10.10
Sociogram showing rejection.

be corrected easily, or a more serious one that will require a lot of time and counseling. The important thing is that a problem has been identified before it can disrupt the team.

Figure 10.11 shows another type of sociogram, one that deals with comparisons. In this example, twelve players have been listed. Again, you can ask whatever question you want, but it must force the players to compare all the members of the team. For example, you could ask such questions as: "Which of your teammates has the best attitude?" "Which of your teammates is the best athlete?" or "Which of your teammates demonstrates the greatest leadership qualities?"

Each player then goes across the form horizontally, comparing every player with every other player. In the example here, we begin with Ann at the top left of the form on the vertical scale and compare her with everyone else across the top, working from left to right. If she is better than Louise, we put a plus sign in the square. If she is not as good as Karen, we put a minus sign in that square, and so on all the way across. Then we go to Betty and repeat the process all the way across the form, and then on to each person until the entire form is completed. It is essential that the order of names listed on the vertical scale be reversed from left to right on the horizontal scale.

Once the forms have been completed, all the plus signs for each individual are totaled and all the minuses are totaled. Be sure to total both across and down. These scores are then combined for each player to represent the player's total score. When these are put in rank order, a clear picture emerges of how the players see their teammates relative to the question that was posed. Because there are twelve people represented on the sample sociogram, a perfect score for an individual

Figure 10.11
Sociogram for obtaining players' evaluations of each other on specific qualities.

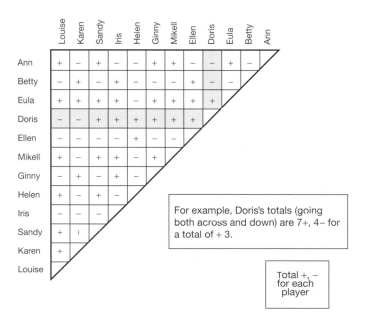

For example, Doris's totals (going both across and down) are 7+, 4− for a total of + 3.

Total +, − for each player

would be 11 (since Ann is not compared to Ann, or Karen to Karen, for example). The results of this exercise in rank order are:

Eula	9+,2−	=	+7
Doris	7+,4−	=	+3
Mikell	7+,4−	=	+3
Sandy	7+,4−	=	+3
Ginny	6+,5−	=	+1
Louise	6+,5−	=	+1
Ann	5+,6−	=	−1
Iris	5+,6−	=	−1
Karen	5+,6−	=	−1
Ellen	4+,7−	=	−3
Helen	4+,7−	−	3

If the question for the sample sociogram had dealt with leadership, for instance, it would be quite clear that the players recognize Eula as the top leader on the team. As a result, she should be given a leadership role. At the same time, Ellen and Helen were perceived as lacking leadership qualities. Therefore, you might elect to work with these players to improve this particular quality. Of course, if you gave this form to the team five times and asked five different questions, the rank order could be different each time. Therefore, the results for each question are very specific.

The advantages of sociograms are that they are relatively easy to use, they do not take a lot of time, the blank forms can be duplicated beforehand, and the players will be frank because they do not sign their names. This is an excellent way to gain a lot of insight into how the players feel about each other, and it helps you learn more about the personalities on the team.

Intangibles

Evaluating players is less difficult in sports where there are tangible factors on which you can rely. For instance, scores in golf, the height of a crossbar in the high jump or pole vault, time in various running events, or the results of a singles match in tennis are clear-cut. The players, by their accomplishments, determine who will participate in the next scheduled event. This takes a lot of the decision-making process off your shoulders.

In team sports such as field hockey, football, volleyball, basketball, and soccer, the responsibility for and difficulty in picking the right players increases. This is because qualities such as agility, quickness, balance, courage, desire, competitive spirit, physical toughness, and mental toughness play a greater role in the process. While all of these qualities are extremely important, they are difficult to measure and, at best, are all subjective. Nevertheless, every possible effort should be made to try to recognize these qualities, or their absence, in each individual on the team. The sooner these unknowns become known, the sooner the best lineup can be determined.

An intangible that many coaches believe to be the most important of all is attitude, because without a good attitude nothing else will matter. A "good attitude" can be defined in a number of ways, but basically it means that a youngster is teachable, cooperative, willing to abide by the rules, and anxious to work hard to become a better athlete. In short, such players are coachable.

Attitude problems can cause conflict on a team and, if left unchecked, can permeate the entire squad and ruin a season. Attitude problems must be dealt with immediately and directly because they normally will not go away on their own. An attitude problem can spread like a rotten apple in a barrel and could result in dismissing someone from a team. If a problem is severe enough, it can even carry over into the next season as well. This can be a very steep price to pay for not paying attention to this factor in evaluating players. An athlete with a great attitude is an "asset" in an athletic event; an athlete with a poor attitude is an "asset" on the bench. Think about it.

Challenge

Another possibility for evaluating athletes is to initiate or develop methods by which individuals can challenge the person playing ahead of them. The main advantage is that it can help eliminate grumbling by substitutes or members of the second or third team. When people have a chance to challenge, they either succeed or fail, and in either case the results are their own doing, not that of a coach. Consequently, if they fail, they cannot blame anyone else, and they should be satisfied that at least they had a fair chance to show what they could do. Challenging is an excellent way to recognize desire and also to keep players on the first team from becoming complacent. Challenge is used frequently in individual sports like wrestling, golf, and track, but it can also be used in team sports like softball or basketball. Some coaches limit this method to preseason only and then use performance in actual contests for evaluating athletes the rest of the season.

WRITTEN TESTS

There is another consideration for you in the teaching process, and that is written tests for the players during preseason practices. In Chapter 9, classroom meetings and written tests on notebook material were mentioned, but written tests can go beyond this. There is some question about how effective athletes can be if they do not know what they or their teammates are supposed to be doing on each play or in certain situations in a contest, or if they cannot describe in writing the skill they are attempting to perform.

For example, when a baseball or softball coach teaches defense against a sacrifice bunt, the easiest way to find out if a player knows what everyone is supposed to do is to have each player draw the whole play. If a football coach wanted to know whether all the players understood the basic team defense with pursuit angles and responsibilities, the easiest way to find out would be to have each player draw the entire defense, showing these elements of the total picture.

Generally speaking, it makes little difference what skill level individual athletes have if they don't understand a play or the execution of a skill. The question you must ask is, if players don't know what is going on, can they possibly be of any help to the team, or will they hurt the team with mental mistakes?

If you decide that written tests are a good idea, you must then decide what constitutes an acceptable passing grade and what to do with athletes who score lower than that grade. Once again, unless some price has to be paid for failing to meet this requirement, the value of the exercise is questionable.

You may be tempted to dismiss this concept because you don't believe youngsters can handle it. This assumption is not true. The important point to keep in mind is that youngsters generally work up to whatever level is expected of them. It is therefore your duty to require, lead, push, and motivate athletes to do more than they themselves think they are able to do—to exceed the limits they put on themselves. Of course, you must be astute enough to be reasonable in the process.

Testing is not an unreasonable requirement for athletes. Among the advantages of written tests:

1. They force athletes to put what they know in writing, thereby reinforcing the learning process.

2. They indicate very clearly whether or not the players know what is going on.

3. They are an excellent tool for evaluating your teaching.

4. They provide information helpful for preparing practice plans.

5. They can be used to determine who will play in the games, meets, or matches.

6. They can be used as motivation to enhance learning and understanding.

7. They can help players become "smart" players.

8. They can be one of the criteria for cutting a team.

TEAM MEETING

The last task to be accomplished before the first practice is a team meeting, as described in Chapter 9.

This is the time to address players' expectations of coaches. Coaches spend a lot of time telling athletes what is expected of them, but rarely, if ever, do coaches take the time to find out what the players expect of coaches. To assume you know what athletes' expectations are can be a serious mistake, and a costly one in terms of a team's or an athlete's performance. If you and your players are to go into any competition united by common goals and respect for each other, it makes sense to make sure you all know what you expect of each other. Appendix E is a questionnaire designed to elicit this information for you.

Everything in this book so far has been intended to get you to this precise point: the moment when you face your players just before the first practice and are able to say to them, "We are ready. We coaches have been working on this season since the last one ended; we have made many decisions and have agreed on many plans. Now the fun begins."

With careful attention to detail and organization regarding every aspect of the program, you have taken a giant step toward a successful season. The whole staff knows exactly what they want to do, what they must do, and the best way in which to do it. Now the many long, tedious hours involved in your planning will come to fruition.

DISCUSSION QUESTIONS

1. Many coaches feel that the best assistants should be coaching on the lower levels to ensure the teaching of sound fundamentals to young athletes. What is your opinion, and why?

2. Should every team have training rules? Why?

3. What are your ideas on discipline?

4. Is your appearance as a coach important, and why? How about the appearance of your staff?

5. What is the importance of having a practice plan?

6. What are your thoughts on cutting players at the high school level? At the junior high level?

7. How important is team unity? How can you, as a coach, encourage and develop it?

8. What is the process of acclimatization? Of what value is it?

9. Which quality in an athlete seems more valuable to you—desire or ability? Why?

10. Why is the game the best way to evaluate an athlete—or is it?

11. What are the advantages of having team captains? What are the disadvantages?

12. "Don't take anything for granted where high school athletes are concerned." What does this mean?

13. Interpret this statement: "The first team should never lose in practice."

14. What does "stack the deck" mean in regard to drills?

15. Give some examples of ways in which coaches can "stack the deck" in drills.

16. How will you expect your team to dress when traveling to an away contest? Why?

17. What kinds of awards would you give your team, if any? Why?

18. Of what value are team goals?

19. Of what value are individual goals for athletes? How can coaches use these goals?

20. Why should a time limit be placed on staying in the locker room after practice?

21. What two critical factors contribute to the possibility of heatstroke?

22. "Repetition is the mother of learning." What implications does this have to conducting practice?

23. Describe mental rehearsal and its implications.

24. List the four principles of player evaluation.

25. What does the term "coach killer" mean?

26. What advantages are there in using sociograms?

27. What are some intangibles to consider in evaluating athletes?

28. What is the primary purpose of a depth chart?

29. What is the basic purpose of a master schedule?

30. Define constant competitiveness.

31. Define range of correctness in teaching skills. What does this concept imply?

32. Is it of any importance for coaches to know what the players expect of them? Why?

11

ISSUES, PROBLEMS, AND CONCERNS IN ATHLETICS

From the beginning, organized competitive athletics have generated controversy through questionable actions of teams, coaches, or individual athletes. There is little reason to believe the future will be any different. In the normal course of events, certain issues are resolved; others no longer matter; new ones appear; and a few seem to have been with us forever.

Some ongoing issues have never been satisfactorily resolved, even though rule books grow thicker. Blue-ribbon panels of experts have been and continue to be organized to make recommendations or offer solutions. It seems that the only things that really change over time are names, faces, and places rather than any significant behaviors. Part of the difficulty is that there are no clear-cut solutions, nor is it easy to get any clear consensus on some issues. Consequently, it is up to individual coaches like you to simply be aware of what some of these problems/issues are and to decide on what seems to be an honorable solution. If you have an opportunity to debate these issues with other coaches or people preparing to become coaches, this is an excellent way to clarify your own thinking. The overriding factor should always be the question, "What is best for the athletes and for athletics—what is the right thing to do?"

Of all the factors demanding the attention of coaches, surveys have shown that the ones most coaches struggle with more than any others are:

- Parents

- Attitude of athletes

- Discipline

- Drug abuse

- Officiating

Every situation is unique, so these problem areas might vary somewhat from school to school—but not much.

PARENTS OF ATHLETES

It is interesting to see parents reported as a top concern, and it's discouraging at the same time. These are the people who should be your greatest supporters, not one of your biggest problems. Parents will get involved one way or another—you need to involve them the way *you* want and not leave this situation to chance. Strategies for minimizing parental problems can be found in Chapter 3.

The following comments from coaches on the high school level illustrate potential problems with parents:

- Parents often impose unreasonable expectations on their children and the coaches.

- Parents look to place blame on coaches for their children's lack of success rather than admit these children simply are not great athletes.

- Parents have attacked the coach verbally right after a game.

- Parents operate on a 4-1 plan in basketball. That is, they want you to play the four best players *plus* their own. In baseball this would be an 8-1 plan, in football a 10-1 plan.

- Parents question the coach's decisions regarding a starting lineup, strategy, and substitutions.

- Parents who are unhappy with a coach often take their complaint directly to the principal or superintendent rather than discuss the matter with the coach.

- Parents' only concern is their child's playing time—or lack of (the eternal problem).

- Parents frequently take the side of their children in a dispute with coaches— even though they know only one side of the story.

- Parents criticizing a coach in front of their children put the youngsters in a squeeze between coach and parent, which can cause real problems.

- Parents blame the coach for not getting their youngster an athletic scholarship.

- If parents get angry at a coach, they will probably stay angry as long as the coach is at that school.

On the other side of the coin, more and more parents are complaining about their children being verbally harassed by coaches through criticism, language abuse, swearing, and mental abuse causing mental stress, which they charge causes a loss of self-confidence.

Make no mistake about it; this is an area of great importance to all coaches simply because of the emotional factor, which does not exist in any other issue. Emotion frequently rules out or gets in the way of logic, thus making it more difficult to arrive at an amicable solution between parent and coach when a problem arises.

There are no easy answers to satisfy this potential problem area with parents and no magic pill or potion that will make you wiser. The first factor that can dull the arrows of criticism by parents (or anyone else) is for the team to win a lot; the second is to develop a great deal of good diplomacy; and the third is to work hard at getting parents to buy into your program . . . and then cross your fingers.

ATTITUDE OF ATHLETES

Athletes' attitudes continue to be a big concern among coaches, as the following comments from an earlier survey indicate:

- Youngsters don't have realistic goals, sometimes because of pressure they get from their parents.

- Their work ethic is not good.

- They have no drive or ambition.

- They lack dedication and commitment.

- They quit easily if they aren't on the "first team," aren't playing a lot, or are getting scolded by the coach.

- Their main concern is for "I" and "me" rather than the team.

- They lack self-discipline.

- They lack mental toughness.

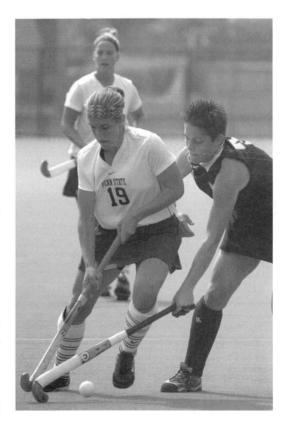

It is a good bet that there is a strong connection between these attitudes and the parent problem. As the old saying goes, "The acorn does not fall far from the tree."

PART-TIME COACHES

Historically, only full-time professional employees of a school district were permitted to coach a scholastic athletic team. In many states across the country now, this is no longer the case. With more athletic teams in the schools, primarily because of Title IX, there are many more coaching vacancies than teachers willing to accept coaching assignments. School officials often find it difficult to get faculty members already on the staff to accept coaching assignments or to hire new teachers for specific openings who are willing and able to coach. Most of those who decline cite lack of interest, long hours, low pay, and family responsibilities. As a consequence, part-time, uncertified coaches are a reality in many of our schools. These people might be certified teachers, physical educators, former athletes, or none of the above.

Many school administrators do not like the idea of using part-time coaches because of three main concerns. The biggest of these concerns is legal implications. If a part-time person with no coaching certification is employed, the coach and the school could face an expensive lawsuit in the event of serious injury to an athlete that a prudent professional could have prevented. The remedy, of course, is coaching certification, or at least workshops for people who want to coach but have had no professional preparation. Experience as a player is not a substitute for professional preparation.

Because a part-time coach is not in the school building except at practice time, communication creates a second main concern. Finally, the lack of a coach's visibility in the school can encourage some athletes to behave in ways they would never consider if they knew the coach was right around the corner.

In spite of these concerns, the practice of hiring part-timers has become widespread simply because there seems to be no alternatives except to eliminate some athletic teams—not a satisfactory possibility.

DRUGS

One of the most serious concerns in all of athletics is drug abuse—primarily a health issue. The use of any drug becomes abuse when it is medically unsupervised. No one can be certain of the extent of drug abuse in sport, but there is no doubt that it exists. Along with the increase of drug use in athletics arises the inevitable confusion between fact and myth. For example, are certain pills harmful while others are not? Do drugs really help increase athletic performance? Do they cause liver and bone damage? Will they increase strength? An in-depth study of this area is more properly a function of the medical profession or of classes in physiology and drug abuse in athletics. Consequently, this is not a lengthy discourse in an attempt to make you an expert in drug abuse among athletes. Instead, here are some simple guidelines for you to consider in dealing with this issue:

1. As a high school coach, chances are you will be dealing with a greater number of drug users than coaches at other levels. One reason, of course, has been the absence of drug testing at the high school level. However, there is a move to introduce testing into high schools in some areas of the country. As expected, these efforts are already being challenged in the courts. Such testing might serve as a deterrent.

2. High school athletes see drugs as a training consideration. Many believe that various drugs will make them stronger, bigger, or more aggressive, and thus better athletes.

3. Every coach should make an effort to become as knowledgeable as possible about drug use and abuse in order to deal with this problem intelligently and accurately. You can do so through exercise physiology courses taken as an undergraduate or graduate student, as well as through workshops, discussions with health educators or medical professionals, materials from the NCAA and other governing bodies, or extensive reading in journals or textbooks such as *The Steroids Game* by Charles Yesalis and Virginia Cowart.

4. You must include the use and abuse of alcohol, tobacco, steroids, other drugs, and diet supplements in team policies that you establish at the outset of every season.

5. Impress upon your athletes that the supposed benefits from taking drugs are nonexistent or marginal at best. Your athletes also need to know that the dangers are real, although in the case of steroids the severity is still in question.

6. You must take the initiative and encourage athletes to focus on safe, alternative ways of getting bigger and stronger, such as carefully supervised weight training.

7. Become a health educator for your players. Teaching the potential harmful effects of drug abuse should be an important part of coaching your team. Your primary concern in this matter should be the physiological effects of drug use on the human body.

8. Learn enough about the topic to recognize the signs of drug abuse in an individual.

Drugs commonly abused can be classified into three major groups, according to the effect on the user: stimulants, depressants, and hallucinogens, many of which can be purchased over the counter. This ease of availability compounds the problem.

Stimulants

The symptoms of abuse of stimulants include (a) restlessness, (b) involuntary trembling, (c) enlarged pupils, (d) dry mouth, (e) higher blood pressure, (f) sweating, (g) aggressive behavior, (h) inability to sleep, and (i) headaches.

The danger associated with stimulants is that they can induce a false feeling of "all's well" when, in fact, the user is completely fatigued. Stimulants short-circuit feelings of exhaustion, requiring the body to use up its reserves. As a result, the individual might experience sudden and total collapse.

Depressants

The symptoms of abuse of depressants or tranquilizers include (a) slurred speech, (b) staggering, (c) drowsiness, and (d) decreased heart rate. The danger associated with depressants is that people taking large amounts lose control of body functions and become restless, hostile, and quarrelsome. (Alcohol is the most widely used depressant.) Reality is distorted, and a user can easily take an overdose, not realizing the effect the drug is having. Overdoses can cause death.

Hallucinogens

Hallucinogens are not usually associated with sport. Most youngsters do not believe that drugs such as LSD and marijuana will enhance performance the way that they believe stimulants or tranquilizers will.

Steroids

Perhaps the chief concern in the overall drug picture is the widespread use of steroids among athletes, all of whom are looking for that edge or that one special thing that will make them champions. Steroids differ from the other three drug groups in that they are natural hormonal products. Many athletes have begun taking high doses of them in hopes of rapidly building up their strength and endurance.

The problem is that the effects of steroids have never been resolved to everyone's satisfaction. There does not appear to be any consensus on the benefits (if any) and possible side effects of these drugs. The evidence indicates that, although strength and size may be enhanced through the use of steroids, there are many risks that certainly outweigh any possible advantage. Until the medical profession clarifies all the ramifications of steroid use, it would be appropriate to discourage their use by athletes.

Common use of steroids has not brought much enlightenment about their effects, at least on normal physiology. Medical researchers have done comparatively little work to separate the psychological effects from the physiological ones. The fact that there is still much dispute over steroids is due to a combination of circumstances. The manufacturers of anabolic steroids do not assume any responsibility for how the substance is taken because it does not come under jurisdiction of the Food and Drug Administration. As far as the governing bodies of sport are concerned, the use of any kind of drug is contrary to their standards of ethics, and that is where their study of the question normally begins and ends.

Until such time as researchers have settled the question of drug use on the physiology of the body, the question of ethics looms large. In the true spirit of sport competition, athletes are expected to participate to the best of their natural ability and to win or lose on that premise. To some, the use of artificial aids such as stimulants and steroids violates this principle, and therefore violates the basic code of ethics in sport.

Even though amphetamines and steroids are taken because athletes believe the drugs will improve their performance, both drugs also provide a psychological lift. To this extent, then, they are no different from marijuana, heroin, and other drugs used to achieve euphoria.

There are several warning signs of steroid use you should recognize. The first is a drastic increase in lean body weight (muscle); the second is a change in behavior, such as compulsive weightlifting or extreme aggressiveness; the third is the sometimes prolonged recovery from relatively minor injuries like an ankle sprain, especially when some of these other signs are present.

Some other suspected side effects of steroid use are:

Musculoskeletal
- Broadening of shoulders in males and females
- Enhanced strength, mass, and performance
- Muscles become stronger than bones and tendons can handle (which can lead to fractures, tears, and other injuries)
- Deepening of voice in males and females
- Premature male pattern baldness in males and females
- Severe acne

Cardiovascular
- Possible thrombotic stroke

In Males
- Production of female hormones
- Increased aggression
- Long-term feminization (nonmale characteristics develop)
- Development of female nipples and breasts
- Higher risk of prostate diseases
- Liver damage

In Females
- Increased aggression
- Permanent enlargement of the clitoris
- Menstrual difficulties
- Permanently decreased breast size
- Male appearance, which might also affect reproduction capability

If an athlete exhibits any of these signs, pass this information on to the team physician at once.

Alcohol

The most abused drug and thus the number one drug problem is alcohol. Alcohol dependence is the most serious drug problem among young people today, in spite of whatever advice coaches or parents give to youngsters. Studies have shown that peer pressure has the greatest impact on teenagers' values and behavior. When we get right down to it, peer pressure might be more of an excuse than a cause. As a consequence, your role in educating youngsters regarding alcohol use becomes more difficult. If you use alcoholic beverages yourself, your effectiveness in influencing youngsters' attitudes toward drinking can become more complicated.

The reason athletes drink is immaterial. The plain fact is that they do, and some to alarming degrees. You need to recognize this situation and address the issue before a problem surfaces to force you to take some kind of action—possibly difficult and unpleasant.

Alcohol is a toxic poison to the cells of the nervous system, and no individuals can do their best work after having drunk even one beer. Accurate measurement of eye movements and study of enzyme systems clearly show that this effect lasts from 24 to 48 hours.

Physiologists also tell us that alcohol and heat do not mix. Alcohol affects the body's temperature-control system, and even though a cold drink of alcohol might feel good going down, it does not cool the body. It actually does the reverse. Alcohol requires energy to be metabolized, and this energy cannot be divided between muscular effort and the burning of alcohol. An athlete who drinks has to rob Peter (athletic performance) to pay Paul (alcohol oxidation). Mixing athletics and alcohol is like burning a candle at both ends with a blowtorch.

The American Medical Association has stated that alcohol and athletics do not mix, and scientific experiments reinforce this conviction. Studies show that not only is there a definite loss of skill, but also a marked drop in physical capacity following the use of relatively small amounts of alcohol.

The point is that there is not one shred of scientific evidence to show that the use of alcohol will make anyone a better athlete or a better anything, for that matter. All the known evidence points to the contrary. This fact in itself should be enough of a selling point to help in educating youngsters—particularly those who have any degree of self-motivation to achieve and excel.

Youngsters should know that it does not take a mature person to drink. Rather, it takes a mature person not to drink when everyone else is.

Tobacco

You will be doing your athletes a huge favor if your training rules prohibit the use of tobacco in any form. Using tobacco products is not a sign of maturity or being "cool"; quite simply, it is a sign of a lack of intelligence, at least in this regard.

Over 50,000 studies have documented the dangers of tobacco use since the original surgeon general's report on smoking was released a number of years ago. Cigarette smoking alone has been linked to heart disease, throat cancer, lung cancer, and emphysema. Evidence also shows a connection between smokeless tobacco and oral cancer.

Smoking reduces the body's ability to deliver oxygen to the working muscles, and that reduces the functional capacity of the body (ability to perform work).

Smoking increases carbon monoxide levels in the cardiovascular system, increasing the chances for respiratory complications as well.

One final fact: 30 percent of all cancer deaths in America are related to smoking. There is a reason for health warnings on tobacco products!

When you look at all the possible outcomes of using any of these drugs, it is clear that they do not offer one single health benefit to any human being. Along with all the other roles, every caring coach should be a good health teacher as well, and in these matters education is definitely the key.

EATING DISORDERS

Many athletes face a difficult paradox in their training. They are encouraged to eat to provide the necessary energy sources for performance, yet they often face self- or coach-imposed weight restrictions. Emphasis on low body weight or low body fat may benefit performance only if the guidelines are realistic, the caloric intake is reasonable, and the diet is balanced. The use of extreme weight-control measures can jeopardize the health of the athlete and possibly trigger eating disorders. Although these problems are much more prevalent in women, eating disorders also occur in men.

It has been suggested that stress, whether from participating in athletics, striving for athletic success, or pursuing social relationships, may trigger psychological problems in susceptible individuals. Eating disorders can be triggered in such individuals by a single event or by comments from a person important to the individual. In athletics, such triggering mechanisms might include offhand remarks about appearance or constant badgering about an athlete's body weight, body composition, or body type.

Eating disorders often experienced by athletes and the associated warning signs include:

1. **Anorexia nervosa**—Self-imposed starvation in an obsessive effort to lose weight and to become thin.
   Warning signs: Drastic loss in weight; a preoccupation with food, calories, and weight; wearing baggy or layered clothing; relentless, excessive exercise; mood swings; and avoiding food-related social activities.

2. **Bulimia**—Recurring binge eating usually followed by some method of purging such as vomiting, diuretic or laxative abuse, or intensive exercise.
   Warning signs: Excessive concern about weight, bathroom visits after meals, depressive moods, strict dieting followed by eating binges, and increasing criticism of one's body.

3. **Bulimarexia**—Anorexia nervosa with the practice of one or more bulimic behaviors.

It is important to note that the presence of one or two of these warning signs does not necessarily indicate the presence of an eating disorder. Absolute diagnosis should be done by appropriate professionals.

To reduce the potential of an eating disorder, decisions regarding weight loss should be based on the following recommendations:

1. Weight loss should be agreed on by both the coach and the athlete with consultation with appropriate medical and nutritional personnel.

2. A responsible and realistic plan should be developed by all individuals involved.

3. Weight-loss plans should be developed on an individual basis.

If a problem develops, thorough medical evaluation of the student suspected of an eating disorder is imperative. Education about eating disorders is a good preventive measure.

The NCAA project "Nutrition and Eating Disorders in College Athletics," which includes videotapes and written supplements, should be reviewed by athletics administrators, coaches, medical personnel, and student-athletes (*The NCAA Sports Medicine Handbook*).

BLOOD-RELATED INJURIES

Infections with the hepatitis B virus (HBV) and the human immunodeficiency virus (HIV) have increased at an alarming rate over the last decade among all levels of society. These diseases have the potential for catastrophic health consequences. Consequently, this concern demands the utmost attention of coaches, team doctors, and trainers. Unless you are very lucky in your school, you will probably fill all three of these roles and thus be totally responsible for knowing the correct way to deal with this critical issue. The following recommendations have been set forth in *The NCAA Sports Medicine Handbook*.

HBV has a much more likely transmission with exposure to infected blood—to open wounds and mucous membranes. The risk of transmission for HBV or HIV on the field is considered minimal; however, most experts agree that the specific epidemiologic and biologic characteristics of the HBV virus make it a realistic concern for transmission in sports with sustained close physical contact, such as wrestling. HBV is considered to have a potentially higher risk of transmission than HIV.

If an athlete develops acute HBV illness, it is prudent to consider removal of the individual from combative, sustained close-contact sports (such as wrestling) until loss of infectivity is known.

The Individual's Health

In general, the decision to allow an HIV-positive student to participate in athletics should be made on the basis of the individual's health status. If the athlete is asymptomatic and without evidence of deficiencies in immunologic function, the presence of HIV infection in and of itself does not mandate removal from play.

The decision to advise continued athletic competition should involve the student, the student's personal physician, and the team physician. Variables to be considered in reaching the decision include the youngster's current state of health and the status of his or her HIV infection, the nature and intensity of the training, and potential contribution of stress from athletics competition to deterioration of his or her health status.

Disease Transmission

Concerns about transmission in athletics focus on exposure to con-taminated blood through open wounds or mucous membranes. Precise risk of such transmission is impossible to calculate, but epidemiologic and biologic evidence suggests that it is extremely low. There have been no validated reports of transmission of HIV in the athletics setting; therefore, there is no recommended restriction of student-athletes merely because they are infected with HIV.

The following recommendations are designed to further minimize risk of blood-borne pathogen transmission in athletic events and to provide treatment guidelines for caregivers:

1. Pre-event preparation includes proper care for existing wounds, abrasions, cuts, or weeping wounds that may serve as a source of bleeding or as a port of entry for blood-borne pathogens. These wounds should be covered with an occlusive dressing that will withstand the demands of competition. Likewise, care providers with healing wounds or dermatitis should have these skin areas adequately covered to prevent transmission to or from a participant. Athletes should be advised to wear more protective equipment on high-risk areas, such as elbows and hands.

2. The necessary equipment and supplies important for compliance with universal precautions should be available to caregivers. These supplies include appropriate gloves, disinfectant bleach, antiseptics,

designated receptacles for soiled equipment and uniforms, bandages or dressings, and a container for appropriate disposal of needles, syringes, or scalpels.

3. When an athlete is bleeding from an open wound, the bleeding must be stopped and the open wound covered with a dressing sturdy enough to withstand the demands of activity before the individual may continue participation in practice or competition. Participants with active bleeding should be removed from the event as soon as is practical. Return to play is determined by appropriate medical staff personnel. Any participant whose uniform is saturated with blood, regardless of the source, must have that uniform evaluated by appropriate medical personnel for potential infectivity and changed if necessary before return to participation.

4. During an event, athletes should be aware of their responsibility to report a bleeding wound to the proper medical personnel.

5. Sterile latex gloves should be worn for direct contact with blood or body fluids containing blood. Gloves should be changed after treating each individual participant, and after glove removal, hands should be washed.

6. Any surface contaminated with spilled blood should be cleaned in accordance with the following procedures: With gloves on, the spill should be contained in as small an area as possible. After the blood is removed, the surface area of concern should be cleaned with an appropriate decontaminate.

7. After each practice or game, any equipment or uniforms soiled with blood should be handled and laundered in accordance with hygienic methods normally used for treatment of any soiled equipment or clothing before subsequent use.

8. All personnel involved with sports should be trained in basic first aid and infection control, including the preventive measures outlined.

For more information, contact NCAA Sports Sciences, 6201 College Boulevard, Overland Park, KS 66211-2422.

BOOSTER CLUBS

The issue of a booster club can be a big concern to a new coach. If a booster club is already in operation, you will have to live with it, whether you want to or not, because trying to disband it could create tremendous public relations problems. If no booster club exists, you will have to decide whether to try to get one organized.

There are three basic types of clubs: a community booster club that serves many facets of the community, an athletic booster club that exists solely to support high school athletics, and separate booster clubs for specific athletic teams in the school.

There is no question that booster clubs can serve many useful functions and give a great deal of aid, especially when a school is attempting to establish a new athletic program or expand an existing one and funds are limited. The contributions of these clubs can range from outright financial support to providing banquets, transportation home after practice, and manual labor on the athletic facilities. At no time should booster clubs become a personal tool solely to give you money for clinics, or gifts of any kind, such as a new automobile for your own use. Favors can cause a lot of problems, including negative feelings among other coaches and faculty within the school. Bad feelings can also arise when booster clubs support only one or two athletic teams and ignore all the rest, which is not unusual.

This can become a serious problem, not only for the coaches, but for the school district as well. Giving aid (especially financial) to a specific team is a violation of Title IX because it violates the equality factor for all the teams. Violations occur because many people do not fully understand Title IX and its purpose. In other words, if a gift is accepted by any coach or school official for a particular team it could end up being shared by several teams in order to meet the conditions of Title IX. This is where the trouble occurs.

Human nature being what it is, when an organization begins giving financial support to a team or coach and starts paying some of the bills, eventually the people in that organization will want some say, not only in how that money will be spent but in how the program should be run and—in time—who the coach should be. More than one high school coach has lost a job because the booster club became dissatisfied. Since the members of the club are taxpayers and often leaders in the community, they can exert very powerful influence over a superintendent or board of education.

To help a booster club remain a group of boosters, you should take an active role in the club to help provide leadership and to channel interest and enthusiasm in the proper direction. Booster clubs become disenchanted not only with coaches but also with directors of athletics or school administrators who they believe are squelching the athletic program. In such situations you have to attempt to calm the overzealous and exercise the greatest diplomacy to prevent a wholesale purge that can create community factions harmful to everyone concerned.

Booster clubs generally consist of four kinds of people: those who have a genuine interest in high school athletics; those who have a special interest—a son or daughter participating in sports; those who enjoy being on the fringe of athletics by associating with the coaches; and the sharpshooters who are frustrated coaches and attend meetings so they can challenge you, the coach. It is to your advantage to identify these groups as quickly as possible to help in dealing with them. Whether booster clubs are a tremendous help to high school athletic teams or whether they create problems depends on the leadership of the officers and, ideally, of the coaches and athletic director.

MEN COACHING GIRLS' AND WOMEN'S TEAMS

One of the unforeseen things that has occurred since the passage of Title IX–mandated equal opportunity for both sexes in all walks of life, including athletics,

is that even though the growth in girls' and women's athletic teams has been phenomenal, the number of women actually coaching does not seem to be keeping pace.

The biggest concern, as mentioned earlier in this book, is the lack of a proper role model for girls and women when their coach is male. The concern of women in the profession is that this situation perpetuates the stereotype of males being in charge as leaders and females playing the role of followers. The answer to this is clear—encourage more young women to enter the coaching profession.

PLAYERS QUITTING

The ease with which youngsters quit athletic teams today is both alarming and distressing to many coaches. When players quit it plays havoc with the way the coach organizes the program and the team, especially if a number of youngsters quit over a period of time during the season.

There was a time not too many years ago when quitting a team was almost unthinkable to a high school athlete. It just wasn't done, because not many boys and girls wanted to be branded a quitter. The word had too many negative implications. One of the basic lessons coaches attempted to teach was "Don't quit; quitters never win."

Maybe it isn't fair to point a critical finger at youngsters who quit teams. After all, quitting or failing to live up to obligations seems to be the style today. This lack of commitment is in evidence everywhere. Looking out for number one seems to be the way to go today. Marriages are falling apart at an all-time high; men and women opt to live together without getting married because they don't want to make a commitment. Many programs on TV show people who are committed to nothing of any real purpose except life in the fast lane and doing only what is "good for me."

Coaches who break contracts to move on to higher-paying jobs or more prestigious positions and professional athletes who continually demand to be traded or to have legal contracts renegotiated also demonstrate lack of commitment and obligation.

What we are suggesting is that there seems to be a great need for youngsters today to learn what it means to make a commitment, or to honor an obligation to something or someone. What better place to teach this lesson than in athletics?

Athletics is full of opportunities for youngsters to learn what commitment means—commitment to finish a task once they take it on, to be at practice every day, to observe coaches' rules, to observe rules of the game, to support teammates, to give an honest effort regardless of circumstances, and never to give up or quit.

The initial part of this lesson should occur when parents give their children permission to try out for a high school team. The youngsters should clearly understand that they are about to make a commitment to themselves, their teammates, and their coaches. If they make such a commitment, they have an obligation to fulfill it. Thus, if they choose to try out for a team, they must agree to complete the season, except for extenuating circumstances, and to not quit of their own volition. Quitting is not one of the characteristics or qualities we admire in our society, nor is it a quality of successful people. It has been said that we really never fail in any task until we quit trying.

Some believe that it is a mistake for youngsters to stay on a team if, once they try out, they find they don't like it. We do not accept this notion. If we believe there is carryover value in adult life from lessons learned in an athletic arena, youngsters need to learn that not every commitment they make or obligation they have in life will always be easy or just plain fun. Some obligations may be downright unpleasant or a struggle. But that doesn't mean that they can simply walk away from these commitments.

Quitting is like telling a lie. The first few times might be difficult, but it gets increasingly easy the more it is done.

Don't Quit

When things go wrong, as they sometimes will,
When the road you're trudging seems all uphill,
When the funds are low and the debts are high,
And you want to smile, but you have to sigh
When care's pressing you down a bit—
Rest if you must, but don't you quit.

Life is queer with its twists and turns,
As every one of us sometimes learns,
And many a person turns about
When they might have won had they stuck it out.
Don't give up though the pace seems slow—
You may succeed with another blow.

Often the goal is nearer than
It seems to a faint and faltering man;
Often the strugglers have given up
When they might have captured the victor's cup;
And learned too late when the night came down
How close they were to the golden crown.

Success is failure turned inside out
The silver tint of the clouds of doubt
And you never can tell how close you are,
It may be near when it seems afar;
So stick to the fight when you're hardest hit
It's when things seem worst that you mustn't quit.

Quitting something that is not easy can become habit all too quickly. Those who learn to face up to fulfilling obligations and commitment through participation in athletics will find it easier to face themselves in a mirror each morning; they will feel better about themselves because they were strong enough to persevere; and they will have learned a valuable lesson that will strengthen them for the inevitable difficult situations facing them later in life.

The ability or willingness to recognize and honor a personal commitment is an honorable trait and one to be admired. Athletics is the perfect place to learn this important lesson of life. As such, it should be a high-priority goal in every coach's teaching.

SPECIALIZATION

There is a strong trend for some coaches to encourage young people to give up participating in several sports in order to concentrate on only one—the sport those coaches just happen to coach. Their selling point, of course, is that specialization, possibly beginning in the upper elementary grades, will automatically make youngsters much better athletes when they finally make the high school varsity. On the other side of the coin, a large number of coaches oppose this idea and encourage athletes on their teams to participate in other sports. Naturally these two views come into conflict within an athletic department.

One of the practices manifested by specialization is an organized off-season strength-training program. The problem is that some youngsters give up other sports so they can participate in the weight program with the hope or suggestion that this will make them better in a particular sport. Whether any pressure has been exerted by a coach in this situation does not really matter, because other coaches in the school will assume it was. This situation can create a lot of hard feelings within the coaching ranks—especially if the number of athletes and level of talent is critical in a given situation.

Specialization in itself might not be bad. The motivation behind a choice is important, however. The decision to give up other sports to concentrate on one can occur because coaches encourage or strongly support it, because parents encourage it, because coaches hint that it would be best for a youngster, and, of course, because the athletes themselves decide it is what they want to do.

There are three basic problems with all of these reasons. The first is that attempting to specialize does not guarantee success in a sport, and therefore the youngster could be cheated out of some positive experiences in other sports by deciding to specialize.

The second problem is the animosity that can arise between head coaches in the same school when one believes the other has influenced a fine athlete to give up one sport to concentrate on another. Unless a school has an abundance of good athletes, the loss of a single athlete can seriously affect a particular team, which certainly affects its coach. So this becomes a matter of professional survival and undue influence on young boys and girls for what could be the selfish reasons of a coach. The last thing any athletic department needs is conflict between head coaches within the school.

The third problem surfaces when a student of junior high age decides to specialize in a single sport only to find out later he or she made a bad choice. Every coach recognizes the tremendous changes that occur in every youngster from ages 12 to 18 and how those bodily changes affect physical skill and strength. Youngsters need to understand that it might be smart to participate in a variety of sports until they find out which ones they like best and which ones they are best suited for in the high school years. There is no need to hurry.

Another phenomenon in this area is the vast proliferation of summer sports camps. Name an activity and a camp probably exists for that activity somewhere in this country. Many such camps are on college campuses, but not all are. Basically, they are money makers for the organizers plus recruiting tools when held on college campuses.

Secondary school athletes are frequently encouraged to attend these camps by their coaches, presumably to become better at a particular sport. The rationale is that youngsters who don't go will fall behind those who do. It is fairly safe to say there is an element of pressure involved that often leads to specializing in a single sport.

It seems that there is no beginning or end to any sport season anymore—each has become year-round practice.

RELIGION

Another issue facing some athletic programs today involves practice or game play on religious days. There are those who believe Sunday, for example, is a religious day and family day. There are those who don't or who believe attending an athletic event on a Sunday with their family is appropriate.

The key is to make certain you are not in violation of school policy by scheduling an event on a Sunday or some kind of religious holiday. If you disagree with school policy, whatever it is, you will have to reconcile this conflict in your own mind.

Another related factor that could draw criticism to coaches and their teams is prayer in association with an athletic contest. It has become traditional for some coaches to require or allow their athletes to pray before an athletic contest or individual competition, sometimes in full view of the spectators. Some people argue that this practice has no place in public-school sport, and certainly not where everyone has to watch.

Whether religion in sport is right or wrong is not the point here. The point is that you should be aware that controversies exist. Rather than make an issue of religion and sports, it would seem appropriate to discuss the matter with the principal, athletic director, and athletes before making any decisions.

CROWD CONTROL/BEHAVIOR

Another problem that needs close attention is crowd control. This problem can easily be narrowed down to the fans at football games, basketball games, and wrestling matches. On the high school level, with increasing frequency fans are testing their limits of decency—throwing objects on a basketball floor and hurling insults at officials, opponents, coaches, and individual players, along with racial slurs and obscene language. This kind of conduct might be a microcosm of society, but that is no excuse.

Fans have a right to yell and scream, *but* the price of a ticket does not give them a right to direct profanity and abusive language at an official or opponent. Far too many spectators treat opponents as the enemy instead of guests. Can you imagine being invited to someone's home only to be verbally abused with obscenities and trash talk for two hours or more? Sounds ridiculous, doesn't it, but that is exactly what is happening in athletic arenas all across the country. You are in a position to change this at your school.

Many city leagues have abandoned night football as a way to prevent trouble during and after games. This policy usually cuts down on the size of the crowd, which also reduces the gate receipts, which then creates financial problems.

Basketball teams have often had to play games in locked, empty gymnasiums because of previous fights and riots involving spectators. The excitement of combat between two wrestlers and the proximity of the spectators to the action can also create dangerous mob spirit.

Normally, it is not the responsibility of coaches to control crowds. This job falls to school officials and other authorities, including the police. But coaches do have an inescapable responsibility for their actions during a game and their effects on spectators. There is no question that a coach who raves and screams on the sidelines can incite a crowd. Such behavior probably occurs more readily in basketball and wrestling, again because of proximity. More often than not, the fans take their cue from the coach when the officials' decision goes against their team. As a matter of fact, so do the players on the team. There is no question that coaches, by their actions on the sidelines, can be a large contributing factor to ugly crowd behavior.

When spectators begin to get out of hand, a courageous coach can do a great deal toward bringing them back to their senses. A coach might prevent a riot by stopping the game and using the public address system to tell the fans to stop abusing officials or the other team, or the game will be forfeited. Obviously, doing so takes a lot of courage, but courage should be a quality of every coach. As Abraham Lincoln once said, "To sin by silence, when they should protest, makes cowards of men."

YOUTH SPORTS PROGRAMS

Programs of the Little League type can become troublesome for high school coaches. The main difficulty is that these programs are usually organized outside the school by nonschool personnel and are dominated by adults who are not trained as teachers. The first mistake these adults make is to assume that children are miniature adults. As a result, the programs are organized from an adult point of view, with little or no regard to what the children need or want.

Often the adults involved in such programs insist they are qualified to coach because of their personal participation in sport somewhere, sometime. The logic in this statement is comparable to that of individuals claiming to be qualified surgeons because they once had an appendectomy. This is nonsense.

Many successful big-time coaches have denounced Little League–type sports. Joe Paterno of Penn State was highly critical of them in his book, *Football My Way*. In Coach Paterno's opinion, youngsters sometimes get a distorted view of themselves and their ability because of the publicity they receive—and so do many parents.

Far too often Little League–type athletic programs are, in reality, adult recreation programs. The adults make the rules, choose the teams, direct practice, decide who will play, get most excited over officials' decisions, determine when and how long practice will be, and get into fights—verbal and physical—over something that occurs when 8-year-old children are playing a game. Adults also choose all-star teams and organize banquets for these children. It is doubtful that any of this is of any real concern to an 8- or 9-year-old youngster—or of any value, for that matter.

Included in this issue is the desire of some townspeople and some coaches in various communities to establish tackle football programs for school-age children. Some of the volunteer "coaches" believe this is how little children learn to be tough. In reality this is how some little children learn to dislike the game, because they find out that playing tackle football can hurt, and not many youngsters enjoy playing games that hurt.

The medical profession's input must also be considered. For example, many doctors agree that preadolescent bone growth is more rapid than muscle development, so that temporarily the bones and joints lack the normal protection of covering muscles and supporting tendons. During this period, a youngster is particularly susceptible to dislocations of joints and to bone injuries, especially to the epiphyses, or ends of long bones. In a survey of some 400 orthopedists, approximately 75 percent agreed that athletic competition was not good for young adolescents and that body contact sports should be eliminated for this age group. Many people in the medical profession have also expressed concern over injury to the elbow associated with pitchers in Little League baseball. This injury usually occurs as a result of youngsters trying to throw hard curve balls.

Besides the physical dangers for a preadolescent involved in competitive sport, there are also emotional ramifications. Muzafer Sherif, a social psychologist, conducted what has become known as the "Lord of the Flies" experiment. He took a group of 11-year-old boys to an isolated camp and divided them into two groups. They competed against each other every day in baseball, football, and tug-of-war. The entire emphasis was on winning. What began as fun and games quickly turned to hostility. Best friends were at each other's throats even when brought together for meals and movies. The situation did not get better until they joined in cooperative efforts that served everyone's mutual benefit. Sherif's conclusion was that competition alone is not inherently antagonistic to human behavior, but when winning becomes all-important to children, watch out!

The fundamental basis for good youth sports programs is intelligent supervision based on sound principles of physical education. Properly conducted, such leagues are not harmful. Improperly conducted, they can be dangerous.

A White House conference on children made the following recommendations concerning youth sports programs:

1. That adults avoid exploiting youth by pressuring them into highly competitive organized activities for which their minds and bodies are not adapted; that they recognize children as individuals rather than as projects in leisure-time pursuits.

2. That schools and communities cooperate in designing out-of-school programs to provide constructive leisure-time activity consistent with sound principles of child development, and to counteract pressures for competitive athletics promoted by groups with good intentions but limited knowledge of the physical and social needs of children.

3. That competitive sports for preadolescents . . . supervised by trained and qualified leaders . . . be further investigated as to their value for children.

It would seem that the main implication for you as a high school coach is to think carefully about all the ramifications before suggesting the start of a youth program for a particular sport. If such a program already exists, you should attempt to provide intelligent leadership to keep the program and the adults involved in it from exploiting the children who participate. Unfortunately, too many adults involved won't want your advice or expertise. In their minds, they already know the best way to teach skills, as well as fundamentals. The real problem arises when people in these programs teach skills/techniques that are different from those taught by coaches of school teams. This puts athletes in a real squeeze because they don't know whom to please.

The argument that "children will play the game anyway so why not have adults step in to teach them the right way and make it more fun" is not valid. When children organize their own games, they set all the rules and limits to suit themselves. They know what they want and what they can do better than some adult who might be looking for a vicarious experience through children.

Bad experiences in these programs can hurt participation in high school athletics. If children learn early in life to dislike a game, for any reason, they tend to give it up completely. In their minds it just isn't worth it to them, so they look elsewhere for something that will be more fun.

Another side of this issue is the effect that a lot of success might have on youngsters when they try out for high school athletic teams. Some coaches blame attitude problems directly on this factor. When youngsters have early success in sport, it can also become a problem for the parents. The athletes and their parents often assume that the same kind of athletic success will occur when these youngsters become members of the high school varsity. Sometimes this is the case—often it is not. What these folks fail to take into consideration, for example, is the "early bloomer" effect that a particular young athlete might enjoy at age 12. By the time these early maturers get into high school, some of their peers may have outgrown them and may even have become better athletes. When parents and athletes fail to recognize this fact, a lot of frustration can set in, and problems can result.

A safe alternative to all of this could be a Saturday morning program for elementary school children, organized by you, the high school coach. In the program, the members of the high school team can serve as coaches, with the only adult involved being you. In this manner a real educator (you) can design, conduct, and control a great program in which the youngsters can learn to enjoy playing the game (the number one priority), whatever the game may be. You should also consider eliminating individual statistics, publicity, all-star teams, banquets, and awards. This would place the emphasis back on play/fun.

The only legitimate justification for any kind of youth sport programs should be to teach young people to enjoy athletics for enjoyment's sake. Fundamentals and strategy can be taught later. Because youngsters mature physically at varying rates, fundamentals and strategy should be a secondary concern. Some children are simply not ready to learn certain fundamentals. When adults keep insisting they try, a boy or girl can develop a feeling of failure and frustration, which can turn into dislike for the game. For preadolescents, fun is the name of the game—period.

OFFICIALS AT ATHLETIC EVENTS

The relationship between coaches and officials should be one of mutual respect. Their shared concern for the fair and safe conduct of an athletic event should provide a common bond. Unfortunately, this is not always the case. Tremendous antagonism often develops instead, particularly in the heat of competition when coaches' emotions are so involved.

One of the most interesting things about coaches' reactions to officials is how they vary from one situation to another. Sometimes an official makes an error in favor of one coach, who sees the error but remains quiet. But if the same official later makes a similar error against that coach's team, the coach frequently goes wild.

When you coach the perfect game, you can expect an official to be perfect also. Until then, keep in mind that officials are human, too, and that mistakes will occur—some in your favor and some not in your favor. Mistakes are part of most athletic events on every level. You need to understand this fact and have enough self-control so that you don't embarrass yourself and your athletes by having a temper tantrum over what you believe is a bad call. Temper tantrums only make you look foolish and upset your players.

A number of factors are basic to officiating in any sport. You have the right to expect officials to

- Be in good physical condition

- Know the rules

- Know the intent of the rules

- Be in the proper position to make calls

- Be fair and impartial (you should be happy with officials who don't care who wins)

- Control the contest

- Understand the "game"

- Give you an explanation for any unusual call

- Keep from developing "rabbit ears"

- Refuse to be intimidated by any coach

- Never lose their cool

On the other side of the coin, officials expect you, the coach, to

- Avoid trying to intimidate officials
- Make sure officials know where to dress and where to go at halftime (when appropriate)
- Provide security after the contest
- Have the team ready to begin at the time agreed on
- Make sure you have enough auxiliary officials present—timers, scorekeepers, etc.
- Provide time to inspect equipment
- Alert them to special events like Homecoming and Parents Night
- Point out any special ground rules
- Have captains prepared
- Control your own players, bench, and fans
- Question calls properly rather than yelling and cursing
- Know the rules and their interpretations
- Question an official's knowledge of a rule when warranted, but not to question a judgment call

If you ever feel the need to criticize officials, the best time to do so is after a win. If you criticize after a loss, you will appear to be looking for an excuse by blaming the loss on officials, whether you say so or not, and you will look bad in the eyes of a lot of people.

Until officials are permitted to shoot a basketball, run a race, swing a bat, spike a volleyball, block and tackle, or coach your team, they cannot win or lose games for you—that is up to you and your players. I'll bet you don't believe this. Well, consider the basketball coach whose team shoots about 30 percent, loses, and then blames the officials; or a softball team that commits five or six errors in a game, loses, and then complains about the umpires. This is ridiculous, and a poor example for athletes. Think about it.

TITLE IX—EQUITY

A short history lesson is in order here. To begin with, competitive athletics for women is *not* a modern day discovery. High school girls played varsity basketball at Union High School in Western Pennsylvania in the 1920s. They were also awarded varsity letters at the same school. Some went on to play professional basketball for the Westinghouse Company in Pittsburgh in the mid-1930s. These professional teams traveled all over the country competing against other women's professional teams. The onset of World War II in 1941 hastened the demise of these teams.

At about that time, leaders in women's physical education (and others) decided that competitive sports for women should be abolished because participating in them wasn't "ladylike" and indeed could be harmful to their physical well-being. Thus began the "play day" era, in which fun, socialization, and absence of competition became the order of the day.

In a play day for volleyball, for example, a school might invite girls from three other schools to participate. Girls from each school would be mixed so that every team was made up of players from each school. They would then play their games, followed in all likelihood with cookies and punch.

When Title IX became law in the early 1970s, its intent was to provide equal opportunity for women *and* men in any federally funded institution. It was not meant to be solely for women and sport, but folks soon discovered its implementation certainly did include these two and the door was once again open for women to become involved in competitive sport.

Male coaches were fearful their programs would suffer. A number of female physical educators also resisted because they felt that the very idea of competitive athletics, scholarships, recruiting, and the emphasis on winning was a contradiction to their philosophy of sport that prevailed at that time. They didn't want to make the same mistakes as men, they said.

A great debate ensued, with the issue of gender equity at the forefront. The key questions seemed to revolve around the definition of equity. Did it mean an even number of teams for men and women? equality in funding? equality in coaches' salaries? a required percentage of participants for both men and women according to overall enrollment? And should football, because of squad size and cost of equipment, be excluded from all of this?

After 32 years of existence, lawsuits, and efforts to bring athletic departments into compliance with the intent of Title IX, significant, if not perfect, progress has been made. One primary concern remaining is scheduling of practice facilities equally and fairly. Doing so takes a lot of imagination and cooperation on the part of everyone.

You need to know that Title IX exists so you can get a clear understanding of what it is and what its purpose is.

LEGAL LIABILITY

The purpose of this section is to alert you to some basic information about legal liability in coaching and to offer some suggestions to help you avoid legal problems. A number of books are available on legal liability in athletics, physical education, and recreation—check with your librarian. It would be a good idea for you to at least skim one of these books in order to get a better understanding of this serious, complicated topic.

Lawsuits are a way of life in today's society, and no one, including coaches, is exempt. This is a fact. Whether you are being paid to coach or are a volunteer, you are legally responsible for what occurs in the program or the part of the program in which you are involved. Not only are coaches being sued regularly, but so are the schools, athletes who cause an injury, and their parents. The attitude seems to be "Since there was an injury, someone is going to pay, and we'll get ours from somebody."

You really don't need a year-long course on legal liability unless you intend to become a "locker-room lawyer." What you do need is to understand your basic legal responsibilities to the athletes and, most important, preventive measures that will allow you to avoid legal difficulties. You have heard it before— an ounce of prevention is worth a pound of cure, and it most certainly holds true in this matter.

When speaking of legal liability in athletics, one need be concerned only with the area of torts. A *tort* is a legal wrong that results in direct or indirect injury to an individual or an individual's property and for which payment for damages may be obtained by court action.

Claims of Negligence

When an injury occurs in athletics, the plaintiff (or injured party) may allege that the injury was caused or aggravated as a result of the coach's negligence. *Negligence* in this sense can be an act of either omission or commission. In other words, negligence can be a factor either in what you did or did not do. The critical question that must be answered is, should the coach, through reasonable prudence and foresight, have anticipated danger or injury to a student under the particular set of circumstances in question? If the answer to this question is yes, then the coach has been negligent in the performance of his or her duties.

Several factors that commonly contribute to negligence claims in athletics are

1. *The absence of protective measures.* A coach is expected to anticipate the hazards involved in any activity and to take whatever steps may be necessary to protect the safety of the athlete.

2. *Poor selection of activities.* A coach must select activities appropriate to the age, size, and skill of the student. Failure to do so can lead to serious injury and constitutes an act of negligence.

3. *Unsafe conditions of facilities and equipment.* Before using any practice area, a coach should always examine it carefully to be sure it is free of

hazards. Such things as broken glass or holes on playing fields often lead to serious injury. No athlete should be allowed to use a piece of equipment until you have examined it to ensure its safe operation and freedom from defect.

4. *Inadequate supervision.* The question of supervision involves both a qualitative and quantitative judgment. Coaches must be knowledgeable in the specific activity they are supervising, and must then provide supervision during the course of the activity. There are two kinds of supervision—general and specific. General supervision means the coach must be within the area, overseeing the whole activity. Specific supervision means the coach must be at a specific location of an activity, such as the high bar in gymnastics. Under *no* circumstance should athletes be permitted to play or practice without proper supervision (or a signed physical card).

5. *Inadequate control measures.* Closely tied with the question of supervision is that of control measures. The actions of one youngster or a group should never be allowed to create a hazardous situation for others. Horseplay not only impedes learning—it often leads to injury.

6. *Poor judgment.* The area of a coach's judgment is rather broad and can encompass a wide variety of situations in which the coach fails to apply common sense and prudent judgment and a student suffers harm as a result. Examples would include

   a. Asking a student to assume an unreasonable risk; for instance, activities designed primarily to build "courage."

   b. Failure to apply proper first aid, or exceeding the limits of first aid.

   c. Punishing a youngster with excessive running or other physically demanding exercises or drills.

7. *Failure to warn.* Warning players of their potential for injury is essential. However, coaches frequently ignore this warning for fear it will have a negative effect on players—particularly in a contact sport. Nevertheless, parents and players both should be informed about the risks involved and should be given written material describing ways in which injuries can be avoided.

These are, in general terms, some of the areas that frequently give rise to negligence claims. The list may appear formidable, but remember that a good coach who has a genuine concern for the welfare of students will rarely neglect their well-being. A few minutes of careful planning, preparation, and common sense are usually all that are necessary to ensure safety.

Defenses Against Negligence Claims

Several defenses against negligence claims can be used in legal actions. The best defense, of course, is providing the extra ounce of care that prevents an accident from happening in the first place. Sometimes, however, an accident occurs despite the most conscientious efforts. In such cases, the following defenses are often employed:

1. *Proximate cause.* The element of proximate cause must be proven in any case involving negligence. It is not sufficient to merely allege that a coach was negligent in his or her duties. One must prove additionally that this negligence was the cause of the damage that occurred to the student.

2. *Act of God.* An act of God is an accident that is attributable to forces of nature, such as lightning striking a student or a limb of a tree falling on a student. If, however, a prudent person could have foreseen the likelihood of such an occurrence, then an act of God is not a valid defense.

3. *Contributory negligence.* Contributory negligence attributes part of the blame for an injury to the injured party. It usually arises when a player was injured while doing something that he or she had clearly been warned not to do. In some states, proof of contributory negligence constitutes sufficient cause for dismissal of a negligence claim. The courts are beginning to turn, however, to a concept of *comparative negligence*, whereby the youngsters are liable only to a degree to which they caused their own injuries, and the coach can still be held liable in part. In cases where student negligence is present, the coach is still liable for a settlement if some percentage of liability is determined by the courts.

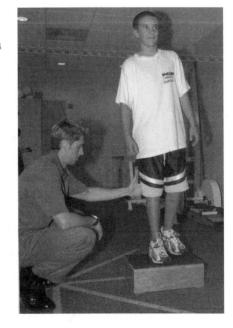

4. *Assumption of risk.* In the past, courts ruled that anyone who participates in sports and physical activities assumes that there are certain dangers built into the very nature of the activity. Since coaches cannot protect students from such built-in dangers, they cannot be held liable for their occurrence. This is no longer totally the case, as courts now have begun to make exceptions to this when athletes allege improper supervision, inferior equipment, or some other failure to conform to reasonable standards. The amount of risk that a student can be expected to

assume varies with age and skill level. A prudent coach will be sure the students are made aware of the dangers in an activity, as well as the techniques by which the dangers can be minimized. Assumption of risk is defensible only if you have proof that you did in fact warn the athletes before the occurrence.

You need to understand that while you can lessen the odds of getting sued, there does not seem to be any foolproof way to totally avoid a lawsuit.

The danger of accidental injury is always present when it comes to sport. Although you can never completely avoid it, you can minimize it by taking a few simple precautions:

1. Know your athletes. Be aware of their abilities and health needs, and plan your practices accordingly. Keep written practice plans on file.

2. Be sure your equipment is safe and in good condition. Be sure to secure all equipment when not in use (attractive nuisance) to prevent injuries through unauthorized use.

3. *NOCSAE (National Operating Committee on Safety in Athletic Equipment)*. Protective equipment (helmets, face guards, pads) must carry current NOCSAE certification. Coaches and athletic directors who use noncertified equipment would be liable for damages if injury occurs.

4. Carefully organize and supervise your team. The better the planning and organization, the less likelihood for injury.

5. Provide thorough instruction in both performance and safety techniques.

6. Put all safety procedures in writing and require all athletes and their parents to sign the document to indicate that they have read it.

7. Describe techniques for performing potentially dangerous skills in writing and give these instructions to the players.

8. Use training films to show correct technique.

9. Should an accident occur:

    a. Administer first aid only—do not practice medicine.

    b. Get professional medical assistance as soon as possible.

    c. Keep an accurate record of the exact circumstances surrounding the accident. This is particularly useful in the event of a lawsuit, since memory tends to dim with time.

EMPHASIS ON WINNING

One criticism leveled at coaches over the years is the charge that all coaches are governed by a win-at-all-cost mentality. Generalizations are usually dangerous and unfair simply because of what they are—generalizations. And so it is in this regard. Don't ever apologize for wanting your team to win, but don't stay in coaching if you want your team to win at any cost.

All teachers have an inescapable obligation to push, plead, insist, coax, demand, and expect all students under their care to strive to become the best they are capable of becoming—whether the focus be math, English, band, or sport. To create or tolerate an atmosphere in which young people learn that mediocrity is acceptable in sport or life would be a flagrant abdication of a teacher's basic obligation to youngsters.

There is a deep tendency in human nature to become precisely what we imagine or picture ourselves to be: we determine either self-limitations or unlimited growth potential. The German philosopher Goethe said, "If you treat individuals as they are, they will stay as they are. But if you treat them as if they were what they could be and ought to be, they will become what they ought to be." The message here is that players need to be encouraged, by coaches, to always strive to go higher and to understand that they can be greater than they think. Obviously this encouragement has to be carefully tempered and realistic, or we will have a nation of psychological wrecks.

We believe that striving to win is important. Please note that we said striving to win, not winning itself. As we stated earlier in this book, there is nothing in the world wrong, sinister, or evil in teaching youngsters to play to win or to strive to be the best. On the contrary, we see winning as one of our primary objectives. It is only when rules, written or unwritten, are violated, or when athletes who end up in second place see themselves as failures, that this notion is corrupted.

All athletes have a responsibility to themselves, their teammates, and their opponents to play to win. In the true spirit of competition we should expect this attitude of all participants, and it should bring out the best skills and efforts required for any game. In the process, the opportunity exists for players to learn the importance of team play, cooperation, and selflessness, all of which are necessary when a group is attempting to realize some specific accomplishment—in this case, victory.

All athletes also owe it to themselves to strive to win in order to fully experience the sense of joy and satisfaction that comes from being completely spent from sheer effort while clutching the prize.

We need to teach young athletes to play the game in such a way that if they come up short on the scoreboard, it is because they were *beaten* rather than because they *lost*. There can be no sense of failure in this case. Disappointment, yes, but failure—absolutely not.

Losing means we ourselves were at fault by playing poorly. It should be unacceptable to coaches and to athletes as well—and it will be if they are being taught to play to win. Being satisfied with less than their best effort in any endeavor is *not* a desirable value for athletes to learn through participation in sport.

There are those who rationalize losing by saying they did their best. The danger in this mentality is that it provides a convenient excuse for a poor effort and can lull athletes into a comfort zone. They react by saying, "Why are you getting upset, Coach? So I came in last . . . but I did my best!" Certainly this statement could be true, but I submit the notion that very few of us, if any, are able to say with any degree of certainty what our best is—mentally or physically. Most youngsters in sport quite simply have no idea what their best is, and it is up to coaches to help them realize that their dreams should always be just a little greater than their grasp. You can do this through the challenge of striving to win—that is why opponents exist. The pressure of competition does not, as some would have us believe, destroy us. Instead, it reveals us.

One of the things coaches and administrators of sport have hung their hats on for years is the claim that the lessons learned through sport are really preparing young people for life. These lessons include respect for rules, commitment, perseverance, self-discipline, and the will to win.

It is therefore important for you to help players develop a competitive spirit to help them learn how to respond to challenge, to attempt to instill the will to win,

and to impress upon them that all of this can and must be done without compromising their honor and integrity. At the same time, they must learn that if and when they come up on the short side of a scoreboard, the world will not end—the sun will still rise tomorrow.

It was once said that if we aim at the moon and fall short, we'll still be among the stars. Not a bad motto for youngsters to carry out of school, is it?

CONFLICT WITH AN ADMINISTRATOR

It seems that everybody is an expert in athletics today, whether ever having participated or not. After all, everyone watches TV and hears the announcers analyze an entire game, including the players; thus, we have couch potato experts who think they know more than coaches—and many high school principals fall in this same mindset.

It is rather unusual for a principal to tell a teacher how to teach, but not so unusual for a principal to tell a coach how to coach or to overrule a decision made by a coach in disciplinary matters. This can become a gigantic problem. Let me describe one real-life situation to you. Put yourself in place of this coach to see how you might respond in the same or similar circumstances.

High school team "A" was scheduled to play its biggest game of the year against a strong opponent in the last game of the season. To add some motivation, the coach of team "A" decided to have the players wear black jerseys (not the school color) because "tough" people wear black, he believed. The players were not aware of this plan. After pregame warm-up in their regular jerseys, the team went into the locker room and discovered the black jerseys hanging on their lockers. This made a real impact on the team, and the athletes really got fired up as they put on their new jerseys.

The team then waited until the last minute to make their dramatic appearance. Naturally, everyone was completely surprised. The game started, and the principal of school "A" came down out of the stands, confronted the head coach, and demanded that the players remove the black jerseys at once in favor of their regular ones. The coach pointed out that the game had begun and changing jerseys at that point was not possible, and so the game continued without interruption.

At halftime, the coach was met at the lockerroom door by the principal and athletic director and was ordered to remove the black jerseys for the second half and have the players wear their regular ones.

When the head coach told the team about the order, they objected strenuously and said they did not want to comply. The head coach asked the assistants what they thought, and they responded that they would support the head coach's decision. He then decided to ignore the order of the principal and allow the team to keep the black jerseys on, as this seemed so important to the team. Naturally the principal was livid that a coach would have the audacity to disobey him.

Two weeks later the coach was fired.

STRESS AND BURNOUT

There is no doubt that coaches work in a stressful atmosphere. It is important that you not only recognize this situation but also understand that you are susceptible to stress. You need to know its causes, the problems associated with it, and ways to deal with it.

Stress is defined as the body's physical, mental, and chemical response to circumstances that frighten, confuse, threaten, or excite us. Stress can be caused by a happy event as well as an unhappy one, and the effects on the body can be the same in either circumstance. For example, winning a particularly crucial athletic event can be as stressful as losing it.

Not all stress is bad, and life without stress would be dull, uninteresting, and without much challenge. Some people deliberately seek out stressful situations in which to immerse themselves for sheer excitement and challenge. But everyone has a maximum tolerance for stress, which should be recognized in order to stay within that limit. Some symptoms of stress are emotional tension, anxiety, insecurity, nightmares, phobias, irritability, and short temper. Studies have shown that some people are more prone to stress and stress-related diseases.

These high-risk individuals are labeled as Type A personalities, and they may have a tendency to develop premature heart disease.

Figure 11.1 is a self-evaluation tool for Type A behavior. Circle the number that most closely represents your own behavior. If you score high in the direction of the asterisks, you have a definite disposition toward a Type A personality. When and if stress becomes chronic, burnout occurs. *Burnout* is physical, emotional, and attitudinal exhaustion. Some symptoms of burnout are high blood pressure, constant fatigue, depression, sleeplessness, headaches, stomach ulcer, excessive drinking, overeating, undereating, or change in sexual behavior. Any or all of these can be a tip-off to the onset of burnout. Job burnout, which is brought about by unrelieved work stress, is characterized by depleted energy reserves, lowered resistance to illness, increased dissatisfaction with the job, and decreased efficiency.

For coaches, a great deal of stress arises from a lack of job satisfaction or from other factors surrounding the job: salary, promotions, relationships with fellow teachers and the principal, negative feedback from parents and critics, attitude problems with athletes, winning, losing, and job insecurity all create stress.

Figure 11.1
Are you a Type A?

*Never late	5 4 3 2 1 0 1 2 3 4 5	Casual about appointments
Not competitive	5 4 3 2 1 0 1 2 3 4 5	*Very competitive
*Anticipates what others are going to say (nods, interrupts, finishes for them)	5 4 3 2 1 0 1 2 3 4 5	Listens well
*Always rushed	5 4 3 2 1 0 1 2 3 4 5	Never feels rushed (even under pressure)
Can wait patiently	5 4 3 2 1 0 1 2 3 4 5	*Waits impatiently
*Goes all out	5 4 3 2 1 0 1 2 3 4 5	Casual out
Takes things one at a time	5 4 3 2 1 0 1 2 3 4 5	*Tries to do many things at once; thinks what he is about to do next
*Emphatic speaker	5 4 3 2 1 0 1 2 3 4 5	Slow, deliberate talker
*Wants good job recognized by others	5 4 3 2 1 0 1 2 3 4 5	Cares about satisfying himself no matter what others may think
*Fast (eating, walking, etc.)	5 4 3 2 1 0 1 2 3 4 5	Slow in doing things
Easygoing	5 4 3 2 1 0 1 2 3 4 5	*Hard driving
Hides feelings	5 4 3 2 1 0 1 2 3 4 5	*Expresses feelings
*Many outside interests	5 4 3 2 1 0 1 2 3 4 5	Few interests outside work
Satisfied with job	5 4 3 2 1 0 1 2 3 4 5	*Ambitious

It is important to recognize these factors and to deal with them directly instead of merely trying to treat the symptoms of stress. Several stress management techniques can help prevent serious problems:

1. *Know your own body.* It is important to be aware of physical and mental changes. Changes in how you handle emotions, frustrations, anger, or pleasure can be the first clue to the onset of stress.

2. *Manage your time.* Work overload and conflict between the demands of a job and personal or family needs are common sources of occupational stress. Too often, too many things need to be done, and therefore the time people have for doing what they would really like to do is cut down. Each person should learn to set priorities in order to use time more efficiently. Be aware of such time robbers as visitors, phone calls, and meetings, and try to keep them to a minimum.

3. *Conduct a stress inventory.* Make a list of the things that cause the most stress in your life. Then break them down so that you can deal with small parts rather than the whole in an effort to resolve some of the stress.

4. *Avoid stress.* It is impossible to avoid stress completely, but it is possible to avoid stressful situations to a degree, once they have been identified.

5. *Alter your own behavior.* Make an effort to change your response to the stressor. If you can't change the circumstances, change yourself. In this way you can control a potentially stressful situation better, thereby reducing the degree of stress.

6. *Exercise.* There is no doubt that enjoyable exercise has both physiological and psychological benefits and is therefore an excellent technique for dealing with stress. Coaches frequently become so involved in their jobs and in teaching others to play a game that they forget to take time for themselves to participate in some form of recreational exercise. You should schedule some time each day for relaxation and recreation, and refuse to give up that time. Indulging in regular, enjoyable exercise can be very healthy for the mind as well as the body.

7. *Communicate.* Efficient communication—both talking and listening—can help reduce stress on the job. One of the best ways to relieve conflicts with administrators and colleagues is to talk over your concerns with them and listen to their points of view. A problem might not be resolved to everyone's satisfaction, but discussing it is far better than keeping it to yourself. That only adds to the stress factor and can eventually lead to other problems. Communicating with colleagues can also be a good way to reduce stress. Sometimes coaches think they are the only ones in the world with a particular problem or concern, and such thinking can cause a lot of stress. In

talking with other coaches, in and out of school, they often discover they are not alone in this regard and may, in the process, pick up some ideas on how to deal with the problem.

Job burnout affects all professions; however, research indicates that coaches, teachers, principals, and counselors seem to suffer a higher incidence than others. Part of the reason may be that the teaching profession deals with intangibles, and there is no finished product a teacher can point to and say, "I did that." In addition, public support and public opinion of the profession is frequently negative, causing some teachers to question their own value. This too can contribute to stress and burnout. It is most important that you recognize what stressors are, what they can do to you, and how you can deal with them.

> I have done what I can and I have done what I must. Tomorrow will take care of some of it and, with a little bit of luck, time will take care of the rest.
> —Katherine LaMancusa, *We Do Not Throw Rocks at the Teacher*

There is no limit to the problems, issues, and concerns associated with any and all athletic departments. Those presented here apply to secondary school athletic programs, in varying degrees, nationwide, and appear to be the most critical issues facing coaches at this time. The point of this chapter is to alert you to some possibilities so that you can think about them and plan for them before they become serious. These considerations should become part of your having a plan for everything. Remember—it is far easier to be a "fire preventer" than a "fire fighter."

DISCUSSION QUESTIONS

1. How do you view youth sports programs? Support your opinion.

2. How would you attempt to convince a board of education that it should not drop interscholastic athletics?

3. Should an athlete's lifestyle be of any concern to a coach? Why?

4. Define tort.

5. When the sole purpose in sport is to win, a "game" becomes an all-or-nothing experience. Explain this.

6. What are some ways coaches can avoid the possibility of lawsuits?

7. What techniques do you believe would be most successful for discussing drug abuse with your players?

8. Do coaches have any obligation to athletes regarding the use of steroids? If so, what is it?

9. What is the number one drug problem throughout society?

10. What is it that you need to understand about Title IX?

11. The earlier boys and girls begin competitive sport in school, the better athletes they will be in senior high school. Do you agree with this statement? Why?

12. Have any people in the class had their fathers or mothers as coaches? Describe this experience.

13. If the attitude of high school students toward sports is a problem in your school, what could you as a coach do to change it?

14. Define burnout.

15. List several ways a coach can deal with stress.

16. What is a stressor?

17. When is "assumption of risk" defensible in a lawsuit?

18. How would you respond to athletes who told you they wanted to take steroids in order to become better athletes?

19. List several advantages and disadvantages of hiring part-time coaches.

20. What are your views on specialization of high school or junior high school athletes? Support your position.

21. How would you deal with an obvious eating disorder in one of your athletes? What might you do to prevent this disorder from occurring?

22. What are the implications in the "Lord of the Flies" experiment?

23. If the use of alcohol were a problem among your athletes, what are some ways you would deal with it?

24. What do you consider to be the number one issue in sport today?

25. How will you plan on dealing with athletes who tell you they want to quit the team?

26. React to the statement, "Game officials do not lose games for you."

27. What do you see as your most important consideration in the area of legal liability?

28. Striving to win is the most important thing in athletics. Do you believe this? Why?

You have picked an exciting way to earn a living. I sincerely hope that the ideas and suggestions in this book will help smooth out some of the rough spots you might face as you begin a career in coaching.

May coaching be everything you ever hoped it would be. I hope you become the greatest coach your sport has ever seen. Good luck!

This final chapter is very short, but it deserves careful consideration. It is a collection of ideas, thoughts, and axioms gathered from a vast number of sources over many years. Most of these items are the direct result of lessons learned through coaching experience, mistakes, and success.

The following list is presented as a means of helping you avoid some of the pitfalls that coaches, including the authors, have encountered in the past.

COACHING POINTS

1. Always keep in mind that you are a role model, whether you want to be or not; so live your life accordingly.

2. No game is worth winning if you have to compromise your integrity to do so.

3. Remember that no matter what you think, someone will think differently.

4. Never criticize members of your team to the news media.

5. Do not blame your team publicly for losing an athletic contest.

6. Do not bad-mouth officials to the news media.

7. Always praise an opponent to the news media.

8. Do not blame officials when your team loses.

9. Try to keep coaching in perspective. The world does not revolve around you and the team you coach.

10. If an athlete comes to you with a complaint, listen carefully. Don't become defensive or resentful.

11. Don't try to be a "pal" to your athletes—this is asking for trouble.

12. Never date a student or, worse yet, one of your athletes.

13. If you get in trouble, you will soon find out who your friends are.

14. Pay attention to those who pat you on the back the hardest when you are winning. The same people will probably be wielding a knife when you start losing.

15. If someone in the community is criticizing you, don't ignore it—meet that person face-to-face to clear the air.

16. Treat your athletes the way you would want another teacher to treat your daughter or son.

17. Never take *anything* for granted where youngsters are concerned.

18. Remember that even the most carefully prepared plans often go wrong.

19. Lucky breaks do happen—so do bad ones.

20. Do not allow your athletes to blame a teammate for a loss. This can rip a team apart.

21. Don't just tell people they did something wrong—tell them how to do it properly.

22. Most games are games of mistakes; normally the team or athlete who blunders the least will win.

23. Just a few courageous and determined athletes can make an immense difference.

24. If you don't have better athletes, and more of them than your opponents, you will never win consistently.

25. Athletes win athletic events, not coaches.

26. Some athletes fight with great courage in the heat of competition— some do not.

27. Desire is more important than skill.

28. One of your first tasks is to determine who the "gamers" are and make sure you get them into competition.

29. High morale is essential to victory.

30. The time to scold a team is when they play poorly but luck out and win anyway.

31. Do not scold your team or athletes after they have lost and when their spirits are low.

32. Teach the value of a good work ethic by demonstrating it yourself.

33. As a season progresses, a team gets better or worse—it never stays the same.

34. Take care of the little things, and the big things will take care of themselves.

35. You will never get bored coaching; if you do, it is time to get out.

36. Have a reason for everything.

37. Always let your athletes know "why."

38. In a deadlock of opinion, the head coach always has one more vote than the whole staff combined.

39. Create an atmosphere where students aspire to be a part of the team you coach.

40. Teach your athletes more than just physical skills.

41. Decide what a great coaching situation would be for you. Someday you will be asked this question in an interview.

42. Be a confidence-builder for your athletes.

43. High school athletes frequently look for shortcuts in preparing themselves to play—don't let this happen.

44. There are only two ways athletes can prepare for an athletic contest—your way or the wrong way.

45. Don't ever settle for mediocrity in any part of your program.

46. Leave no stone unturned in an effort to get the athletes to believe in you and what you are trying to do for them.

47. Practice doesn't have to be drudgery.

48. No pain, no gain is a myth.

49. The real test of your coaching ability is not the scoreboard but whether you are able to get 100 percent out of your players.

50. The only happy players on the team are the starters or those who get a lot of playing time.

51. The toughest problem in picking players is to figure out what they'll do in the actual competition.

52. An attitude problem can destroy a team if ignored.

53. Use a youngster's proper name or nickname all the time. Derogatory names are insulting.

54. Do not curse at your players.

55. Let your players know you have faith, and trust, in them.

56. Establish good habits for players and insist they be practiced at all times.

57. Don't take yourself too seriously.

58. Don't be afraid to laugh it up when warranted.

59. Remember, losing can become a habit.

60. Losing can cause a lot of problems.

61. Be positive in your coaching, not just a critic.

62. Don't ignore the "down-the-liners."

63. Don't let an athlete leave the locker room dejected.

64. In the locker room athletes should be good friends with their teammates.

65. Don't accept "I did my best" after a loss. None of us knows what our best is.

66. Never accept an excuse or alibi—there is no room for excuses in athletics.

67. While coaching is your chosen profession, remember that no matter what the sport, it is still just a game to most high school athletes.

68. High school athletes rarely hurt as much or as long as you will after a disappointing loss.

69. When things are going badly (losing) for the team, resist the temptation to make sweeping changes or resort to gimmicks to straighten things out. Usually this approach will not work in the long run. You always need good athletes to win consistently, not experiments or gimmicks.

70. Underclass players find ways to lose; seniors find ways to win.

71. Don't interfere with your opponents when they are in the process of destroying themselves.

72. Before you can win an athletic event, you first have to keep from losing it. (The value of preparation)

73. When victory seems imminent, that's the time to "buckle your helmet strap."

74. You are never as good as you think you are when you win—and never as bad as you think you are when you lose.

75. Only a fool commits an act without first considering the price of that act.

76. The harder you work, the harder it is to surrender.

77. No superior has the moral right to direct you to cheat.

78. You only get real deterrence when people know there is a price to be paid.

79. It's what you learn after you know it all that counts.

80. Excellence costs a lot, but mediocrity eventually costs more.

81. An army of deer led by a lion is more to be feared than an army of lions led by a deer.

82. Success is never final.
    Failure is never fatal.
    The only thing that counts is courage.
    —*Winston Churchill*

83. Be honest.

84. Always choose the difficult right over an easier wrong.

85. Don't whine and make excuses.

86. Pay attention to what's best for the team versus what seems best for you.

87. Don't pursue happiness—pursue excellence.

88. On the fields of friendly strife
    Are sown the seeds which in other years
    Bear the fruits of victory.
    —*Gen. Douglas MacArthur*

Figure 12.1
A coaching creed.

A COACHING CREED

Be a resource person able to assist the athlete to develop his/her athletic potential and self-dependency.

Recognize individual differences in athletes and always think of the athlete's long-term best interests.

Aim for excellence based upon realistic goals and the athlete's growth and development.

Lead by example. Teach and practice cooperation, self-discipline, respect for officials and opponents, and proper attitudes in language, dress, and deportment.

Make sport challenging and fun. Skills and techniques need not be learned painfully.

Be honest and consistent with athletes. They appreciate knowing where they stand.

Be prepared to interact with the media, league officials, and parents. They too have important roles to play in sport.

Coaching involves training by responsible people who are flexible and willing to continually learn and develop.

Physical fitness should be a lifelong goal for all. Encourage athletes to be fit all year, every year and not just for the season.

DISCUSSION

Rather than listing questions to be answered, I recommend that each of the coaching points be used for discussion and debate. Through this technique you should be able to better understand the meaning of these points and their ramifications.

TOURNAMENT SCHEDULING

One of the first and most important steps in organizing competition is selecting the tournament best suited to the sport. In many sports, only one form of tournament is suitable; others may adapt to more than one system.

Certain factors will determine the type of tournament to be used. Among these are the number of entries, the time allotted for playing, the facilities that are available, and the advantages and disadvantages of each tournament structure. Also, in each individual case problems and situations will arise that have some bearing on the choice of format.

SEEDING

Seeding, where it is possible, can play an important role in elimination tournaments. A seeded team or player is considered to be highly rated in skill and a

definite contender for the championship. The purpose of seeding is to prevent the highly skilled entries from eliminating each other in the early rounds. This is accomplished by placing the seeded teams or players in separate brackets. Thus the glamor and excitement mounts as the top teams are pitted against each other in the final rounds. The final goal is to have the championship round between the two best entries, the semifinals between the four best entries, and so on, depending on the size of the tourney.

Two of the main objections to seeding are (1) matching the inferior player with a superior player, which usually ends in defeat for the former; and (2) creating dissatisfaction and resentment on the part of players who are paired with a seeded opponent. However, if superiority is evident among certain entries, these teams or players should be seeded to guarantee a better outcome of the tournament.

Generally, two out of every four entries are seeded. But in many cases the number of seeded teams will depend on the situation. When seeding is not practiced, entries are placed by drawing lots.

BYES

Whenever a team is awarded advancement into the next round without having to compete against an opponent, it is considered to have received a *bye*. If there are seeded players or teams in the tournament, they should be awarded the byes. If the original number of contestants is an exact power of two (2, 4, 8, 16, 32, etc.), byes are not required. When the total number of contestants does not balance out to an even power of two, byes are used to make up the difference. If there were only 13 teams, the number of byes to be used would be 16 minus 13, or 3. A team that is awarded a bye automatically advances to the second round.

In elimination tournaments, if there is an even number of byes, they are divided equally and placed half at the top and half at the bottom of the bracket. The position of byes as used in round robin tournaments will be taken up in the discussion on that type of tournament.

PRELIMINARY QUALIFYING ROUNDS

Where there are a great number of contestants, it may be necessary to conduct preliminary qualifying rounds to cut down the field. The teams that play in this "pretournament" tournament are drawn by lot or chosen because of poor or unknown ability. The latter method of selection prevents losing superior entries in the qualifying rounds. After the necessary number of rounds are completed to reduce the field to the desired number, the regular elimination tournament can be charted and scheduled.

SINGLE ELIMINATION TOURNAMENTS

Single elimination tournaments are charted in bracket form. As the quickest method of determining a winner, the single elimination tournament has the disadvantage of providing fewer opportunities for contestants to play.

The number of games to be played to complete the tournament can be figured simply by subtracting 1 from the number of entries. For example, with 16 entries, 15 games will be played (16 − 1 = 15). The total number of rounds required should be the same number as the power to which 2 must be raised to equal the number of entries. For example, with 8 contestants, two must be raised to the third power, indicating there will be three rounds. When there are only 13 contestants, this total must be raised to 16, the next highest power to two. Thus, as $16 = 2^4$, there will be four rounds, as shown in the diagram opposite.

To calculate the number of games to be played in round 1, subtract the number of byes from the number of teams and divide by two (13 − 3 = 10, divided by 2 = 5 games). As explained previously, the seeded teams are awarded the byes.

Single Elimination Tournament

ROUND I	ROUND II	ROUND III	ROUND IV

```
A
BYE      A
B              A
C        B
D                    A
E        D
F              D
G        G
H                          A
BYE      H                 CHAMPION
I              H
J        J
K                    K
BYE      K
L              K
M        L
                     D
                     H
                     THIRD PLACE
                     D
```

No. of entrants	16		SEEDED TEAMS	FINAL STANDINGS
No. of contestants	13		1—A	1st—A
No. of byes	3		2—K	2nd—K
No. of games	15		3—H	3rd—D
No. of rounds	4		4—D	4th—H
No. of round I games	5		5—M	

If time permits, an interesting preliminary game to the championship contest is a playoff for third place. This gives the losers in the semifinals an opportunity to play again and allows more teams to participate in the placement laurels.

CONSOLATION TOURNAMENTS

Aside from the regular elimination tourney, a consolation tournament may be conducted with losers from the first round of play. This arrangement enables every entry to play in at least two contests. Weaker teams who may have drawn a seeded team in the first round, and teams who have traveled long distances are given a second chance to compete.

The diagram on page 302 illustrates the consolation bracket. In order to equally balance the total number of entries, three byes are used (8 entrants − 5 contestants = 3 byes). From this point, the tourney is conducted like a single elimination tournament, ending with a special consolation champion.

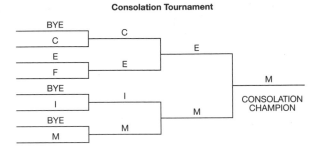

Consolation Tournament

DOUBLE ELIMINATION TOURNAMENT

The double elimination tournament requires a much longer period of play than the single elimination tournament. Each team must be defeated twice before being eliminated from further competition. As shown in the following diagram, the championship bracket is carried on in the usual manner, with the defeated teams dropping into the losers' bracket. The teams that win out in both brackets are matched for the championship.

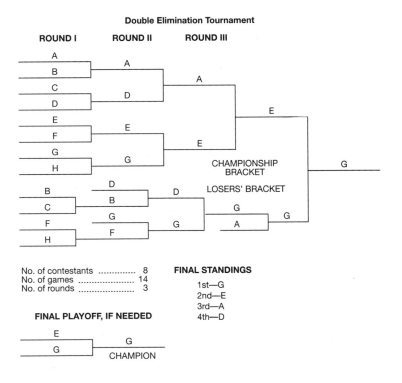

If team E had defeated team G in the diagram, the tournament would have been over, since team G had been defeated previously. With team G winning, team E suffers its first defeat, and a rematch between the two must be held to determine the champion.

The number of games to be played in a double elimination tournament is determined by subtracting 1 from the number of entries and multiplying by 2. Add 1 to this total for a possible championship playoff. If byes are needed in the losers' bracket, they should be arranged to avoid matching entries that drew a bye in the championship bracket. Also, avoid pairing entries that have met in earlier rounds.

ROUND ROBIN TOURNAMENTS

Requiring a longer period of time for completion, the round robin tournament provides more participation for every contestant than any other type of tourney. Every player or team competes against every other player or team, which stimulates interest throughout the playing season.

The final outcome of such a tournament is decided on a percentage basis. The winner is determined according to the percentage of victories, which is obtained by dividing the number of victories by the number of games played. The team with the second-best percentage is awarded second place, the team with the third-best percentage third place, and so on. As an added incentive during the playing season, team percentages should be posted from time to time. This tends to add to the competitive atmosphere of the tournament.

Before a schedule is charted, the total number of games to be played must be determined. This can be done either by applying the formula for number of games, with N representing the number of entries, or by recording the number of entries (6, 5, 4, 3, 2, 1), then canceling the highest number, and then adding the remaining figures (5 + 4 + 3 + 2 + 1 = 15 games to be played).

There are many different methods of arranging and charting round robin tournaments. One of the most common methods is to arrange the teams in vertical columns, depending upon whether there is an even or odd number of teams.

Team 1 plays Team 4

Team 1 plays Team 4

Team 2 plays Team 5

Team 3 plays Team 6

With an even number of entries, the position of No. 1 remains stationary while the other numbers revolve clockwise or counterclockwise until the original combination is reached.

ROUND ROBIN TOURNAMENT SCHEDULE

4-TEAM SCHEDULE

FIELD OR COURT

A	2-1	4-2	4-1
B	3-4	1-3	2-3

5-TEAM SCHEDULE

FIELD OR COURT

A	1-4	3-1	5-3	2-5	4-2
B	2-3	4-5	1-2	3-4	5-1

6-TEAM SCHEDULE

FIELD OR COURT

A	2-1	3-4	6-4	5-3	5-6
B	4-5	6-1	2-3	6-2	1-3
C	3-6	2-5	1-5	4-1	4-2

7-TEAM SCHEDULE

FIELD OR COURT

A	1-6	4-2	2-7	5-3	3-1	6-4	7-5
B	2-5	5-1	3-6	6-2	4-7	7-3	1-4
C	3-4	6-7	4-5	7-1	5-6	1-2	2-3

8-TEAM SCHEDULE

FIELD OR COURT

A	5-6	3-4	7-8	7-5	1-3	3-6	8-2
B	3-8	1-7	6-2	6-1	4-2	4-5	7-3
C	4-7	8-6	4-1	2-3	5-8	2-7	1-5
D	2-1	2-5	5-3	8-4	6-7	8-1	6-4

9-TEAM SCHEDULE

FIELD OR COURT

A	1-8	5-3	2-9	6-4	3-1	7-5	4-2	8-6	9-7
B	2-7	6-2	3-8	7-3	4-9	8-4	5-1	9-5	1-6
C	3-6	7-1	4-7	8-2	5-8	9-3	6-9	1-4	2-5
D	4-5	8-9	5-6	9-1	6-7	1-2	7-8	2-3	3-4

10-TEAM SCHEDULE

FIELD OR COURT

A	2-1	10-4	6-9	10-6	5-3	1-9	7-3	5-6	8-4
B	5-8	1-7	7-8	2-5	6-2	10-8	6-4	1-10	9-3
C	4-9	8-6	3-1	3-4	7-10	2-7	5-1	2-9	6-1
D	3-10	9-5	4-2	1-8	8-9	3-6	8-2	4-7	7-5
E	6-7	2-3	5-10	9-7	4-1	4-5	9-10	3-8	10-2

11-TEAM SCHEDULE

FIELD OR COURT

A	1-10	6-4	2-11	7-5	3-1	8-6	4-2	9-7	5-3	10-8	11-9
B	2-9	7-3	3-10	8-4	4-11	9-5	5-1	10-6	6-2	11-7	1-8
C	3-8	8-2	4-9	9-3	5-10	10-4	6-11	11-5	7-1	1-6	2-7
D	4-7	9-1	5-8	10-2	6-9	11-3	7-10	1-4	8-11	2-5	3-6
E	5-6	10-11	6-7	11-1	7-8	1-2	8-9	2-3	9-10	3-4	4-5

12-TEAM SCHEDULE

FIELD OR COURT

A	6-9	11-3	5-8	10-11	12-8	4-2	8-1	9-3	4-7	7-12	1-9
B	3-12	10-4	2-11	9-12	4-5	5-12	9-7	6-1	3-8	6-2	10-8
C	4-11	8-6	12-1	8-2	3-6	7-10	10-6	7 5	1-11	9-10	2-5
D	5-10	9-5	6-7	1-5	2-7	6-11	2-3	8-4	12-10	4-1	3-4
E	2-1	1-7	3-10	6-4	10-1	8-9	12-4	11-12	2-9	5-3	11-7
F	7-8	12-2	4-9	7-3	11-9	1-3	11-5	10-2	5-6	8-11	12-6

13-TEAM SCHEDULE

```
FIELD OR COURT
A  1-12  7-5   2-13  8-6   3-1   9-7   4-2   10-8  5-3   11-9  6-4   12-10 13-11
B  2-11  8-4   3-12  9-5   4-13  10-6  5-1   11-7  6-2   12-8  7-3   13-9  1-10
C  3-10  9-3   4-11  10-4  5-12  11-5  6-13  12-6  7-1   13-7  8-2   1-8   2-9
D  4-9   10-2  5-10  11-3  6-11  12-4  7-12  13-5  8-13  1-6   9-1   2-7   3-8
E  5-8   11-1  6-9   12-2  7-10  13-3  8-11  1-4   9-12  2-5   10-13 3-6   4-7
F  6-7   12-13 7-8   13-1  8-9   1-2   9-10  2-3   10-11 3-4   11-12 4-5   5-6
```

14-TEAM SCHEDULE

```
FIELD OR COURT
A  2-1   13-14 4-7   7-12  11-5  2-11  5-3   1-9   7-8   10-13 14-6  8-4   12-10
B  3-14  1-7   5-6   8-11  12-4  3-10  6-2   10-8  14-1  11-12 2-5   9-3   13-9
C  6-11  8-6   12-1  9-10  13-3  4-9   7-14  11-7  2-13  1-5   3-4   10-2  14-8
D  4-13  9-5   13-11 1-3   14-2  5-8   8-13  12-6  3-12  6-4   10-1  11-14 2-7
E  5-12  10-4  14-10 4-2   8-1   7-6   9-12  13-5  4-11  11-9  12-13 3-6
F  7-10  11-3  2-9   5-14  9-7   1-13  10-11 14-4  6-9   8-2   12-8  6-1   4-5
G  8-9   12-2  3-8   6-13  10-6  14-12 4-1   2-3   5-10  9-14  13-7  7-5   1-11
```

15-TEAM SCHEDULE

```
FIELD OR COURT
A  1-14  8-6   2-15  9-7   3-1   10-8  4-2   11-9  5-3   12-10 6-4   13-11 7-5   14-12 15-13
B  2-13  9-5   3-14  10-6  4-15  11-7  5-1   12-8  6-2   13-9  7-3   14-10 8-4   15-11 1-12
C  3-12  10-4  4-13  11-5  5-14  12-6  6-15  13-7  7-1   14-8  8-2   15-9  9-3   1-10  2-11
D  4-11  11-3  5-12  12-4  6-13  13-5  7-14  14-6  8-15  15-7  9-1   1-8   10-2  2-9   3-10
E  5-10  12-2  6-11  13-3  7-12  14-4  8-13  15-5  9-14  1-6   10-15 2-7   11-1  3-8   4-9
F  6-9   13-1  7-10  14-2  8-11  15-3  9-12  1-4   10-13 2-5   11-14 3-6   12-15 4-7   5-8
G  7-8   14-15 8-9   15-1  9-10  1-2   10-11 2-3   11-12 3-4   12-13 4-5   13-14 5-6   6-7
```

16-TEAM SCHEDULE

```
FIELD OR COURT
A  2-1   14-15 2-7   11-16 13-9  5-12  6-4   10-1  7-8   10-13 14-4  3-10  6-15  11-5  14-12
B  3-16  1-7   4-5   10-2  16-6  4-13  8-2   12-8  1-15  11-12 15-3  4-9   7-14  10-6  2-9
C  4-15  8-6   12-1  12-15 12-10 3-14  7-3   11-9  16-14 4-1   16-2  5-8   8-13  9-7   16-10
D  5-14  10-4  16-8  13-14 2-5   6-11  9-16  13-7  4-11  5-3   1-9   6-7   9-12  8-1   15-11
E  6-13  9-5   13-11 6-1   3-4   7-10  10-15 15-5  3-12  7-16  13-5  16-12 10-11 14-2  3-8
F  7-12  11-3  14-10 7-5   1-11  8-9   11-14 14-6  2-13  6-2   10-8  15-13 1-3   15-16 4-7
G  8-11  12-2  15-9  9-3   15-7  16-1  12-13 16-4  5-10  8-15  12-6  14-1  4-2   13-3  5-6
H  9-10  13-16 3-6   8-4   14-8  2-15  1-5   2-3   6-9   9-14  11-7  2-11  5-16  12-4  1-13
```

17-TEAM SCHEDULE

```
FIELD OR COURT
A  1-16  9-7   2-17  10-8  3-1   11-9  4-2   12-10 5-3   13-11 6-4   14-12 7-5   15-13 8-6   16-14 17-15
B  2-15  10-6  3-16  11-7  4-17  12-8  5-1   13-9  6-2   14-10 7-3   15-11 8-4   16-12 9-5   17-13 1-14
C  3-14  11-5  4-15  12-6  5-16  13-7  6-17  14-8  7-1   15-9  8-2   16-10 9-3   17-11 10-4  1-12  2-13
D  4-13  12-4  5-14  13-5  6-15  14-6  7-16  15-7  8-17  16-8  9-1   17-9  10-2  1-10  11-3  2-11  3-12
E  5-12  13-3  6-13  14-4  7-17  15-5  8-16  16-6  9-16  17-7  10-17 1-8   11-1  2-9   12-2  3-10  4-11
F  6-11  14-2  7-12  15-3  8-13  16-4  9-14  17-5  10-15 1-6   11-16 2-7   12-17 3-8   13-1  4-9   5-10
G  7-10  15-1  8-11  16-2  9-12  17-3  10-13 1-4   11-14 2-5   12-15 3-6   13-16 4-7   14-17 5-8   6-9
H  8-9   16-17 9-10  17-1  10-11 1-2   11-12 2-3   12-13 3-4   13-14 4-5   14-15 5-6   15-16 6-7   7-8
```

18-TEAM SCHEDULE

```
FIELD OR COURT
A  2-1   15-16 3-4   6-11  9-16  13-5  17-11 7-5   1-11  7-8   10-13 14-2  18-8  5-14  6-4   12-8  16-14
B  3-18  1-7   2-5   8-9   10-15 14-4  5-6   8-4   12-10 16-1  11-12 15-18 2-7   6-13  9-18  17-3  17-13
C  5-16  8-6   12-1  7-10  11-14 15-3  2-9   11-18 13-9  17-15 1-3   16-17 4-5   7-12  10-17 14-6  18-12
D  4-17  9-5   13-11 1-17  12-13 12-6  4-7   10-2  14-8  18-14 4-2   8-1   3-6   9-10  11-16 15-5  2-11
E  6-15  14-17 14-10 18-16 4-1   17-18 3-8   9-3   15-7  2-13  5-18  9-7   1-13  8-11  12-15 16-4  5-8
F  7-14  11-3  15-9  2-15  5-3   10-8  18-10 12-17 16-6  3-12  6-17  11-5  14-12 18-1  13-14 13-7  4-9
G  8-13  12-2  16-8  3-14  7-18  1-9   14-1  13-16 17-5  4-11  7-16  10-6  17-9  4-15  1-5   18-2  3-10
H  9-12  13-18 17-7  4-13  6-2   11-7  15-13 14-15 18-4  5-10  8-15  12-4  16-10 3-16  8-2   10-1  6-7
I  10-11 10-4  18-6  5-12  8-17  16-2  16-12 6-1   2-3   6-9   9-14  13-3  15-11 2-17  7-3   11-9  1-15
```

In the case of an odd number of entries, a bye is placed at the top of the second column. With this arrangement, all numbers revolve, with the first number drawing the bye or "open date" in each round.

Team 1 draws a bye

Team 2 plays Team 5

Team 3 plays Team 6

Team 4 plays Team 7

When teams do not have home fields or courts, a round robin schedule should be adjusted so that each team plays approximately the same number of games on each field or court.

The following diagrams might help to clarify round-robin tournament scheduling.

Example: (Even number of teams = 8)
Even number of teams will have one less number of rounds (8 teams = 7 rounds)

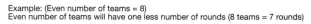

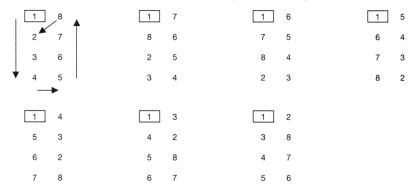

Example: (Odd number of teams = 7)
Odd number of teams has same number of rounds (7 teams = 7 rounds)

THIRTY RULES FOR GETTING THINGS DONE THROUGH PEOPLE

1. Make people on your staff want to do things. Making people *want* to do things is a much more skilled and subtle process than selling them on doing it and is usually more effective.

2. Study assistants and determine what makes each tick. Most experts say that knowing one's personnel is the main tool of leadership.

3. Delegate responsibility for details to assistants. Delegating responsibility is the essence of leadership.

4. Be a good listener. Always give the other person the right-of-way when you both start to speak at the same time. A good leader must be careful not to develop the "executive syndrome," whereby she listens to an assistant for two minutes and then tunes her out.

5. Criticize constructively. Make sure all the facts are clear. Then suggest a constructive course of action for the future. Better still,

   have the person being corrected suggest his or her own corrective action. Constructive criticism should be preceded by praise.

6. Criticize in private. Criticizing an individual in public will create resentment through embarrassment or humiliation.

7. Praise in public. Make certain that the praise is deserved and that everyone involved is included.

8. Be considerate. Nothing contributes more to building a strong, hard-working, and loyal staff than a considerate boss.

9. Give credit where it is due. The leader who takes credit for the work of a subordinate is something of a tyrant. Credit for new ideas belongs to the person who developed them.

10. Avoid domination. The effective leader thinks of the staff as working with him, not for him. A dominant leader sometimes stifles people with initiative.

11. Show interest in and appreciation of the other fellow. It is a good idea to let assistants know that you are concerned about them and that you appreciate the quality of their work. This will pay great dividends.

12. Make your wishes known by suggestions or requests. Your position may permit you to issue edicts, but there is less chance of resentment when you use suggestions or requests.

13. Be sure to give the reasons for your requests. People want to know both what they are doing and why they are doing it.

14. Let your assistants know about your plans and programs even when those plans are in an early stage. As a rule, the sum of the ideas of your assistants and your own will be better than yours alone.

15. Never forget that the leader sets the style for his people. If you are careless, late for meetings, or unenthusiastic, your assistants can be expected to follow suit.

16. Play up the positive. For most people, praise provides better motivation than criticism.

17. Be consistent. A leader who flies off the handle or gyrates wildly in mood, reaction, and manner bewilders his or her staff.

18. Show your people that you have confidence in them and that you expect them to do their best. People in general tend to live up to what is expected of them, and if goals and standards are realistic, most are able to do a first-rate job. Leaders who show that they have confidence in their staff and expect high standards of efficiency usually get what they expect.

19. Ask your assistants for their counsel and help. This gets a staff involved. The goals of the group become their goals. Since people tend to consider their own goals important, they approach goals they have participated in formulating in a more conscientious manner.

20. When you are wrong or make a mistake, admit it. No person expects a leader to be absolutely perfect. No leader loses face when he admits he was wrong—if he isn't wrong too often. By admitting mistakes, a leader gains the confidence of a staff in his fairness and honesty.

21. Give courteous hearing to ideas from your staff. Even fantastic ideas deserve a full hearing. No idea should be disparaged or ridiculed.

22. If an idea is adopted, tell the originator why. If the originator knows why you approve of an idea, then her line of thought is reinforced. She is likely to apply it to other problems. If the idea is not adopted, tell her why, too. Ideas that are presented and never heard of again discourage additional ideas and produce resentment.

23. Give weight to the fact that people carry out their own ideas best. It is good tactics to deliberately plant seeds of ideas in the thoughts of others. Thus the person who executes the idea will feel that it is his or her own.

24. Be careful what you say and how you say it. You must consider the impact that words and voices have played in the life of the average person. Harshness and curtness, for example, are associated with anxiety, reprimand, disapproval, and hostility. Words can be spoken in an atmosphere of approval, even when you are criticizing an assistant. In any event, effective communication is a major tool of leadership and human relations. Carelessly chosen words or an unintended inflection of the voice can breed unhappiness and misunderstanding. Words, forgotten the moment they are spoken, can cause unproductive days and sleepless nights for those who hear them.

25. Don't be upset by moderate grousing. In small doses, griping serves as a safety valve for letting off steam. Vicious personal griping is another story, and when it is ongoing, it can destroy a staff. In this case, it is up to the leader to find the cause and correct it immediately.

26. Use every opportunity to build up in assistants a sense of the importance of their work. People like to consider their role in any job as an important one. Everyone likes to feel he or she is making some kind of contribution in order to function well. It is the leader's job to ensure that assistants feel this way.

27. Give your people goals, a sense of direction, something to strive for and to achieve. In order to work more effectively, people need to know where they are going, what the goals of the organization are, and why the goals exist.

28. Keep your people informed on matters affecting them. Whenever possible, let your staff know in advance. When people know what is coming and why, they are able to gear their thinking more realistically to the goal.

29. Give assistants a chance to take part in decisions, particularly those affecting them. When people have had a say in a decision, they are much more likely to go along with it enthusiastically. Even if they don't agree, they will go along, since they had a part in it; at least their views were considered.

30. Let your people know where they stand. Perhaps the most devastating work situation that can be devised is one in which people don't know where they stand with the boss. They must know what you expect. The task of evaluating personnel is among the most difficult human relations problems with which any leader must deal. As a very general rule, evaluations that involve both praise and criticism are the most effective form of long-range motivation. But the criticism must be constructive.

Source: The University of Pittsburgh School of Business Administration

TWELVE POINTS OF SUCCESSFUL LEADERSHIP

1. *Be tough*—Mentally, morally, spiritually, psychologically.

2. Your desk is not your place of business—go where the action is. Leave your footprints over the whole organization.

3. Be a "fire preventer" not a "fire fighter" where problems are concerned.

4. Clarify the make-or-break activities in your program and make them top priority.

5. Be sensitive to the people with whom you work.

6. Do not take anything for granted.

7. Do not tolerate incompetence.

8. Do not alibi or accept alibis—just fix it.

9. Do not procrastinate—don't put off tough decisions.

10. Recognize good things your coaches and athletes do.

11. Be honest.

12. Be consistent.

PARENTS' EXPECTATIONS OF COACHES: A QUESTIONNAIRE

If the players' and parents' expectations are important to you (and they should be), you may want to use this questionnaire as a tool to gather data. Chances are many coaches believe they know what the youngsters and parents expect. This could be a serious mistake—the matter needs some careful thought.

In order to help make your youngsters' athletic experience more meaningful, it is important that we know not only what they expect of their coaches but what you expect as well. This information can help all of us avoid some misunderstandings throughout the season.

There will be no attempt to identify you on this form, so feel free to be as open and honest as you like. Thank you.

Please answer the following questions by circling the number that most closely corresponds to your expectations: *Do not sign this form.* (1, strongly agree; 2, agree; 3, disagree; 4, strongly disagree)

I expect the coach to:	Strongly Agree	Agree	Disagree	Strongly Disagree
1. Enforce team rules strictly.	1	2	3	4
2. Refrain from using tobacco in any form.	1	2	3	4
3. Be a positive role model.	1	2	3	4
4. Teach responsibility and self-control.	1	2	3	4
5. Take an active interest in my child's classroom performance.	1	2	3	4

6. Involve me in policy decisions that affect the team.	1	2	3	4
7. Ask for my opinion about my child's playing time.	1	2	3	4
8. Have formal educational credentials.	1	2	3	4
9. Have a successful win-loss record.	1	2	3	4
10. Get my youngster an athletic scholarship.	1	2	3	4
11. Be a full-time member of the faculty.	1	2	3	4
12. Teach the desire to win.	1	2	3	4
13. Teach my youngster to be aggressive.	1	2	3	4
14. Refrain entirely from using profane language or swearing.	1	2	3	4
15. Refrain from using abusive language if it embarrasses my child.	1	2	3	4
16. Present a neat (well-dressed) appearance even when away from school.	1	2	3	4
17. Present a personal example of physical fitness.	1	2	3	4
18. Instruct me about the recruiting process.	1	2	3	4
19. Be a strong disciplinarian.	1	2	3	4

20. Teach my youngster to strive to win in every competition.	1	2	3	4
21. Push my youngster to be the best athlete he or she can possibly be.	1	2	3	4
22. Teach that mediocrity is unacceptable.	1	2	3	4
23. Never yell at my son or daughter.	1	2	3	4
24. Give everyone a chance to play in the game.	1	2	3	4
25. Educate my youngster about drug, alcohol, and tobacco use.	1	2	3	4
26. Berate officials when he or she thinks they have made a mistake against my child.	1	2	3	4
27. Impress upon my child that winning is all that counts.	1	2	3	4
28. Avoid teaching values.	1	2	3	4
29. Always have a winning record.	1	2	3	4
30. Hate losing.	1	2	3	4
31. Let me know if my youngster has personal, drug, or alcohol problems.	1	2	3	4
32. Teach respect for authority.	1	2	3	4
33. Teach respect for an official's call even if the call was wrong.	1	2	3	4

34. Teach values for everyday life.	1	2	3	4
35. Psych out (upset) an opponent if it helps the team to win.	1	2	3	4
36. Intimidate the officials if it helps us to win.	1	2	3	4
37. Penalize my young-ster for missing games or practice.	1	2	3	4
38. Stress commitment to any task under-taken.	1	2	3	4
39. Fully instruct my youngster about the college recruiting process.	1	2	3	4
40. Teach proper nutrition.	1	2	3	4
41. Be willing to accept calls at home to talk about any team-related matter.	1	2	3	4
42. Lead the team in prayer before athletic contests.	1	2	3	4

Source: Contributed by Mike Morse

PLAYERS' EXPECTATIONS OF COACHES: A QUESTIONNAIRE

In order to help make your participation on this team more meaningful, it is important that we know what you expect of your coach(es).

There will be no attempt to identify you on this form, so feel free to be as frank and honest as you like.

Answer the following questions by circling the number which most closely corresponds to your expectations. *Do not sign this form.* (1, strongly agree; 2, agree; 3, disagree; 4, strongly disagree)

I expect the coach to:	Strongly Agree	Agree	Disagree	Strongly Disagree
1. Enforce team rules strictly.	1	2	3	4
2. Refrain from using tobacco in any form during practices or games.	1	2	3	4
3. Be a positive role model.	1	2	3	4
4. Teach responsibility and self-control.	1	2	3	4
5. Take an active interest in my academic performance.	1	2	3	4
6. Make winning our number one goal.	1	2	3	4
7. Get me an athletic scholarship.	1	2	3	4

8. Bend rules to win.	1	2	3	4
9. Teach me to be aggressive in everyday life.	1	2	3	4
10. Refrain entirely from using profanity (swearing) at all times.	1	2	3	4
11. Present a neat, well-dressed appearance at all times.	1	2	3	4
12. Present a personal example of physical fitness.	1	2	3	4
13. Be a strong disciplinarian.	1	2	3	4
14. Teach me to strive to win every time I compete in a game.	1	2	3	4
15. Push me to be the best athlete that I can possibly be.	1	2	3	4
16. Teach me that mediocrity is unacceptable in athletics.	1	2	3	4
17. Never yell at me.	1	2	3	4
18. Educate me about drug, alcohol, and tobacco abuse.	1	2	3	4
19. Berate officials when he or she thinks they have made a mistake against our team.	1	2	3	4
20. Avoid teaching values.	1	2	3	4
21. Hate losing.	1	2	3	4
22. Teach respect for an official's call even if the call was wrong.	1	2	3	4

23. Psych out an opponent if it helps the team to win.	1	2	3	4
24. Intimidate the officials if it helps us to win.	1	2	3	4
25. Penalize me for missing practice.	1	2	3	4
26. Stress commitment to any task undertaken.	1	2	3	4
27. Fully instruct me about the college recruiting process.	1	2	3	4
28. Teach proper nutrition for athletes.	1	2	3	4
29. Be willing to accept calls at home to discuss my personal or team concerns.	1	2	3	4
30. Be a buddy.	1	2	3	4
31. Socialize with me at parties.	1	2	3	4

Source: Contributed by Ray LaLonde

SAMPLE BASKETBALL PRACTICE PLAN—MONDAY

PRACTICE #5

3:30-40 Chair Shooting

3:40-45 Stretching

3:45-50 Drive and shoot

3:50-4:00 Kansas City [64]

4:00-4:05 H20

4:05-4:20 Shooting [perimeter and post]

> Perimeter
> -run the gauntlet W offensive move on the last person
> -boss drill-square up and power lay up
> -V-cut/L cut boss drill w/defense-power lay up
> -V cut/L cut, escape dribble middle 1-2 dribbles, jumper
> -jab series
> -3's power leg back
>
> posts
> -power lay up from the timeline
> -@ block
> -drop step baseline and middle
> -show and go
> -step through
> -short corner-jumper and drive from circle concept
> -high post-jumper and drive from circle concept

4:20-25 Footwork [H20]

4:25-35 3-3 balance and contain

4:35-40 Full CT. Steer

4:40-5:00 4-4 shell [pass and position] [Person with ball penetrates/Stop the ball reversal]

5:00-10 H20/Freethrows

5:10-25 Shooting off screens [down/back] Review

5:25-35 5-0 $1/_2$ court [pick and roll] H20

5:35-50 5-5 start $1/_2$ court go full [make it take it]

5:50-6:00 Yoders

Things to work on: Vision series/post defense/close out/transition/block out/secondary/3 screens/circles/feed the post

SAMPLE BASKETBALL PRACTICE PLAN—TUESDAY

PRACTICE #6

3:40-50 Huskie Shooting

3:50-55 Stretching

3:55-4:00 Two Ball Drill

4:00-4:00 Figure 8 to 2-1/5 person/3-2/2-1

4:05-4:15 Cincinnati

4:15-20 H20

4:20-25 Pop back/contest

4:25-30 Steer [side]

4:30-40 Close out 1-1 [roll ball]/2-1 close out

4:40-55 4-4 shell drill [emphasis on hands/ball pressure] start no hands

4:55-5:10 4-4 shell [no hands to convert]

5:10-20 Free throws [20?]

5:20-30 Feed post [2-1/2-2] Perimeter 3's power leg back

5:30-40 5-0 Motion a [answer Jess question]

5:40-55 5-5 Motion [Start $1/_2$ court-go full court] Start with get 10 - flat ball

5:55-6:05 Yoders

Things to work on: *Secondary* [start with] *3-3 close to convert*/3-3 screens to convert/*post defense*/ball screens/*block out*/traps/Breaking press

1 Mo	Knake
2 Char	Billi
3 Bo	Steph
4 Liz	Jen
5 Mick	Jess

SAMPLE BASKETBALL PRACTICE PLAN

8:00-8:10	Pre-Practice
8:10-8:15	Dribble
8:15-8:20	5 on 0 Basic
8:20-8:35	*STANCE*

    1. Push-Footfire-Push-Footfire-Push   35 seconds

    2. 6-6   1 minute

    3. Full Ct. Close   Out F.T. $1/_2$ F.T. Base 2X

    4. 6 Man Slide 2X   Over Screen   35 seconds

    5. Close Out Wing—Trace—Push Corner 2X   35 seconds

8:35-8:40	Fresno D Footwork
8:40-8:50	Alley Drill w/Charge
8:50-8:55	Drink
8:55-9:00	2 Line Passing
	Close Out Passing

9:00-9:10	Shoot	*Perimeter*	*Post*	*Morphs*
		Curl	Post Moves	Curl/Square
		Square	Square	3's
		3's		Square Step High Post
		Inside Dribble		

9:10-9:25	*Perimeter*	*Morphs*	*Bigs*
	Close Out 1 on 1	Close Out 1 on 1	Post D—Jucare
	Stagger 1 on 1	Post D—Jucare	Cross Screen/Duck In
		Cross Screen/ Duck In 2 on 2	

9:25-9:40   4 on 4 Shell

    1. Jump To Ball

    2. Help Side Screen

    3. Rotation

9:40-9:55   4 on 4 Cut Throat

    2 pts-stop

    3 pts-charge

    Drive to Paint—Switch D

SAMPLE BASEBALL PRACTICE PLAN

WEEK 4
PRACTICE DAY 16

3:30 P.M.	TEAM MEETING (S/H HANDOUTS)
	STRETCHING/AGILITY/ABS
4:15 P.M.	LONG TOSS – ALL POSITIONS
4:40 P.M.	IF/OF – DOUBLE CUTS (THROWS) THIRD BASE
	P/C – BULL PENS
	PAST BALL DRILLS 1 – 2 – 3
	CATCHERS PICK CALLS
5:15 P.M.	POP FLY PRIORITIES
	"MINE BEFORE YOURS"
5:40 P.M.	POSITION – BASERUNNING
	PITCHERS CONDITIONING

SAMPLE FOOTBALL PRACTICE PLAN

Period	Time	Coach 1	Coach 2	Coach 3	Coach 4	
1	9:15	PURSUIT	PURSUIT	PURSUIT	PURSUIT	1
2	9:20				BUMP DRILLS	2
3	9:25	DISCIPLINE	DISCIPLINE	STANCE & STEPS	SOFT DRILL	3
4	9:30	TAKE-OFF	TAKE-OFF	JAM DRILL		4
5	9:35	6 PT PUNCH	6 PT PUNCH	CAN READS	MAN TO MAN	5
6	9:40	SHED	SCRAPE	4 CONE ANGLE TACKLE		6
7	9:45	BLOCK REACTION	SCOOP	MATCH DRILL	RELEASES	7
8	9:50		DROP	2 MATCH WITH # 1	WEAVE DRILL	8
9	9:55	ZONE BLITZ REVIEW	ZONE BLITZ REVIEW	SKELLY	SKELLY	9
10	10:00					10
11	10:05					11
12	10:10	FG BLOCK	FG	FG BLOCK	FG BLOCK	12
13	10:15	MOVEMENT	2 MAN SLED	UNDER DRILL	1/2 ASS DRILL VS.	13
14	10:20		SPLL		WITH SAFTIES	14
15	10:25	PASS PURSUIT	PASS RUSH	BALL DRILLS		15
16	10:30			SKELLY	SKELLY	16
17	10:35	1 ON 1 PASS RUSH	1 ON 1 PASS RUSH			17
18	10:40					18
19	10:45	COUNTER	PUNT	PUNT	PUNT	19
20	10:50	TEAM APART	TEAM APART	TEAM APART	TEAM APART	20
21	10:55					21
22	11:00					22
23	11:05					23
24	11:10	SECURE	SECURE	SECURE	SECURE	24
25	11:15	MEET	MEET	MEET	MEET	25
26	11:20					26

PHOTO CREDITS

Chapter 1
opposite page 1: courtesy Penn State Sports Media Relations; page 3: photo by Brad Taylor; page 5: courtesy Northern Illinois University; page 6: courtesy Centre Daily Times, photo by Craig Houtz; page 8: courtesy Penn State Sports Media Relations; page 10: courtesy Penn State Sports Media Relations; page 13: courtesy Penn State Sports Media Relations

Chapter 2
page 18: courtesy Centre Daily Times, photo by Craig Houtz; page 23: courtesy Northern Illinois University; page 25: courtesy Northern Illinois University; page 29: courtesy Penn State Sports Media Relations; page 32: courtesy Penn State Sports Media Relations; page 35: courtesy Northern Illinois University; page 38: courtesy Northern Illinois University; page 41: courtesy Northern Illinois University; page 43: courtesy Centre Daily Times, photo by Nabil K. Mark

Chapter 3
page 46: photo by Jan Bortner; page 49: courtesy Northern Illinois University; page 52: courtesy Penn State Sports Media Relations; page 55: courtesy Centre Daily Times, photo by Craig Houtz; page 56: photo by Bill Simon; page 57: courtesy Northern Illinois University; page 59: courtesy Penn State Sports Media Relations; page 63: courtesy Cheryl Norman; page 64: courtesy Brian Segrist; page 67: courtesy Penn State Sports Media Relations

Chapter 4
page 70: courtesy Penn State Sports Media Relations; page 73: courtesy Penn State Sports Media Relations; page 76: photo by Kristy Shaner; page 82: courtesy Penn State Sports Media Relations; page 85: courtesy Northern Illinois University; page 86: courtesy Penn State Sports Media Relations; page 88: courtesy Centre Daily Times, photo by Craig Houtz; page 91: photo by Colin Scott; page 93: courtesy Centre Daily Times, photo by Craig Houtz; page 95: courtesy Sharon Walker, Muskingum College; page 101: courtesy Penn State Sports Media Relations

Chapter 5
page 104: courtesy Centre Daily Times, photo by Nabil K. Mark; page 106: courtesy Penn State Sports Media Relations; page 109: courtesy Penn State Sports Media Relations; page 111:courtesy Centre Daily Times, photo by Craig Houtz; page 114: courtesy Northern Illinois University; page 117: courtesy Penn State Sports Media Relations; page 121: courtesy Northern Illinois University

Chapter 6
page 124: courtesy Penn State Sports Media Relations; page 129: courtesy Penn State Sports Media Relations; page 132: courtesy Northern Illinois University; page 133: courtesy Penn State Sports Media Relations; page 137: courtesy Northern Illinois University

Chapter 7
page 140: courtesy Penn State Sports Media Relations; page 143: courtesy Penn State Sports Media Relations, photo by Dave Shelly; page 146: courtesy Penn State Sports Media Relations

Chapter 8
page 154: courtesy Northern Illinois University; page 157: courtesy Northern Illinois University; page 158: courtesy Alan Erdley; page 161: courtesy Penn State Sports Media Relations; page 163: courtesy Penn State Sports Media Relations; page 166: courtesy Penn State Sports Media Relations; page 168: courtesy Centre Daily Times, photo by Michelle Klein

Chapter 9
page 170: courtesy Ron Pavlechko; page 174: courtesy Penn State Sports Media Relations; page 181: courtesy Michael D. Sabock; page 182: courtesy Penn State Sports Media Relations; page 193: courtesy Penn State Sports Media Relations; page 196: courtesy Northern Illinois University; page 206: courtesy Sports Information, Northern Illinois University; page 210: courtesy Michael D. Sabock; page 212: courtesy Northern Illinois University; page 214: courtesy Sandy Sabock

Chapter 10
page 216: courtesy Penn State Sports Media Relations; page 222: courtesy Penn State Sports Media Relations; page 222: courtesy Northern Illinois University; page 228: courtesy Penn State Sports Media Relations; page 232: courtesy Northern Illinois University; page 238: courtesy Penn State Sports Media Relations; page 247: courtesy Northern Illinois University; page 248: courtesy Michael D. Sabock; page 252: courtesy Penn State Sports Media Relations

Chapter 11
page 256: courtesy Centre Daily Times, photo by Misha T. Kwasniewski; page 259: courtesy Penn State Sports Media Relations; page 266: courtesy Northern Illinois University; page 270: courtesy Northern Illinois University; page 275: courtesy Penn State Sports Media Relations; page 277: courtesy Penn State Sports Media Relations; page 280: courtesy Dan Sabock; page 283: courtesy Kevin Sabock; page 286: courtesy Penn State Sports Media Relations

Chapter 12
page 292: courtesy Northern Illinois University

Appendix A
page 299: courtesy Northern Illinois University

Appendix B
page 307: courtesy Penn State Sports Media Relations

INDEX

A

abilities, 25;
    of players, 247–48
accountability, 4
ACT scores, 167
Adams, Henry, 105
administrators:
    assistant coaches and, 129–30;
    becoming, 44;
    on coaching, 24;
    conflicts with, 286–87;
    cooperation with, 26;
    ethics and, 14–15;
    frustration with, 27;
    honesty with, 14, 51;
    loyalty and, 14;
    objectives of, 51,
    relationship with, 47–52;
    responsibilities of, 48–50
advice:
    giving, 116–17;
    receiving, 64;
    students and, 13–14
alcohol, 263–64;
    as depressant, 262
ambition, 26,
    of assistant coaches, 134–35;
    athletes versus, 58;
    wives and, 146
American Alliance of Health, Physical
    Education, Recreation and Dance, 51–
    52
American Medical Association, 264
American Red Cross, 230
amphetamines, 263
anorexia nervosa, 265
anxiety, 116
assistant coaches, 39–40;
    administrators and, 129–30;

ambition of, 134–35;
athletes rapport with, 136–37;
brainstorming with, 138;
considerations for, 129;
flexibility of, 139;
goals of, 127;
hiring, 125;
interviewing for, 127–29;
as liaison, 137–38;
motivation by, 138–39;
philosophy of, 126–27, 134;
playing experience of, 135;
qualities of, 131–39;
relationship with, 61;
responsibilities, 130;
willingness to work, 138
athletes:
    assistant coaches and, 136–37;
    attitude of, 163, 259;
    band performers and, 62;
    conduct, 52–53, 232;
    eligibility of, 167;
    goals of, 184, 220–21;
    with HIV, 267;
    individual, 86–87;
    off-season correspondence with,
        185–91;
    parental pressure on, 91;
    personal appearance of, 163;
    physical examinations of, 195;
    placement of, 94;
    practice policies and, 224;
    press and, 65;
    qualities of, 82, 92;
    recruiting suggestions for, 159–61;
    recruitment of, 63;
    relationship with, 58;
    schoolwork, 52;
    self-image of, 111;
    selfishness of, 20;

ABOUT THE AUTHORS

Sports have played a major part in the life of **Ralph Sabock**. Through personal participation in sports and seventeen years of active coaching on the high school, military, and college levels, he has a wealth of practical coaching principles to pass on to those preparing to become coaches. Dr. Sabock has coached football, baseball, wrestling, and track and field.

Upon receiving his Ph.D. at The Ohio State University, he joined the faculty at The Pennsylvania State University where he taught courses in the professional preparation of young men and women coaches. He has authored numerous articles, conducted a number of workshops dealing with coaching, and was responsible for the graduate program in Sports Administration at Penn State University. An annual Penn State indoor track meet is named for Sabock and Dutch Sykes in honor of their thirty-plus years of service officiating at this meet.

Michael Sabock is the son of Dr. Sabock. He has been an assistant football coach at Northern Illinois University for over twenty years and during that time has coached every position on the defense. In addition to his coaching, he also serves as the recruiting coordinator. Sabock is a graduate of Baldwin-Wallace College in Ohio where he participated in football and track. He earned his Master's degree in sports administration from Kent State University.

He spent five years coaching on the high school level and one year as a graduate assistant defensive backfield coach under Joe Paterno at Penn State University before becoming a member of the staff at Northern Illinois University.